D1713189

Dwight R. Daniels
Hosea and Salvation History

Beihefte zur Zeitschrift für die alttestamentliche Wissenschaft

Herausgegeben von
Otto Kaiser

Band 191

Walter de Gruyter · Berlin · New York
1990

Dwight R. Daniels

Hosea and Salvation History

The Early Traditions of Israel
in the Prophecy of Hosea

Walter de Gruyter · Berlin · New York
1990

Library of Congress Cataloging-in-Publication Data

Daniels, Dwight R. (Dwight Roger), 1956—
    Hosea and salvation history : the early traditions of Israel in
the prophecy of Hosea / Dwight R. Daniels.
    p.   cm. — (Beihefte zur Zeitschrift für die alttestamentliche
Wissenschaft, ISSN 0934-2575 ; Bd. 191)
    Revision of author's thesis (doctoral)—University of Hamburg,
1987.
    Includes bibliographical references and index.
    ISBN 3-11-012143-3. — ISBN 0-89925-596-5 (U.S.)
    1. Bible. O.T. Hosea—Theology.   2. History (Theology)—
Biblical teaching.   I. Title.   II. Series: Beihefte zur Zeitschrift für
die alttestamentliche Wissenschaft ; 191.
    BS 1565.6.D35   1990
    224'.606—dc20   90-43910
                                                              CIP

Deutsche Bibliothek Cataloging in Publication Data

Daniels, Dwight R.:
Hosea and salvation history : the early traditions of Israel in the
prophecy of Hosea / Dwight R. Daniels. — Berlin ; New York : de
Gruyter, 1990
    (Beihefte zur Zeitschrift für die alttestamentliche Wissenschaft ;
    191)
    Zugl.: Hamburg, Univ., Diss., 1987
    ISBN 3-11-012143-3
NE: Zeitschrift für die alttestamentliche Wissenschaft / Beiheft

ISSN: 0934-2575

Printed in Germany
Printing: Werner Hildebrand, Berlin 65
Binding: Lüderitz & Bauer, Berlin 61

FOR

SUSAN

PREFACE

The present study is a revised version of my doctoral dissertation, which was accepted by the University of Hamburg in the summer of 1987. I would like to thank my mentor, Prof. Dr. Klaus Koch, for his undaunted willingness to discuss the issues and for his insightful criticisms and suggestions. From his active interest in the study and from his seminars and lectures I have learned a great deal and have no doubt incurred a debt which cannot be repaid. Prof. Dr. Bernd Janowski was the secondary reader of the dissertation and made several helpful comments. He, too, has taken an active interest in my academic progress, for which I am grateful. I would also like to thank Prof. Dr. Otto Kaiser for his acceptance of the manuscript for publication in the BZAW series, as well as for his helpful suggestions. Thanks also go to Dr. Uwe Gleßmer who wrote the special character fonts and made the necessary adaption of the corresponding existing fonts. His investment of time and effort has been quite selfless and is much appreciated. Lastly, I would like to extend a special word of thanks to my wife Susan who has accompanied me throughout my theological pursuits and whose patience has been put to the test more times than I care to remember. For these and a myriad of other reasons this book is dedicated to her.

Hamburg   DRD
Easter, 1990

TABLE OF CONTENTS

CHAPTER 1

INTRODUCTION

One of the main objectives of research into the Old Testament, at least within a Christian context, is the development of an appropriate presentation of its theological content. However, in the current discussion there is no general agreement as to how such a presentation should be approached. One of the central points of contention concerns the proper evaluation of history as a mode of revelation and within the context of Old Testament theology.

A. GOD AND HISTORY IN OLD TESTAMENT THEOLOGY[1]

"The Old Testament is a history book." This oft quoted and now famous statement of Gerhard von Rad[2] has come to typify his conception of Old Testament theology. Actually, von Rad had laid out his position more fully almost a decade prior to this statement.[3] According to von Rad the Old Testament depicts a history of God with men and focuses to such an extent on this history that all its contents are colored by this concern. He therefore advocates a salvation-historical approach to the theology of the Old Testament. Under salvation history he at this point understands a course of history set in motion by the divine Word, created by it and guided by it towards its goal.[4] This history is driven forward by the rhythm of promise and fulfillment related to the salvific gifts which form the foundation of life. In this rhythm the fulfillment, in a "process of glorification," is painted with such vibrant colors that the experienced reality of the conditions inaugurated by the event pale by comparison. The fulfillment hence comes to be understood as only partial, awaiting final consummation in a future saving act. The fulfillment thus becomes itself promise.[5]

Von Rad later altered his use of the term salvation history within the context of the Old Testament. Here according to von Rad salvation history is limited to the span of history beginning with the patriarchs and concluding with the conquest of the land. The great deeds of Yahweh in this period became the foundation of Israel's life and faith.

---

[1]   The focus in what follows is on the Old Testament. For a broader discussion of the issues involved cf. H. Graf Reventlow, *Hauptprobleme*, 65-137.

[2]   "Typological Interpretation," 181 = 25 = "Typologische Auslegung," 23 = 11.

[3]   "Grundprobleme," esp. pp. 227-229.

[4]   Von Rad later altered his use of the term salvation history. In his *Old Testament Theology* the term refers to Yahweh's great acts in history recounted in the historical confessions.

[5]   Here lies the seed bed of von Rad's typological interpretation of the Old Testament. For a presentation of the same idea without resulting in a typological interpretation cf. W. Zimmerli, "Promise and Fulfillment."

Israel's subsequent history came to be seen as qualitatively different because it took place under essentially different presuppositions in that now the human factor is allowed to play a much greater role in determining the course of events. In the "canonical" salvation history, however, Yahweh himself insured that the promise was fulfilled. The inheritance of the land always remained for Israel the high-point of her past history.[6]

The strong emphasis on history in von Rad's position raises two fundamental issues. The first deals with the question of which history is to form the basis of a salvation-historical approach to Old Testament theology, the picture which Israel herself presented of her history or that reconstructed using the methods of modern historical research. Von Rad himself was well aware of the problem and opted for Israel's own confessional presentations.[7] This decision was vigorously challenged by F. Hesse. In his earlier work Hesse retained the idea of salvation history and conceived of it as God's speaking and acting in Israel culminating in the goal of the divine self-revelation in Jesus Christ.[8] If God did in fact act in the history of Israel leading up to Christ, then salvation history must be present "in, with and under" the actual history of Israel as it really happened. Thus, although salvation history is not simply to be equated with the history of Israel, it is nevertheless to be found there, and so the more complete the picture of Israelite history becomes, the better the presuppositions for comprehending salvation history.[9]

In his response to his critics von Rad drew attention to the fact that the very presuppositions of modern historiography render it incapable of perceiving divine action in history.[10] The point is well taken, but it hardly resolves the entire issue. An attempt to overcome the discrepancy was therefore undertaken by R. Rendtorff,[11] who formulated the problem quite clearly. The implication of von Rad's position is that history must be theologically abandoned, whereas the implication of F. Hesse's position is that (large portions of) the Old Testament itself must be theologically abandoned.[12] Rendtorff, however, argues that the alternative is more apparent than real. When one seeks to illuminate Israel's witness to her history, one finds that it is indissolubly coupled with tradition. And when one pursues Israel's history, one discovers that this too is indivisibly connected to tradition, so that "the separation of history on the one side and witness on the other side turns out to be invalid, because we encounter both only as tradition."[13] History and tradition can only be distinguished when history is inadequately understood as merely a sequence of *bruta facta* limited to political and military events. The distinction

---

[6]   *Theology* I, 121-126 = *Theologie* [1]I, 127-132.

[7]   *Theology* I, 107-111 = *Theologie* [1]I, 113-117.

[8]   "Erforschung der Geschichte Israels," 2.

[9]   "Erforschung der Geschichte Israels," 10ff; cf. *idem*, "Kerygma oder geschichtliche Wirklichkeit," 24-26; and *idem*, "Evaluation and Authority," 294-299 = "Wert und Geltung," 81-85 = 275-280.

[10]   *Theologie* [1]II, 9 (not included in the English translation).

[11]   Rendtorff's work occurred within the context of the "Revelation as History" program, on which see W. Pannenberg (ed.), *Offenbarung als Geschichte,* especially the second edition with a *Nachwort* by Pannenberg in which initial reactions are briefly discussed. Again, the focus of the current presentation is on the Old Testament and is limited to a sketch of the primary voices. For further literature with discussion see Reventlow, *Hauptprobleme,* 83-95.

[12]   "Hermeneutik des AT," 36 = 20; cf. *idem*, "Geschichte und Überlieferung," 81-82 = 25-26.

[13]   "Hermeneutik des AT," 36-39 = 20-23, quotation p. 39 = 23; cf. also "Geschichte und Überlieferung," 84-86 = 28-30.

between "external" and "internal" processes, though perhaps necessary on practical grounds, must not be allowed to obscure the fact that history encompasses both.[14]

Although Rendtorff has made some excellent points, he is able to equate tradition and history only because of a good deal of terminological imprecision. Thus, within the space of a single page he asserts that tradition is not tradition about history, but history itself, and then that the tradition about God's activity in history is itself history.[15] But what is the difference between "tradition about history" and "tradition about God's activity in history," especially since he identifies the two when he states that salvation history, by which he means history in which God acts, is nothing other than history?[16] Rendtorff himself appears to have felt this problem. In his later article tradition becomes a *component* of history.[17] Here it is necessary to make a consistent use of qualifiers and to speak of the (entire) history of Israel as composed of various segments, such as her political, legal, cultic, social, and religious histories. Similar distinctions must be made with reference to the various types of tradition which go into making Israelite "tradition" as a whole. Tradition constitutes a part of history because an event is perceived and interpreted within the prevailing conceptual framework informed by the relevant traditions existing at the time of an event's occurrence, and the resulting understanding of an event influences the reaction to it. This reaction is also predicated upon an understanding of the implications of certain actions under certain circumstances, and this understanding, too, is dependent on the prevailing conceptual framework. In the other direction, the experience of an event either confirms the conceptual framework and so serves to stabilize it, or the framework must be altered in light of aspects of the event which were not fully comprehensible. This in turn means that the relevant traditions will be altered or expanded. Herein lies the justification for Rendtorff's statement that history and tradition cannot be fully separated from one another.[18] But it also becomes apparent that the two cannot simply be equated, and this is reflected in the shift in Rendtorff's terminology.

Consequently, Rendtorff again poses the question of the "historicity" of what is reported in the (historical) traditions.[19] He notes that the core of the tradition usually goes back to actual historical facts[20] and concedes that the subsequent development of the tradition resulted in a picture of Israel's history inconsistent with the results of modern historical criticism. The subsequent "interpretation" does not therefore lack "historicity," because it is itself an historical process. Accurate though this statement may be, it fails to address the original question, which dealt not with the nature of the tradition as an historical entity but with the factual historical accuracy of that which is reported in the

14 "Hermeneutik des AT," 39 = 23; "Geschichte und Überlieferung," 91-93 = 35-37.
15 "Hermeneutik des AT," 39 = 23: "Diese Überlieferung ist aber nicht Überlieferung *von* Geschichte ... sondern sie ist selbst Geschichte" and "Vielmehr ist die Überlieferung von Gottes Geschichtshandeln selbst Geschichte" (emphasis original).
16 "Hermeneutik des AT," 40 = 24.
17 "Geschichte und Überlieferung," 86, 88 = 30, 32; cf. also his citation of M. Noth that "the history of the ... tradition is itself a part of the history of Israel" (*Pentateuchal Traditions*, 252 = *Überlieferungsgeschichte des Pentateuch*, 272). Noth's statement originally referred specifically to the history of the Pentateuchal tradition.
18 Cf. also K. Koch, "Der Tod des Religionstifters," 114-115 n. 53.
19 "Geschichte und Überlieferung," 88-89 = 32-33.
20 He is aware of exceptions (*ibid.*, 89 = 33 n. 20) but does not treat them extensively.

tradition.[21] Thus, Rendtorff is unable to reconcile the two positions. In principle he himself opts for the historical-critical picture of Israel's history, but he understands this history as encompassing both the external political events and the various internal processes reflected in the history of her various traditions. The historical-critical method must therefore be appropriately developed to enable it to perform this task.[22]

In light of Rendtorff's considerations, in particular his pointing out that Hesse's position effectively denied large portions of the Old Testament theological relevance, Hesse first distanced himself somewhat from his earlier conception of salvation history *(Theologie der Heilstatsachen)* and then shortly thereafter bid farewell to the idea all together.[23] He now defines the term "salvation history" as meaning that salvation itself has a history of some sort or that it exerts an influence upon history and forms it over a longer period of time.[24] He then proceeds to examine the Old Testament understanding of salvation and comes to the conclusion that salvation is an earthly condition of peace and prosperity which ultimately only Yahweh can grant. This he does unconditionally. Disaster *(Unheil)*, by contrast, is the divine reaction to human action of a sinful nature and so is retribution and punishment. Salvation and disaster are thus mutually exclusive.[25] When one examines Israel's history, it becomes apparent that prior to the Davidic kingdom Israel did not experience salvation in the full sense of the term, and so one cannot properly speak of a history of salvation in this period. With the realization of salvation in the Davidic era Israel looked forward to a history of salvation as guaranteed by the prophecy of Nathan.[26] But the future course of Israel's history failed to live up to expectations. Disaster after disaster befell Israel, and salvation became an eschatological hope for the future.[27] The Old Testament thus does not perceive Israel's history as a history of salvation, and nowhere in the New Testament can the idea of a continuous history of salvation be sustained.[28]

Hesse then focuses on the component "history" in the term salvation history. He lists three possibilities of what it could refer to -- the actual history of Israel; Israel's own view of her history; or a history in, with and under Israel's actual history -- and rejects them all. The second option is rejected for the same reasons that Hesse had given in his earlier work. His own previous position is rejected because one can only say what the salvation history "in, with and under" Israel's actual history is not, but it is not possible to define positively a salvation history so conceived. It can therefore not be reconstructed. With regard to the first possibility Hesse argues that election does not require a continuous series of divine acts. "When God deals with people in a special way not experienced by other people, this expresses itself in an *event*, but need not find expression in a *history*."[29] Continuity belongs to the essence of history, but God's action in history is contingent. It enters history from outside history, "so that here the continuity of events is pierced

---

[21]   Cf. F. Hesse, *Das Alte Testament als Buch der Kirche*, 123-125.
[22]   "Geschichte und Überlieferung," 92-93 and esp. 94 n. 39 = 36-37 and 38 n. 39.
[23]   *Abschied von der Heilsgeschichte.*
[24]   *ibid.*, 7.
[25]   *ibid.*, 11-14.
[26]   *ibid.*, 17-22.
[27]   *ibid.*, 25-27.
[28]   *ibid.*, 31-35.
[29]   *ibid.*, 39 (emphasis original).

through 'from above.'" There can therefore be no history of salvation because divine acts lack continuity, which is the essence of history.[30] Nevertheless, the miraculous is excluded and divine acts in history do not rupture the continuum of Israel's history. "Divine acts ... in it (viz. Israel's history) are just as subject to the laws of causality as they are in every other history."[31] Hesse thus sees God operating punctually in history in a manner which does not violate the law of causality and hence is perceptible only to the eye of faith.

The implication of Hesse's view of the divine activity in history is that it is sporadic and that Israel is essentially left to its own devices in the intervals.[32] It may also be pointed out that when Hesse argues that election need not express itself in a history, he has not demonstrated that this cannot be the case. But the entire conception is dubious. Election *occurs* as an event but *expresses* itself in a unique relationship which necessarily has a history. His conception of salvation is also questionable. Are salvation *(Heil)* and disaster *(Unheil)* as mutually exclusive as Hesse asserts? If so, why is it necessary to qualify the statement and say that salvation "in the full sense" was never present prior to or following the Davidic kingdom?[33] Was it then partially present, and if so, why can this partial salvation not have a history? Does "partial salvation" also exclude "partial disaster"? If so, why then is the salvation only partial? In effect Hesse has set up a straw man to knock down when he defines salvation history as the history of a fully present salvation. Previously, the term was generally used to refer to the history leading up to (full) salvation and not the history of its full presence.

Basic to this more common conception of salvation history is the idea that history is purposeful and moves towards the goal of salvation, and this consciousness of history is often held to be unique to Israel and so distinguishes her from her environment. Von Rad writes, "Israel came to realise that Jahweh had a definite plan for her .... It was God who established among the multiplicity of occurrences the continuity and goal-orientedness in the temporal sequence of events."[34] Similarly Rendtorff: "The consciousness of history as a meaningful, goal-oriented continuity first arose in Israel."[35] Even H. Gese, who sees the beginnings of historical thought already present in Mesopotamian culture prior to Israel, maintains that Israel conceived of her history as predicated upon a divine plan of salvation, a conception for which there is no evidence in Mesopotamian culture.[36]

The conception of salvation history has also been challenged by contesting the idea of a divine plan in history. This approach has been taken by B. Albrektson,[37] who comes to the conclusion that "the phrase 'the divine plan in history' is hardly suitable when we want to define what is typical of the Old Testament view of history as a whole."[38] History

---

30   *ibid.*, 49-56, quotation from p. 54: "so daß hier das kontinuierliche Geschehen 'von oben her' durchbrochen wird."

31   *ibid.*, 58.

32   Cf. the question posed by Rendtorff, "Geschichte und Überlieferung," 90 = 34: "Handelt Gott nur dann und wann und überläßt Israel in der Zwischenzeit sich selbst?"

33   With respect to "Heil," qualifiers such as "vollgültiges," "in ungebrochener Weise," "im Vollsinne des Wortes" are typical in Hesse's argumentation.

34   *Theology* II, 106 = *Theologie* [1]II, 119-120. The second part of the translation is my own.

35   "Geschichte und Überlieferung," 91 = 35.

36   "Geschichtliches Denken," 141-142 = 95-96.

37   *History and the Gods,* Chapter 5: The Divine Plan in History, 68-97.

38   *ibid.*, 89.

is here equated with the entirety of universal history,[39] and plan is to be understood as a *fixed* plan, a specifically conceived and articulated method of doing something, and not merely in the sense of intent or purpose.[40] But here the issue has been dismissed *per definitionem*. "The author tries to argue that one can only speak of a plan in history if all nations were involved in it all the time. We think that most people are content to accept that there is a plan in history ... if an ultimate goal is being reached, however much or little individual nations at a given moment may be affected by this plan. There is no attempt to deny the existence of a plan in this sense."[41]

The second fundamental issue raised by a strong emphasis on history concerns the role of the divine Word in history, especially as a source of revelation. Von Rad held that "if ... we put Israel's picture of her history in the forefront of our theological consideration, we encounter ... the living word of Jahweh coming on and on to Israel forever, and this in the message uttered by his mighty acts."[42] He also maintained that Israel herself subscribed to "the absolute priority in theology of event over 'logos.'"[43] This basic position was adopted by R. Rendtorff, who held that not the isolated word was revelatory but only the event which the word announces, when it is recognized within its tradition-historical context as an act of Yahweh.[44] W. Zimmerli responded that the event was not recognizable in this sense unless the name Yahweh had previously been proclaimed.[45] Rendtorff then took another look at the problem and came to the conclusion that where a word of announcement is proclaimed, this cannot be isolated from the ensuing event. Only the word-event complex as a whole is revelatory. A look at the historical works of the Davidic-Solomonic era, however, indicates that a prior word of Yahweh is not an indispensable prerequisite to recognizing an event as an act of Yahweh.[46] In his study Rendtorff explicitly states that he employs the term "word" to refer only to the prophetic word and related phenomena.[47] When, however, the term "word" is expanded to include tradition, then "word" becomes essential to comprehension because the historiographers of the Davidic-Solomonic era stood in the tradition of the understanding of history as the work of Yahweh, as Rendtorff himself recognizes.[48] At this point the considerations link up with those previously discussed in connection with history and tradition.[49]

---

[39]   *ibid.*, 87.
[40]   *ibid.*, 77.
[41]   W. G. Lambert, "Review Article," 173.
[42]   *Theology* I, 112 = *Theologie* [4]I, 125.
[43]   *Theology* I, 116 = *Theologie* [4]I 129.
[44]   "Offenbarungsvorstellungen," 40 = 58.
[45]   "'Offenbarung' im AT," esp. p. 24.
[46]   "Geschichte und Wort," 624-634 = 63-73.
[47]   *ibid.*, 623 = 62.
[48]   *ibid.*, 635 = 74.
[49]   See above pp. 2-4; see also the careful study of R. Knierim, "Offenbarung im AT," esp. pp. 216ff, where the exchange between Rendtorff and Zimmerli is also examined.

B. History in the Proclamation of the Prophets

The broader discussion of the proper evaluation of history for Old Testament theology naturally had repercussions for the approach to the prophets, although the basic issues present themselves in a somewhat different guise. The prophets, of course, were unfamiliar with any historical-critical reconstruction of Israel's history, and so the question of "which history" did not pose itself to them. They knew of Israel's past history only from her own presentation of it in her traditions, especially her historical traditions. This problem is hence non-existent for the understanding of the prophets on their own terms, and of the questions associated with this issue in the larger debate the primary one that remains is whether the prophets conceived of a history of salvation. The discussion of the relationship between history and word also received a specific stamp when applied to the prophets. Since the prophets knew of past history from Israel's historical traditions, the question of primary interest became the role of historical tradition and the word of Yahweh in the development of the prophetic proclamation. Since most conceptions of salvation history include the idea of a final goal,[50] this issue naturally came to be discussed in terms of the prophetic eschatology. This is true even of von Rad's more limited usage. As will be recalled, he employed the term to refer to the events from the patriarchs to the conquest which were confessed in Israel as the foundation of her life and faith. In application to the prophets the idea could also be applied to the new future action of Yahweh since the prophets "shifted the basis of salvation to a future action of God" which would "take exactly the forms of the old one."[51] The prophets took up the old salvific traditions and related them to the coming "eschatological" age typologically. The history recounted in these traditions is now seen to be a preliminary and partial fulfillment of the old promise which will be fully realized only in the coming age. But before the dawn of this new age there comes Yahweh's "great act of demolition" creating a "break which goes so deep that the new state beyond it cannot be understood as the continuation of what went before."[52] Nevertheless, this new age, like the present one, is an age within history. There is thus both typological and historical continuity between the two ages.[53]

An opposing view is advocated by G. Fohrer. According to Fohrer, the prophets up to Ezekiel had no eschatological component in their message. Amos, Isaiah, and Micah proclaim only the total destruction of Israel. Hosea, Jeremiah, and Ezekiel at first preach

---

[50] See above pp. 5-6.

[51] *Theology* II, 118 = *Theologie* [1]II, 132. This conception created a certain tension in von Rad's treatment of the prophets. The future action of Yahweh is seen by Isaiah and Micah in terms of the David-Zion tradition and therefore not in terms of the old saving history as defined by von Rad. In this context he therefore tends to speak rather of "old election traditions" or simply of the "old traditions." This tension has been relieved in the position of K. Koch, who holds that in Judah the canonical saving history was expanded to culminate in the election of David and Zion; cf. K. Koch, *The Prophets* I, 138-140 = *Die Profeten* I, 151-153, and *idem*, "Geschichte," 578-579.

[52] *Theology* II, 115 = *Theologie* [1]II, 129.

[53] *ibid.*, 115-116 = 128-130. A similar view is expounded by H. W. Wolff, "The Understanding of History in the Old Testament Prophets"; cf. also K. Koch, *The Prophets* II, 199 = *Die Profeten* II, 202.

repentance as the only means of averting annihilation, but then as a result of a particular experience during the course of their respective ministries become proponents of a faith in redemption *(Erlösungsglaube)*, a redemption which Yahweh himself will accomplish despite Israel's lack of repentance. When eschatological prophecy does arise in the late and post-exilic periods, history is seen as ending with the beginning of the new age. "The eschatological age of salvation proceeds in eternal historylessness."[54] Neither should the term "salvation history" be used in connection with the prophets. They know of no eternal plan or "rigid, minutely determined program," but only of divine intentions which are tied to individual cases and may even be altered or rescinded. Fohrer proposes to speak rather of a "history of decision" since at every point Israel stood before the decision of further apostasy from Yahweh or return to him.[55]

Fohrer's presentation is not without its difficulties. Leaving aside the questions of whether Amos, Isaiah, and Micah really anticipated nothing more than Yahweh's total destruction of his people and of whether later prophecy actually envisioned a future age of "eternal historylessness," the question of the nature of the redemption envisioned by Hosea, Jeremiah, and Ezekiel, and its relationship to (past) history receives insufficient explication. Does this redemption also issue in an age of eternal historylessness? If so, why is this not eschatological prophecy? If not, does the new age then stand in continuity with the former? Fohrer's rejection of salvation history is based on an understanding of the term similar to that advocated by Albrektson, which was criticized above, and the idea of a series of limited divine goals each opposed by human sinfulness. And yet in his concluding remarks Fohrer sees the entirety of the divine activity in history as aimed at a twofold goal, the rule of God and communion with him. Is this not salvation history, the history of God's activity in establishing salvation?

Turning to the question of the role of historical tradition and the word of Yahweh in the prophetic proclamation, von Rad, building on the studies of E. Rohland and H. W. Wolff,[56] maintained that the prophets were "deeply rooted in the religious traditions of their nation" to such an extent that "their whole preaching might almost be described as a unique dialogue with the tradition by means of which the latter was made to speak to their own day."[57] When von Rad speaks of tradition in this context he means primarily those recollections of Yahweh's salvific deeds on behalf of Israel in the early period of her history. The prophets took up these historical traditions to actualize them and apply them to the Israel of their day. In doing this, however, they differed radically from their contemporaries. One need only recall the words of Amos that Israel's election made the coming disaster inevitable (Amos 3:1-2)![58] The common understanding of these traditions was that they contained a guarantee of salvation and prosperity for Israel. But for the prophets they contained no such guarantee. Israel's historical traditions were not a unilateral insurance of salvation, but also entailed a standard for Israel's life, obligations

---

54   "Prophetie und Geschichte," 487-495 = 273-284, quotation col. 494 = p. 283.
55   *ibid.*, 497-498 = 288-291.
56   E. Rohland, *Die Bedeutung der Erwählungstraditionen Israels für die Eschatolologie der alttestamentlichen Propheten*; H. W. Wolff, "Das Thema 'Umkehr' in der alttestamentlichen Prophetie." Von Rad's approach to the prophets as expressed in his *Theology* can also be seen in his own earlier work, cf. e.g. *Der Heilige Krieg,* 50-68.
57   *Theology* II, 177 = *Theologie* [4]II, 183.
58   Cf. *ibid.*, 179 = 185.

and responsibilities which Israel had failed to live up to. The prophets did not arrive at their interpretation of these traditions as a result of their own reflection and contemplation. Rather, Yahweh revealed to them his intent to judge his people on the basis of the traditions themselves. He "enlightened them and led them from one insight to another."[59] According to von Rad "the prophets did not derive their conviction that Yahweh proposed judgment from any special revelation, independent of his saving acts, but from the old saving traditions themselves."[60] Yahweh thus revealed to the prophets the proper understanding of the traditions, from which his intent to judge became apparent.

G. Fohrer has taken exception to von Rad's view.[61] For Fohrer the prophets are "primarily charismatic" and "lay claim to preaching the living word of God as they received it and not to proclaiming a tradition."[62] Revelation of the divine word is thus primary and occurs without recourse to historical traditions. In order to communicate the word which they received, the prophets may draw upon tradition as one way of making their new insight comprehensible to others, but this is only one among several possibilities and does not mean that they are bound to tradition. This becomes especially apparent in the prophetic interpretation of Israel's history in a manner contradictory to tradition.[63] It is not tradition that is decisive for understanding the prophets but rather "the individual experience of the terrifying and merciful presence of God in those moments of secret experiences ... in which the spirit of the word of God came upon them" and "the living impress of the belief of the Mosaic age, which lived anew in them in a more refined and expanded form."[64]

When reviewing the positions of von Rad and Fohrer, several points remain unclear. Von Rad's position seems to require that Israel's historical traditions were in some way involved in the prophetic reception of revelation, yet in his treatment of this subject he nowhere explicitly defines this role.[65] R. Rendtorff, a staunch proponent of von Rad's view,[66] therefore maintains that the words with which the prophets were inspired were in some way connected with the insights gained in the course of their reflection upon the traditions.[67] This, however, is merely asserted, not demonstrated. Fohrer's efforts on this point are no more satisfying since he merely asserts, but does not demonstrate, the opposite, namely that "the traditions and their interpretations do not belong to these fundamental elements but to the secondary stages in the rise of the prophetic word."[68] Subsequent efforts to resolve this issue have focused on the call narratives as affording the best venue into the direct prophetic experience of God. For M.-L. Henry, who considers the uniqueness of the prophets endangered by an overemphasis of tradition and cult in

---

[59] *ibid.*, 177 = 183.

[60] *ibid.*, 186 = 192.

[61] See especially "Remarks on the Modern Interpretation of the Prophets"; "Tradition und Interpretation im Alten Testament"; and "Prophetie und Geschichte."

[62] "Modern Interpretation," 314 = 25.

[63] "Prophetie und Geschichte," 495 = 286: "Ebenso wird die Gesamtgeschichte Israels in einer Tradition widersprechenden Weise umgedeutet."

[64] "Modern Interpretation," 316 = 27.

[65] This criticism has also been raised by J. Vollmer, *Geschichtliche Rückblicke*, 3.

[66] See especially "Tradition und Prophetie."

[67] "Geschichte und Wort," 641 n. 45 = 80 n. 45.

[68] "Modern Interpretation," 316 = 27.

the understanding of them,[69] sees the call experience as the typically prophetic characteristic. The call experience enables the prophet to enter into a direct relationship with God,[70] and also lifts him out of the sphere of cultic security based on the salvation traditions. In his pre-prophetic days the prophet no doubt shared the common conviction that the traditions cultivated in the cult contained a promise of salvation for Israel. This conviction had to be broken if the prophet was to proclaim a message of judgment. Henry does not deny that traditional and cultic elements are present, for example, in Isaiah's call, but these form the "static background" from which the dynamic prophetic traits must be disassociated.[71] In effect the prophetic call experience causes the prophet to break with tradition. R. Knierim, also investigating the call of Isaiah, interprets the event quite differently.[72] Various traditional elements in Isa. 6:1-4 which can be tied to the conception of the divine council and to the Temple-Zion theology serve to communicate to Isaiah the decision of judgment which has been reached in the council. Isaiah is then subsequently called to proclaim this message (v. 8ff). Because the fact of judgment was perceived by Isaiah in the traditional elements, when proclaiming this message "Isaiah was not of the opinion that he had actualized these theological traditions by himself but he would say that they were actualized for him in his vision by Yahwe."[73] But it is not at all clear that, beyond the mere fact that a decision had been made in the divine council, the initial portion of Isaiah's vision also communicated to him that the decision was one of judgment. Neither does Henry's relegation of the traditional and cultic elements to a "static background" seem a proper evaluation of the situation.[74]

An approach similar to that of Henry is pursued by J. Vollmer.[75] He, too, sees the call experience as causing the prophet to break with tradition. In his call the prophet is informed that the salvific implications of the historical traditions are no longer valid. Vollmer goes beyond Henry by employing this view as a means of comprehending the prophetic view of history. He interprets the prophets as viewing Israel's history from its end. This is not meant in any eschatological sense. Rather, the single word of the prophetic message is the annihilation of Israel. This is what the prophet has to proclaim and to ground, and his use of historical traditions is therefore only to illuminate and substantiate this message.[76]

This brings us to a consideration of Fohrer's second decisive factor for comprehending the prophets, "the living impress of the belief of the Mosaic age." Fohrer does not develop this idea, so that one wonders not only what exactly is to be understood under "the living impress of the Mosaic age," but especially how the prophets came to possess it if not through the cultivation and application of the corresponding traditions. The question also arises as to why only the belief of the Mosaic age is of importance. Why should other periods, and practically speaking that means the traditions relating to these periods, not

---

[69]   *Prophet und Tradition*, 2-3.
[70]   *ibid.*, 21.
[71]   *ibid.*, 26, 28.
[72]   "Vocation of Isaiah," 64-67.
[73]   *ibid.*, 67.
[74]   Cf. the criticism of R. Clements, *Prophecy and Tradition*, 37-38.
[75]   *Geschichtliche Rückblicke.*
[76]   For Amos, *ibid.*, 44; for Hosea, *ibid.*, 118-119; for Isaiah, *ibid.*, 129-130.

also have had an influence on certain prophets? Fohrer does not address himself to this issue, which is a decided weakness in his position.

In his recent two-volume work K. Koch has introduced the term "metahistory" into the discussion of an adequate appreciation of the prophets and their conception of the divine activity in history. For the prophets reality is not limited to empirically observable events. Rather, they are also aware of various forces generated by human behavior as well as of active powers in nature and society which derive from God. Metahistory is the explanation of the interaction of these three components (which together comprise suprahistory) as the determining factor behind the course of historical events. Only at the metahistorical level can meaning be discerned in the empirical events of history.[77]

What are the implications of this conception for the issues of concern in the present study? First it should be noted that one of the primary active forces through which Yahweh is at work in history is his word. It is an efficacious word (cf. e.g. Isa. 9:7 [8]; 55:10-11).[78] But how are the prophets aware of the other forces which Yahweh has imparted or which have accrued through human behavior? Here a keen knowledge of Israel's history with Yahweh is indispensable. This history saw not only the establishment of the institutions through which Yahweh imparted certain active forces to Israel, but also Israel's response, its use or abuse of these forces in its conduct. In practice this means a keen knowledge of Israel's historical traditions coupled with an astute perception of Israel's current condition. Thus, the question whether word *or* historical tradition is the primary feature of the prophetic proclamation becomes a false alternative. "Two parallel fields of experience provide the foundation for their preaching: their secret (extra-sensory) experience of visions and spoken messages ... and ... the general experience of the Israelites in their own history."[79] Both are integral to the message of the prophet for his particular moment in history.

C. HISTORY IN HOSEA

From the foregoing review of the history of research it is apparent that with respect to the prophets some fundamental questions remain open. Can one legitimately speak of salvation history in connection with the prophets, and, if so, in what sense? What is the relationship between past and present history and the future envisioned by the prophets? Is it one of continuity or discontinuity? How is the prophetic use of historical tradition to be evaluated? Is it integral to a proper understanding of the prophets, or do these traditions constitute nothing more than one among several sources of illustrative material? Research must be open to the possibility that these questions must be answered differently for different prophets. We have chosen to consider Hosea. In his prophecies Hosea makes particularly extensive reference to history, and this large body of relevant material promises to facilitate the investigation and provide it with a broad foundation.

---

[77]   *The Prophets* I, 4-5 and esp. 70-74 = *Die Profeten* I, 14-15, 82-85.

[78]   *ibid.*, 71 = 82.

[79]   *The Prophets* II, 194 = *Die Profeten* II, 197.

1. Previous Research

Modern research into Hosea's relationship to and use of historical traditions may reasonably he said to begin with the study of Hosea by O. Procksch.[80] For Procksch Hosea's entire proclamation, and therefore also his view of history, is dominated by his marriage experience. Despite his wife's infidelity, Hosea continued to love her and brought her hack to himself. This experience of his love for Gomer despite her adultery revealed to Hosea the love of Yahweh for his people Israel and convinced Hosea that, just as he could not completely reject Gomer, neither would Yahweh completely reject Israel. Yahweh's love would cause him to bring his apostate people back to himself. Because of the centrality of the concept of the love of God for Hosea, he is not so much interested in the external course of Israel's history, where the parallel to his own experience was at best limited, but rather in the internal development of Israel in its relationship with Yahweh. This is Hosea's concern when contemplating Israel's historical traditions.[81] These he knew from the first edition of the Elohistic source (E[1]), probably already in written form.[82] This conclusion rests of course on a view of the Hexateuchal sources which has since been abandoned, but also in part on the reconstruction of the corresponding sections of E[1] on the basis of Hosea.[83]

Procksch's basic analysis of the motivating factors underlying Hosea's use of historical tradition found general acceptance. In his study on "The Historical Orientation of the Prophecy of Hosea," E. Sellin accepted Procksch's view that Hosea was dependent on E[1], which Sellin thought to extend through 2 Kings.[84] He therefore sought to explain various difficult passages in Hosea which had been held to allude to contemporary events by combing this source for historical traditions of the more distant past to which Hosea could be referring. In this attempt Sellin has found little following.

J. Rieger also shared Procksch's view that Hosea's perception of the love of Cod stemming from his marriage to Gomer was central to Hosea's prophecy. It formed the bridge between Hosea's conception of the past and future and led to a certain periodization of history in Hosea's thinking.[85] Rieger differs from Procksch at two points. Unlike Procksch he emphasizes the general course of world history as another motivating factor in Hosea's use of historical tradition. Current events in Hosea's day were anything but favorable for Israel and seemed to stand in contradiction to Yahweh's love for Israel. Hosea therefore took refuge in the traditions of the early period when Yahweh's care for Israel was more evident and projected them into the future.[86] Rieger also sees Hosea as dependent upon oral tradition for his knowledge of Israel's early history. He questions the validity of the division of the Elohistic source into two strands or editions and is less inclined to fill in the gaps in this source from Hosea.

---

[80] *Geschichtsbetrachtung und geschichtliche Überlieferung bei den vorexilischen Propheten.*
[81] *ibid.*, 14-19.
[82] *ibid.*, 118-134.
[83] Cf. e.g. the reconstruction of Gen. 32:25ff, *ibid.*, 119-120.
[84] "Geschichtliche Orientierung," 650.
[85] *Bedeutung der Geschichte,* 100-106.
[86] *ibid.*, 87-90.

Common to all these investigations is the underlying conception that Hosea's use of historical traditions is ancillary to a more fundamental message, namely the basic love of Yahweh for his people. Not even Sellin moves consciously beyond this point. Yet in his presentation a certain tension is perceptible. On the one hand, Hosea is immersed in the history of his people right down to his own day (or at least until the massacre at Jezreel, Hos. 1:4). On the other hand, Sellin cannot help but notice that in passages where Israel's pre-settlement history is treated (11:1ff; 13:4ff) the present sin of Israel seems to recede into the background "as if in the meantime absolutely no history with completely new sins had occurred."[87] Sellin later interprets this fact as indicating that Hosea sees in the present merely a repetition of sins already attested in the earliest history of Israel,[88] depriving an otherwise perceptive observation of any particular meaning. History is still relegated to the role of merely illustrating Israel's repeated sin.[89]

At this point specific work on Hosea gave way for the most part to the more general discussion inaugurated by von Rad, which has been briefly sketched above.[90] In von Rad's own treatment of Hosea the traditions held to be fundamental to Hosea's preaching are those of the old saving history,[91] by which he presumably means those traditions referred to in the historical confessions. He is not specific on this point, but his discussion of Hosea certainly suggests this. Similarly, H. W. Wolff's high evaluation of the role of history in the prophets also found expression in his Hosea commentary,[92] whereas history receives no special emphasis in the commentary of Rudolph, who focuses rather on the decalogue, especially the first commandment, to understand the prophet.[93]

J. Vollmer subsequently reexamined the use of history made by Amos, Hosea, and Isaiah in light of the more general discussion and took a stance, part of which has already been noted,[94] based on Fohrer's argumentation and emphasizing Hosea's discontinuity with tradition. Hosea does not merely reinterpret or actualize the traditions; he declares them null and void.[95] It will be recalled that the further course of the discussion of the prophetic use of historical tradition had centered on the call narratives. This concentration on the call reports is not without its problems. One suspects that occasionally sight is lost of the fact that the prophet's call was only one among many occasions on which the word of Yahweh came to the prophet, leading to attempts to account for all the various aspects of a prophet's proclamation solely on the basis of his call.[96] For Hosea it may be pointed out that no call narrative has been preserved. Vollmer is well aware of this and so interprets the report of Hosea's marriage to Gomer in Hos. 1 as taking the place of a call

[87] "Geschichtliche Orientierung," 619.
[88] ibid., 649.
[89] Cf. the similar evaluation of these traditions as "Anschauungsmaterial" by Rieger, Bedeutung der Geschichte, 114. This is also essentially the position of M. Köckert ("Hoseabuch," 26) who maintains that Hosea is interested in unique historical events only to the extent that they reflect behavior typical of Israel.
[90] See above pp. 7-11.
[91] Theology II, 138-146, esp. p. 140 = Theologie [4]II, 145-153, 147.
[92] Hosea, XIX-XXIII; cf. idem, "Understanding of History." Wolff also associated Hosea with postulated prophetic-levitic opposition circles as the tradents of the traditions drawn upon by Hosea, cf. idem, "Hoseas geistige Heimat," and Hosea, XIV.
[93] Hosea, 254-260.
[94] See above p. 10.
[95] Geschichtliche Rückblicke, 119-124.
[96] Cf. the attempt of R. Knierim, "Vocation of Isaiah," 64-67.

narrative. Yet even so he concentrates on the name "Not my people" as declaring the election tradition null and void and neglects the other events reported in the chapter.[97] Vollmer is also aware that Hosea proclaimed not only judgment but also redemption. This fact in and of itself precludes an understanding of the proclamation of Hosea solely on the basis of his supposed "call" experience. Vollmer consequently divides Hosea's ministry into two periods. At first he proclaimed a judgment of destruction, later a judgment of purification.[98] This reorientation came about as the result of the reception of a new word of Yahweh. Here the revelatory event is conceived of as communicating merely the fact of purification through judgment, whereas it is left up to the prophet to express this message as he chooses. It should also be noted that this conception of the word of Yahweh necessitates that Hosea's prophecies be grouped chronologically according to content. Those announcing a judgment of purification must belong to the latter period of Hosea's ministry.[99] But as the examination of the redaction history of the book will make clear, these prophecies are not to be assigned to a single period.[100] Vollmer's presentation thus proves to be inadequate in accounting for the fact that disaster and salvation occur side by side in Hosea's proclamation throughout his ministry.

It will also be recalled that in the presentation of his position Fohrer failed to specify what exactly he meant by the "living impress of the Mosaic age" and how this was cultivated if not by means of the appropriate traditions. It is revealing that in his defense of Fohrer's position Vollmer also fails to elaborate these points. As we have seen, Fohrer's interpretation requires an absolute prophetic freedom over against tradition. Are the questions raised by the "living impress" thereby rendered irrelevant, or merely discomforting? The question of the probable form of the traditions known to the prophets also becomes in large part unimportant, and Vollmer feels justified in dispensing with this issue.[101] In his treatment of Hosea he assumes that the prophet knew the Elohistic source in its present form.[102] But the freedom of a prophet over against tradition can only be established after an examination of the probable form in which he knew the traditions, so that Vollmer's failure to treat the issue is a decided weakness.

The same must be said even more emphatically of the study by H.-D. Neef. Especially with regard to Jacob (Hos. 12), Neef not only presupposes that Hosea knew the corresponding Genesis accounts, he also refers to them to clarify uncertainties in Hosea's meaning, which in turn requires that the sources J and E already existed in fixed form.[103] This supposition also requires that Hosea's positive view of the wilderness period be explained as a reinterpretation of the divine self-revelation at Sinai.[104] But this

---

[97]   *Geschichtliche Rückblicke,* 119.

[98]   In this conception Vollmer follows in part G. Fohrer, "Umkehr und Erlösung," who sees three periods in the preaching of Hosea: 1) unconditional destruction; 2) repentance as a possible means of averting destruction; and 3) redemption solely on the basis of the divine initiative.

[99]   According to G. Fohrer, "Umkehr und Erlösung," 177-181 = 235-239, these include Hos. 12:10 (9); 3:1-5; and the various units in 2:16-25 (14-23).

[100] See below pp. 23-31, esp. 24-29; cf. also D. Kinet, "Eschatologische Perspektiven," 53-55.

[101] *Geschichtliche Rückblicke,* 6.

[102] See, for example, *ibid.,* 82.

[103] H.-D. Neef, *Heilstraditionen,* 35-47, 232-233.

[104] *ibid.,* 113-119, following H. Gese, "Bemerkungen zur Sinaitradition," 146-149 = 40-43.

interpretation is itself problematic and fails to resolve the entire issue.[105] Unlike Vollmer, however, Neef emphasizes Hosea's complete continuity with the traditions he draws upon. He neither annuls them nor reinterprets them, but continues to see in them salvation traditions in which Yahweh's nature is clearly depicted. Thus for Neef the continuity is grounded in the constancy of the divine essence as one of love and care.[106]

From this brief sketch it is quite apparent that no general consensus on the issues listed at the beginning of this section has been reached for the prophet Hosea. The applicability of the term "salvation history" has not been discussed explicitly in the more recent works on Hosea, and so it will be profitable to take a specific look at this question. Neither has the continuity-discontinuity debate on the prophetic eschatology been resolved. As we have seen, the problem has been approached in terms of the role of historical tradition in the prophetic experience. Attempts to clarify this point have revolved around the question of whether tradition is a primary or secondary feature. In the wake of Fohrer's remarks these terms have been understood chronologically, which has usually led the search for an answer into the realm of the prophetic reception of the word of Yahweh. A satisfactory solution under these conditions would require the reconstruction of both the phenomenon of revelation as experienced by the prophets and the formulation of the content of revelation. But the available resources do not permit such a comprehensive reconstruction. It is therefore necessary to take the discussion out of the realm of the "secret experiences" of the prophets, which have indeed remained a secret as far as the mechanics are concerned, and to focus strictly on the issue of whether historical traditions are a primary feature of the prophetic proclamation, in the present case of Hosea's proclamation. Here we are on firmer ground. This approach is also more in keeping with the prophets' own understanding of their proclamation not as a derivative explanation or elaboration of a more basic and succinct divine word,[107] but as the very word of Yahweh itself. The prophet proclaims the word of Yahweh. This simple statement, however, implies that if historical tradition is a primary feature in the prophetic proclamation, it is also a primary feature of the word of Yahweh as comprehended by the prophet, and recourse to the call narratives becomes unnecessary. The term "primary," therefore, should not be taken in a chronological sense, but rather in the sense of fundamental to the proper understanding of the prophetic message. In this way it will also be possible to examine Koch's understanding of the prophetic argumentation in terms of metahistory. The task therefore becomes to demonstrate that historical tradition forms an integral component of Hosea's proclamation.

How is such a demonstration to be undertaken? It would seem that the most promising approach is to evaluate the role played by historical traditions in shaping both a prophet's underlying conception of Israel's history and his appraisal of the Israel of his own day. In this connection it is not a question of individual references to historical tradition taken in isolation, a procedure not uncommon in the literature, but of their synthesis into a coherent whole in order to discern the foundation of prophetic thought. Of course, it must not be assumed that every prophet shared exactly the same conception of the sweep of history, and so the investigation must adapt itself to the prophet under

---

[105] See below p. 59.

[106] *Heilstraditionen*, 249-255.

[107] This is required by the view advocated by Fohrer and followed by Vollmer, see above pp. 7-8, 10, 13-14. But it is highly questionable whether such a neat distinction can be made.

consideration and the traditions he draws upon. Since Hosea is a prophet from and to the
northern kingdom, his prophecies are free from the influence of traditions concerning
David and Zion. If there was a special royal ideology in the north, which would seem *a
priori* likely, it does not find specific expression in Hosea's proclamation.[108] The
investigation therefore need not be complicated by the need to reckon with influences
from conceivably competing strands of tradition but can concentrate on the traditions of
the early history of Israel.

2. Hosea and Pentateuchal Studies

Research into the origins of the Pentateuch is currently in a state of flux, to put it
charitably. Whereas fifteen years ago the Yahwist was for the most part living comfortably
in his Solomonic or early post-Solomonic home, today he may find himself residing
anywhere from an early monarchic villa to a late exilic or post-exilic condominium. Some
would even deny his very existence. This is not the place for an exhaustive discussion of
the issues and arguments involved, but a look at a few of the more recent major works
in this field is appropriate.

In his book *Der sogenannte Jahwist*, H. H. Schmid advances the thesis that the work
of the Yahwist is to be placed in the general vicinity of the deuteronom(ist)ic work. He
pursues basically two lines of reasoning. First, upon examining a sampling of Yahwistic
passages Schmid finds a basic similarity in theological outlook with the deuteronomistic
corpus. Thus, for example, he sees the basic framework of the book of Judges --
disobedience, tribulation, cry of the people, deliverance -- reflected in the call of Moses
(Ex. 3:7ff) and recurring again in the passages recounting the murmurings of the people
in the wilderness, and seeks to support this structural argument by pointing to similarities
in language.[109] But the structural parallels are not always exact, and the possibility that
both J and Dtr adopted and adapted the general pattern from a common setting within
Israel's cultic or legal institutions is hardly given serious attention. The language also can
rarely be shown to be exclusive to J and Dtr, and where this is likely there is no attempt
to deal with the possibility that the deuteronom(ist)ic phraseology developed over a period
of time.[110] This becomes particularly problematic when the "deuteronom(ist)ic" parallels are
found outside of Deuteronomy. With respect to the Sinai pericope Schmid argues similarly,
though here the efforts to demonstrate similarity of language recede noticeably. The major
burden therefore lies on the structural similarity. The Yahwistic version of the Sinai events
encompasses theophany, law, promise, obligation and the conclusion of a covenant. This
same conception is found in Dtr and, since Schmid subscribes to Perlitt's thesis that this
covenant theology is a deuteronomistic construct,[111] J cannot be dated significantly earlier.

---

[108]   In his stimulating article "Gott und Geschichte im Alten Testament," J. Jeremias gives the impression that,
        in contrast to the Judean view of kingship as a means of realizing divine blessings for people and land,
        Israel saw in the same institution only a danger to its life and faith. However, if we possessed a
        representative sample of northern royal psalms, the northern attitude towards kingship would no doubt
        appear less one sided.

[109]   H. H. Schmid, *Der sogenannte Jahwist,* 24-41, 61-82.

[110]   Cf. the criticism of G. Wallis, review of H. H. Schmid, Der sogenannte Jahwist, 24, on this point.

[111]   L. Perlitt, *Bundestheologie im Alten Testament.*

It should be clear that Schmid's argumentation for the Sinai pericope stands and falls with the validity of Perlitt's thesis.[112]

Secondly, Schmid compares the selected passages of the Yahwist with the classical prophets. His basic position is that the Yahwist seems to presuppose the work of Isaiah and that the pre-exilic prophets are better understood within the context of the flow of tradition leading up to the Yahwist than subsequent to him. In support of the first point Schmid notes the common usage of the term "believe" in Ex. 4 and Isa. 7:9 and compares the problem of the hardening of the heart of pharaoh with Isaiah's commission in Isa. 6.[113] On the broader question of the relation to pre-exilic prophecy, Schmid argues that the integrated theological reflection on the various periods of history and the concomitant "canonical" view of Israel's early history evidenced by the Yahwist is lacking in the pre-exilic prophets and is first found in deuteronom(ist)ic thought.[114] Also, in contrast to eighth-century prophecy, in which the prophet pronounces his message as absolute and unavoidable, the Yahwist presents Moses as a prophet who offers pharaoh an alternative and hence a choice. But this view of prophecy first becomes prominent with Jeremiah, again suggesting a later date for the Yahwist.[115]

J. van Seters also argues for a much later dating of the Yahwist, but whereas Schmid still allows for a previous oral stage, van Seters dismisses this possibility. In his study of the Abraham traditions[116] he argues that there is little evidence of a long history of oral transmission lying behind the traditions. He sees rather a literary process of growth which at any stage could have incorporated folkloristic forms and motifs since these were no doubt current throughout Israel's history. Also, it is a linear literary process, with subsequent stages supplementing and reworking previous ones rather than originally separate sources being combined. For the Abraham traditions van Seters reckons with two pre-Yahwistic stages, the second being utilized by the Yahwist for his presentation of Abraham. The promises of land and numerous descendants have been influenced by royal ideology and are best understood as addressing the hopes and needs of an exilic community yearning to return to and repopulate their land.[117] The Yahwist's work in turn was utilized and redacted by the priestly writer.

It should be pointed out, however, that van Seter's view of the process of growth as entirely literary results as much, if not more, from his presuppositions than from an examination of the texts. In his methodological guidelines he notes that Israel was a literate society and hence the scribal tradition would depend on written documents rather than on oral transmission for the preservation of tradition. He rejects the idea that the various literary strands of the Pentateuch were all dependent on a fixed body of oral tradition and yet composed independently of one another. Rather, "it is much more reasonable to assume that each successive stage of the literary development had access to

---

[112] Schmid himself recognizes Perlitt's thesis as being "von einschneidender Bedeutung" (p. 85) for his argument.

[113] *Der sogenannte Jahwist*, 38-41, 49.

[114] *ibid.*, 31.

[115] *ibid.*, 44-48, cf. also pp. 154-166.

[116] For what follows see J. van Seters, *Abraham in History and Tradition*, especially his conclusions pp. 309-313.

[117] *ibid.*, 269-278.

the previous scribal tradition."[118] This in effect assumes a unilinear and literary development which then becomes the basic operational assumption for the ensuing examination of the texts. It therefore comes as no surprise when this working assumption is "confirmed" in the conclusion.[119] Van Seters' position also envisions a unified scribal tradition throughout Israel, a conception which is better demonstrated than assumed.

In his subsequent book van Seters addresses the broader issue of history writing in Israel, in particular the relationship of his exilic Yahwist and post-exilic priestly redaction to the Deuteronomistic history.[120] Here, too, he subscribes to the same basic model. The Deuteronomistic history was written first. It was then taken up and utilized by the Yahwist in the late exilic period when he set out to write the history of Israel beginning with creation. He therefore only had to make a few additions to the book of Joshua to connect his own work with the Deuteronomistic history, Josh. 24 being his last composition. This work was later redacted and expanded by P, whose last addition is to be found in Judg. 1:1-2:5.

But here again van Seters arrives at his conclusion before examining a single text. He notes that the priestly writer is increasingly viewed as an author and redactor supplementing the earlier Pentateuchal sources and that some scholars now argue for a late date for the Yahwist, perhaps even a post-Dtr date. He then concludes that "to accept these changes would mean to acknowledge that Deuteronomy and the Dtr history were written first. The Yahwist and the Priestly Writer looked upon the conquest as portrayed in Joshua as the fulfillment of their land promise theme, and thus composed the rest of the Pentateuch (the Tetrateuch) in two stages as additions to the earlier history."[121] Not only has the further course of the discussion been predisposed, it has been done by means of a *non sequitur*. Even if for the sake of argument both protases be admitted, it does not follow that the Yahwist knew and supplemented Dtr. The possibility of roughly contemporaneous and yet independent works has been completely overlooked (due to the "guidelines" set forth in his previous book?). When van Seters does turn to the texts, his treatment is quite brief. The crucial passage in his presentation is the story of Rahab and the Israelite spies related in Josh. 2, to which van Seters devotes a single, half-page paragraph. He states that there are "many internal problems," none of which he specifies or treats, choosing instead to focus on the chronological problem which the story as a whole presents in its present context (the three days mentioned in Josh. 1:11; 3:2 he considers insufficient time for the expedition) and the fact that when Jericho is finally taken the intelligence gathered by the spies plays no role. To explain these factors as reflecting an originally independent tradition is "highly speculative and forced" because Dtr would certainly have done a better job of integrating the narrative into his chronological scheme. The chapter must therefore be a secondary literary addition. The references to the Red Sea and the defeat of Sihon and Og indicate that the story is the work of the Yahwist who "contrived" the piece for theological reasons. Van Seters then states his second principle: "if Pentateuchal sources are to be found in Joshua, whether J or P, they are all secondary additions made directly onto the original Dtr work."[122] The choice of

---

[118] *ibid.*, 164.
[119] *ibid.*, 309-312.
[120] *In Search of History,* esp. 324-342.
[121] *ibid.*, 323.
[122] *ibid.*, 325.

vocabulary is revealing: it is a principle that is being applied rather than a conclusion that is being drawn. Also, a connection with the Yahwist is less than obvious. Rahab says that Yahweh "dried up" (הוביש, v. 10) the waters of the Red Sea, an expression not found in Ex. 14. Similarly, the statement that Israel utterly destroyed Sihon and Og in the ban (hiphil of חרם) is also found in Deut. 2:34; 3:6, but not in Num. 21:21-35 (cf. however 21:1-3). And finally, it is dubious procedure to attribute to the Yahwist a chronological blunder of his own contrivance.

A rather different approach is advocated by R. Rendtorff. Whereas Schmid and van Seters both still operate with a Yahwistic source, Rendtorff calls into question the existence of such a source and indeed questions the validity of the documentary hypothesis itself. He argues that although the existence of sources as envisioned by the classical documentary hypothesis is not necessarily incompatible with the tradition-historical approach to the problem, neither is it a necessary stage in the development. The tradition-historical approach begins with the "smallest units" of tradition and traces the process by which these smallest units coalesce into larger units and complexes of tradition. Only when at some stage in the development an overarching redaction of these larger units or complexes spanning the entire Pentateuch can be demonstrated is it legitimate to speak of a source (or sources should more than one such redaction be shown) in the sense of the documentary hypothesis.[123] Rendtorff then turns to an examination of the patriarchal narratives as an example of the growth of a larger complex. His examination focuses largely or, the promises to the patriarchs, and he sees various stages and layers of growth.[124] However, in a cursory glance at the other larger units he finds little evidence of correspondence with the reworking(s) of the patriarchal narratives.[125] It is not until relatively late that a group of "deuteronomically stamped" texts (Gen. 50:24; Ex. 33:1-3a) are added to connect the larger units with one another to form a comprehensive presentation.[126]

It must be said, however, that this is certainly a small "group" to perform such a monumental task. Rendtorff discusses a series of other texts, but it is not clear in every instance which, if any, are to be assigned to the same revisional layer as Gen. 50:24; Ex. 33:1-3a. His summary suggests that none are to be so assigned since only Gen. 50:24 and Ex. 33:1-3a are said to bind together the patriarchal narratives with the traditions recounting Israel's journey from Egypt into the promised land.[127] Also, whereas on the basis of his methodological considerations the argumentation seems to require that only with the "deureronomistically stamped" revision were all the larger units of the Pentateuch combined, Rendtorff later considers it possible that this revision only interpreted a Pentateuch which was otherwise in all its essentials already completed.[128] Regarding the date of this deuteronomically stamped revision Rendtorff is rather hesitant given the current lack of criteria for differentiating within the larger realm of what is often nebulously termed "deuteronomistic." As a possible means out of this dilemma and in any case a fact to be reckoned with is the "silence" of the pre-exilic literature where the

---

[123] R. Rendtorff, *Das überlieferungsgeschichtliche Problem des Pentateuch,* 2-28, esp. p. 18; cf. also pp. 75-79.
[124] *ibid.,* 29-65.
[125] *ibid.,* 65-75.
[126] *ibid.,* 75-79.
[127] *ibid.,* 79.
[128] *ibid.,* 164. Rendtorff has since abandoned this possibility in his *Einführung,* 171-173.

themes of the Pentateuch are concerned.[129] This would suggest a late date. As has been seen, Schmid also draws upon this argument,[130] and van Seters also recognizes its importance.[131] Curiously enough, Hosea has not been consulted in this regard, and this is a serious deficiency.

Rendtorff's approach has recently been taken up by E. Blum.[132] Beginning with the Jacob tradition, he finds three early traditions in the conflict between Jacob and Esau (Gen. 25:21ff*; 27*), Jacob's dream at Bethel (Gen. 28:11ff*), and the contract between Jacob and Laban (Gen. 35:45ff). These coalesced into a Jacob-Esau-Laban story, which was subsequently supplemented by a compositional layer (Gen. 27:40b; 28:10-22*; 29f; 31; 32f) yielding a Jacob narrative (Gen. 25:21ff*; 27-33*). This occurred in the northern kingdom under Jeroboam I.[133] This narrative was in turn expanded and combined with an early version of the Joseph story, also in the northern kingdom, to produce a history of the life of Jacob.[134] This history of Jacob wandered to Judah following the fall of Samaria and was there combined with the Judean Abraham-Lot story sometime prior to the fall of Jerusalem. This initial patriarchal history (*Vätergeschichte 1* = Vg[1]) was reworked during the Exile to underscore and expand the patriarchal promises and the commands to leave Mesopotamia or Egypt and not to settle or return there. This second patriarchal history (*Vätergeschichte 2* = Vg[2]) contained no literary connections with the other pentateuchal traditions.[135] Such connections were first created by the Deuteronomistic redaction which took place in the last third of the sixth century BC[136] This Deuteronomistic edition of the patriarchal history also underwent further redactions, the most important being the priestly layer comprised of El-Shaddai texts and the Toledot framework.

For all their differences in approach and results,[137] the trends represented by these scholars have at least one thing in common: there was no continuous presentation of the early history of Israel prior to the late seventh century BC. This date, of course, is a good hundred years later than the period of Hosea's prophetic ministry, and so the reconstruction of his conception of Israel's history may provide an independent means of examining the validity of these views. Does Hosea's view of Israel's early history indicate that the traditions he drew upon constituted part of a continuous presentation, or does it rather suggest that no such account had yet been formed?

When examining Hosea's relationship to these traditions it will naturally be helpful if not only the general traditions which he used can be determined, but also if information can be gleaned concerning the form in which he knew them. The investigation will therefore also seek to deduce such information where possible. Our efforts in this regard

---

129   *Überlieferungsgeschichtliches Problem,* 169-173.
130   See above p. 17.
131   *Abraham,* 3; cf. also *idem,* "Confessional Reformulation in the Exilic Period," where, however, Jeremiah is the earliest prophet considered.
132   *Die Komposition der Vätergeschichte.*
133   Cf. the summary *ibid.,* 202-203.
134   Cf. the summary *ibid.,* 258-261.
135   Cf. *ibid.,* 339, 345-346, 359-361.
136   *ibid.,* 392-393, 396.
137   Besides the works already cited see the exchange of views in *JSOT* 3 (1977), as well as R. Rendtorff, "Traditio-Historical Method and the Documentary Hypothesis"; J. van Seters, "Recent Studies on the Pentateuch: A Crisis in Method"; and H. H. Schmid, "Auf der Suche nach neuen Perspektiven für die Pentateuchforschung."

may at times appear somewhat speculative, but that is because we have tried to avoid the temptation of merely assuming that Hosea knew the traditions in exactly the same form as we now possess them, As we have seen, this question has in essence remained dormant for more than half a century, much to the detriment of more recent studies which have neglected it. This methodological consideration is also not without significance for testing the extent of the prophet's freedom *vis-à-vis* tradition.

3. The Format of the Investigation

The exegetical portion of the study proceeds for the most part as follows. After the *Translation* of the text with accompanying *Textual Notes* there follows a section on *Form*. Here the isolation of the original unit offered in translation is discussed, its genre examined, and questions of literary criticism treated. There then comes a *Comment* in which each passage has been treated in its entirety, the exegesis generally proceeding line by line. Treatments of individual verses or short passages, be they undertaken for schematic or thematic purposes, can be helpful in clarifying particular details of interpretation and therefore are not without a certain justification. But one is often left wondering how the particular view offered fits within the total context and flow of the unit as a whole. This is particularly true of treatments of the Jacob problematic in Hos. 12, to name a specific example. It is questionable, however, whether one can penetrate to the function of these traditions within Hosea's proclamation when they are treated on the basis of a quick summary of the general tenor of the passage. The entire unit must be thoroughly analyzed. In a final section the *Results* of the exegesis for Hosea's conception of Israel's history and his relationship to tradition are examined.

The selection of passages treated has been confined to explicit references to historical tradition in the interest of establishing a firm foundation. Hosea may be alluding to such traditions in passages not considered in the present study, but the degree of certainty in such instances in necessarily diminished. Such suppositions will have to be tested against the general picture developed on the basis of Hosea's explicit allusions and is a task for further research.

CHAPTER 2

GROWTH AND DEVELOPMENT OF THE BOOK OF HOSEA

The aim of the current investigation is to examine Hosea's use of and relationship to Israel's early traditions concerning her origins and her entry into the land. With this as our stated goal the question arises as to the means by which it is possible to reconstruct and to interpret Hosea's message. Of course, the obvious answer is that this must be undertaken on the basis of the prophecies preserved in the book which bears his name. But it is here that the methodological questions really begin. Aside from the question of "authenticity," which must be examined for each passage, there is also the question of the collection and redaction of the various prophecies proclaimed by Hosea in the course of his prophetic activity, which spanned the three decades from the latter part of the reign of Jeroboam II (*ca.* 755; cf. 1:1, 4) to the beginning of the siege of Samaria (*ca.* 725/24; cf. 13:9-10). How is this redactional process to be conceived and what are the consequences of this conception for interpretation?

The final form of the book of Hosea is a Judean product intended for Judean readers. This can be deduced from two factors. First, although Hosea was most likely a citizen of the northern kingdom and his prophetic preaching was concerned predominately with his own nation, the superscript in 1:1 indicates the period of Hosea's activity by naming the Judean kings who ruled during this time. Of the corresponding Israelite kings only Jeroboam II is mentioned. Second, a series of Judean additions have been scattered throughout the book. These are not without a certain basis in Hosea's proclamation which itself occasionally encompassed Judah (2:2 [1:11]; 4:15; 5:10, 12, 13, 14; 6:4). The additions themselves are easily recognizable. They derive from various periods and are with a few exceptions only loosely integrated into their respective contexts. Thus, 1:7 contains a promise that Yahweh will deliver Judah miraculously without any of the accoutrements of war and probably refers to the deliverance of Jerusalem in 701 BC. On the other hand, 5:5bß; 6:11a; 8:14aß; 10:11[1] reflect negatively upon Judah. Hos. 5:5bß states that Judah, too, has stumbled and so probably looks back on the fall of Jerusalem in 587 BC. This may also be the case for 6:11a, although if the perfect נטע is understood in the sense "has set," then the verse may be understood as anticipating the fall of Judah. A pre-exilic date would then be indicated. The dating of 8:14aß and 10:11* is particularly difficult since it cannot even be said with confidence whether or not they presuppose the existence of Judah as a state. Still, they are perhaps best understood against this background. Then there is the unique substitution of "Judah" for an original "Israel" in 12:3 (2).[2] This

---

[1]   The extent of the addition is uncertain here. It is either limited to "Judah," in which case Ephraim is harnessed so that he may plow, or it includes "Judah must plow." The balance of the bicolon is better served by the first possibility.

[2]   See below p. 34, textual note 3b. Whether 12:1b (11:12b) is Hoseanic or not is difficult to decide with any degree of confidence given the uncertainties, with regard to both text and content, which plague the verse. However, it can be said that the text probably presupposes the Judean state and so is most likely pre-exilic.

substitution is also most comprehensible if the southern kingdom still stands. Even a quick perusal of the passages cited[3] suffices to show that none of them has substantially affected the overall shape of the book.[4] This has led most scholars to conclude that the book was already completed prior to the Judean actualizations of its various parts.[5] If this inference is correct, then the book must have received its essential shape sometime between 722, when in the face of the Assyrian onslaught some of Hosea's disciples, and perhaps even Hosea himself, sought refuge in the south, and 701, when the first Judean addition was inserted.

The book of Hosea itself falls naturally into three sections: chapters 1-3; 4-11; and 12-14.[6] It has long been recognized that Hos. 1-3 belong together. Here and only here does Hosea's family life play an explicit, indeed dominating role. Hos. 4-11 likewise form a separate collection of oracles, as indicated by the new beginning in 4:1-3, an oracle with superscript character for the ensuing chapters, and the concluding formula נאם יהוה "utterance of Yahweh" at the end of Hos. 11.[7] The chapters 12-14 are then left and may be taken as a third collection.

The first collection, Hos. 1-3, has been the object of much recent study. B. Renaud argues for three originally independent units of Hoseanic material encompassing a) 1:2b*-4 (Gomer and children not being "of harlotry"), 6, 8-9; b) 3:1a, 2, 3a, 4; and c) 2:4-7, 10-15. His listing of the material in this order suggests an initial collection having this format, but he is not specific on this point. The material next underwent a deuteronomistic redaction which identified Gomer and Hosea's children with the harlotrous woman and children of 2:4ff and hence is responsible for the present form of 1:2. This redaction also identified the woman of Hos. 3 with Gomer and hence arranged the material in its present sequence to reflect its understanding of Hosea's marital life. The עוד "again" of 3:1 derives from this redaction, along with 3:1b, 3b, 5* (save "and David their king"). The last sentence of 1:4 also stems from this redaction. This edition in turn underwent a priestly redaction which supplied the remainder of these chapters and is responsible for their current form.[8]

L. Ruppert envisions a similar, though somewhat more complex redactional process.[9] A core unit 2:4-7, 10-15, itself composed of two originally independent units redactionally combined by 2:11b, was subsequently expanded by Hosea who added first 2:8-9, 16, 17b,

---

3   Mention should also be made of the reference to "David their king" in 3:5 which, since it conflicts with Hosea's attitude to kingship in Israel (see below p. 74 n. 136 and p. 119), is also most likely a Judean addition.

4   Scholars who reckon with a more extensive Judean redaction will not subscribe to this view. (Jeremias is an exception; see next note.) Since these studies are either limited to Hos. 1-3 (Ruppert; Renaud) or are based in large measure on the results obtained in these chapters (Yee), they shall be dealt with in that context.

5   Wolff, XXVI-XXVII; Rudolph, 26-27; Mays, 16-17; Jeremias, 18.

6   On the basis of essentially the same arguments as follow, the same overall division has been advocated by Wolff, Rudolph, Mays, and Jeremias; cf. also G. A. Yee, Composition, 51.

7   E. M. Good ("Composition," 27, 48-49) fails to ascribe sufficient importance to this formula and so considers Hos. 4-14 to be a single composition (cf. also Andersen-Freedman, 57-59). His view that in Hos. 2 this formula never marks the conclusion of an oracle is mistaken and results largely from his refusal to take form-critical arguments seriously (ibid., 26).

8   B. Renaud, "Le Livret d'Osée 1-3"; cf. also idem, "Osée 1-3."

9   L. Ruppert, "Beobachtungen zur Literar- und Kompositionskritik von Hosea 1-3"; and "Erwägungen zur Kompositions- und Redaktionsgeschichte von Hosea 1-3."

17a, 19; then transposed v. 17 to accommodate v. 18aßb and appended v. 21-22 to v. 19; and finally added v. 23aß-24. Exactly why this composition occurred in stages rather than all at once is not stated. Shortly after 733 the material was redacted by Hosea's disciples who composed 1:2abα* (Gomer and children not "of harlotry"), 3-4, 6abα*, 8-9 and 2:25* (save "in the land"). Levitic circles in Judah around 620 added the harlotry to 1:2, also adding 1:5b and 1:7. They were also in possession of Hos. 3:1a, bαγ, 2-4. Identifying this woman with Gomer, they added עוד "again" and ומנאפת "and adulterous" to v. 1 and composed 3:5abα; 2:1b, 2b to conclude their collection. The final redaction, which added the remainder of the material and gave the composition its current shape, took place in Judah during the exile.

The recent publication of G. A. Yee[10] seeks to delineate the redactional history of the entire book of Hosea, but since the results for chapters 4-14 depend on those obtained for chapters 1-3, we examine them here. If I understand Yee correctly, it all began with a *single* oracle of Hosea which can be traced from 2:4aα through 14:1 (!)[11] and was delivered during the Syro-Ephraimite war.[12] This oracle was written down by a "collector, who was probably a disciple of Hosea,"[13] sometime after the fall of Samaria in 722.[14] His work is limited to 1:2-4, 6abα, 8-9; 2:4aß, 6-7a, in which he reinterprets the wife of 2:4, originally Rachel, as being Gomer; the children, originally the northern tribes, as being Hosea's three children; and 2:18aßb, 21-22a in which he envisions a reunion of Yahweh and Israel, a note of hope lacking in the genuine Hoseanic oracle. There later followed a deuteronom(ist)ic redaction, limited in Hos. 1-3 to 2:10a, 11, 13-15a, but traceable through 10:15, and finally an exilic redaction which gave the book its present shape.

Literary-critical decisions and, to the extent that they impinge upon these, also form-critical decisions have an important impact on one's conception of the transmission and redaction of a given book or portion thereof. In our opinion these authors attribute decidedly too much material to later hands, and hence our understanding of the redaction history of the material differs significantly from theirs. The arguments concerning Hos. 2, in particular v. 16-25, are examined in the section dealing with these verses.[15] As for Hos. 1, the main point of difference is the contention of Ruppert and Renaud that the attribution of Gomer and her children as a woman and children of harlotry is a secondary interpretation imported from 2:4ff.[16] This opinion derives more from our inability to solve "the riddle of Hosea's marriage" (Rudolph) and to determine in what sense Gomer (and her children) was (were) harlotrous than from any serious difficulty in the text. (One need only accept the presence of a zeugma in 1:2.) But ignorance is no grounds for excision, and one can also question whether Hosea's disciples would have mistakenly (or

---

[10] *Composition and Tradition in the Book of Hosea.*

[11] Cf. *ibid.*, 307, where Yee repeatedly speaks of "the Hosean oracle" and "the Hosean saying" in the singular. She also interprets the wife of 2:4ff as being Rachel, Jacob's wife, on the basis of 12:13 (*ibid.*, 124, 305-306).

[12] *ibid.*, 306.

[13] *ibid.*, 307.

[14] *ibid.*, 115, 308. However, cf. p. 102, where a date prior to 722/21 seems to be suggested.

[15] See below pp. 94-98.

[16] See the discussion of Rudolph, 40-49, who also adopts this "solution" and lists predecessors in this view, p. 48 n. 30.

intentionally) identified the woman of Hos. 3 with Gomer when they must have been
familiar with Hosea's family life and have been active at a time when others were also
aware of it.

With regard to Hos. 3, deuteronomistic influence is alleged, though in varying degrees.
The phrase "turning to other gods" is considered deuteronomistic by Ruppert and Renaud
despite the fact that the phrase occurs elsewhere only in Deut. 31:18, 20 (cf. 29:17; 30:17)
and that Deuteronomy prefers the phrases "go after/serve other gods" (Deut. 6:14; 8:19;
11:28; 13:3; 28:14; 17:3; 29:25; 7:4; 11:16; 13:7, 14; 28:36, 64).[17] Hos. 3:5 is said to go
beyond what had been said to the woman in 3:3, which either presupposes a certain
understanding of 3:3b achieved by emending the text,[18] or attributes 3:3b to the same
expansion as 3:5.[19] The reference to "David their king" is for Ruppert an indication of
levitic circles,[20] for Renaud of priestly circles,[21] and for Yee of deuteronomistic circles.[22]
Yee also attributes the factors already mentioned to these circles as well as the notion of
God's love for Israel and the term "the latter days."[23] Yee then attributes all of Hos. 3 to
an exilic redaction because, in the train of Stinespring, she mistakenly poses the question
in terms of the chapter being either "totally original or totally secondary."[24] The alternative,
however, is artificial. Also, the term באחרית הימים ("in the latter days") occurs in
Deuteronomy only twice (4:30: 31:29), and differences in the usage of the term "love" in
Hosea and Deuteronomy have also been noted.[25] Hence, there appear to be no compelling
reasons for attributing significant segments, let alone the entirety of Hos. 3 to a later
hand.

Having thus sketched the most significant differences in the determination of the
genuine Hoseanic material between the most recent studies and our own view, we can now
present our own analysis of Hos. 1-3. Within this first collection the first-person report in
Hos. 3 clearly constitutes a separate unit. It is composed completely in prose and, with the
exception of עוד "again" in v. 1, is fully self-sufficient. The report claims to be from
Hosea's own hand, and there is no reason to doubt that Hosea was indeed its author. This
point, however, makes it unlikely that the third-person report in Hos. 1 also derives from
Hosea since a first-person report would then be expected.[26] Hos. 1:2-9 may have circulated
independently at one time and could have been composed as early as the birth of the
third child. Currently, however, 2:1-3 (1:10-2:1) forms the conclusion to this report. This
is indicated both by its dependence on the names of Hosea's children and the imperative
of 2:4 (2) which signals the beginning of a new complex.[27]

---

17   L. Ruppert, "Beobachtungen," 175; B. Renaud, "Livret d'Osée 1-3," 163-164.

18   Implicit in Ruppert's argument ("Beobachtungen," 174), though nowhere explicitly acknowledged.

19   B. Renaud, "Livret d'Osée 1-3," 164-165.

20   "Beobachtungen," 177.

21   "Livret d'Osée 1-3," 173.

22   *Composition,* 58.

23   *ibid.*

24   *ibid.,* 57, with reference to W. F. Stinespring, "Hosea, The Prophet of Doom."

25   See below p. 121.

26   This consideration remains valid regardless of whether the chapters are variant accounts of Hosea's initial
     marriage to Gomer, successive episodes in their marital life, or reports of Hosea's dealings with two
     different women. On the question in general see, besides the commentaries, H. H. Rowley, "The Marriage
     of Hosea," as usual with a plethora of literature.

27   The imperatives of 2:3 (1) belong with the promise of the preceding verses owing to their positive content.

This complex then continues throughout the remainder of the chapter. It presupposes, especially in 2:23-25 (21-23), a knowledge of the significance of the names of Hosea's children, and its format (disaster - salvation) parallels that of 1:2-2:3 (1). These factors, combined with the fact that the formula וְהָיָה בַיּוֹם הַהוּא "(and it shall be) on that day" occurs only in these chapters (1:5; 2:18, 20, 23 [16, 18, 21]), led Rudolph to the conclusion that 1:2-2:25 (23) is the work of a single redactor.[28] This is possible, although were this the case one might rather expect 2:1-3 (1:10-2:1) to have been placed with the other prophecies of salvation at the end of the chapter. Wolff argues that 2:4-17 (2-15) originally preceded Hos. 3 since both have the same theme. He compares 3:3-4 with the proposed isolation in 2:8 (6), 3:5 with the expected return in 2:9 (7), and 3:1 with the promised love of Yahweh in 2:16-17 (14-15).[29] He is also of the opinion that the rhetorical units of 2:4-17 have been transformed into an indivisible kerygmatic unit so completely that it can scarcely be the work of anyone other than Hosea.[30] But the opposite is in fact the case. The connecting particle לָכֵן "therefore" (v. 8, 11, 16 [6, 9, 14]) greatly facilitates the identification of the original units. Such indications are far less frequent in Hos. 4-14. Also, as the introduction to an independent piece 2:4ff is less than convincing. Some form of preparation for the family imagery would certainly be desirable. This, along with Wolff's desire to retain "again" in 3:1 as original, forces him to postulate the loss of a first-person report of Hosea's initial marriage which must have preceded 2:4ff.[31] This report must then have been suppressed by a disciple of Hosea's responsible for the composition of 1:2-6, 8-9 and the inclusion of 2:1-3, 18-25. But why would a disciple consider it necessary to compose his own account of events which Hosea had already recounted and then to substitute his own report for Hosea's? Why not proceed similarly with Hos. 3 and so avoid the anomaly of a first- and a third-person report? And again, is it not rather to be expected that, if 2:1-3, 18-25 derive from the same redaction, they would be grouped together?

This last point suggests that 2:4-25 (2-23) was composed subsequently to 1:2-2:3 (1). The similarities with Hos. 3 observed by Wolff further suggest that this account was also known to the compiler. It therefore appears probable that the compiler of 2:4-25 not only appended his work to 1:2-2:3 but also concluded the resulting collection with Hosea's first-person report. Concerning the date of this redaction, it may be noted that Hosea's prophecies appear to have been arranged not only according to theme but also on the basis of chronological considerations, and the prophecies contained in Hos. 1-3 are usually assigned to the second half of the reign of Jeroboam II. Hos. 1:4 presupposes that the dynasty of Jehu is still on the throne, and the prosperity of the latter half of the reign of Jeroboam II accords well with the depiction of Israel's luxuriant lifestyle in 2:7, 10-11, 13, 15 (5, 8-9, 11, 13). If, as the current composition of the book implies, Hosea's children influenced only the beginning of his prophetic ministry, then 2:1-3, 23-25 may also be assigned to this period. That, on the one hand, the material of these chapters probably stems from Hosea's early ministry, and, on the other, that they were not utilized in the two subsequent collections (Hos. 4-11 and 12-14) suggests that this collection was completed prior to the other two, perhaps prior to the proclamation of the earliest

---

28   Rudolph, 78.
29   Wolff, 74. He is followed by Mays, 15.
30   Wolff, 39; followed by J. Jeremias, "Eschatologie," 223.
31   Wolff, 74-75.

prophecies contained in Hos. 4:1-5:7. In sum Hos. 1-3 is comprised of three complexes: 1:2-2:3 (1); 2:4-25 (2-23), which go back to two separate redactions within the circle of disciples around Hosea, and 3:1-5, which goes back to Hosea himself.

The second major collection, Hos. 4-11, also contains several complexes. The first five of these may be identified on the basis of introductory imperatives in 4:1; 5:1; 5:8; 8:1; and 9:1. Beginning with 9:10 there then follows a series of complexes characterized by historical retrospections and the boundaries of which are generally apparent. Hos. 9:10-17 builds a complex with the unifying theme of fertility. It is also clear that Hos. 11 forms a separate complex. Unclear is the composition of Hos. 10. At the beginning of the chapter v. 1-8 are held together by the themes of cult and king, at the end v. 11-15 by the imagery of plowing. Somewhat isolated between these two blocks stand v. 9-10, but the prospect of war here and in v. 13-14 makes it appear likely that v. 9-10 belong with v. 11-15. Thus, the second major collection is composed of nine complexes: 4:1-19; 5:1-7; 5:8-7:16; 8:1-14; 9:1-9; 9:10-17; 10:1-8; 10:9-15; 11:1-11.[32]

The composition of Hos. 4-11 has generally been attributed to the circle of Hosea's disciples.[33] This view rests in part on the incorrect attribution of the redaction of 2:4-17 (2-15) to Hosea (see above) and the correct observation that the style of composition in Hos. 4-11 differs greatly from that of 2:4-17. When one compares the two styles, the relative lack of structural and/or connecting particles in Hos. 4-11 is striking. The literary integration of the original oracles has also been more thorough.[34] These factors do indeed point to different redactors for these two collections, and, although absolute certainty cannot be attained, it appears likely that Hosea himself was the redactor of chapters 4-11. The degree of freedom with which the oracles have been welded into literary form points in this direction since such an operation is more conceivable for the prophet himself than for his disciples, all the more so when Hos. 1-2, and especially 2:4-25, are kept in mind. Rudolph's view that the redaction of Hos. 4-14 derives from the same hand responsible for the redaction of Hos. 1-3 owing to the common pattern of disaster followed by salvation[35] is not convincing in light of the distinct differences in style. The disaster-salvation pattern underlies Hosea's own experience (Hos. 3) and will certainly have been passed on by him to his disciples.

The third collection, Hos. 12-14, is also characterized by a combination of historical retrospections (Hos. 12-13) and an introductory imperative (14:2 [1]). The division into constituent complexes may thus be analyzed in the following manner. Hos. 12:3-15 (2-14) is held together by the references to the patriarch Jacob. The role of 12:1-2 (11:12-12:1) in connection with the rest of the chapter is problematic since no direct link with Jacob is apparent. It would seem more likely, then, that these verses constitute the superscript to Hos. 12-14 analogous to 4:1-3 for Hos. 4-11. A second retrospection begins

---

[32]   The same division is advocated by Wolff and Jeremias, each with one unclear point in his presentation. Although Wolff views both 4:1 and 4:4 as beginning a speech (p. XXIV), he also states that in the present literary composition the אך "yet" of 4:4 connects 4:4ff with 4:1-3 (p. 90). Similarly, and at the same time in the opposite direction, Jeremias initially seems to indicate that 4:1-19 constitutes a single literary complex (p. 19), but in his exegesis he treats 4:1-3 and 4:4-19 separately, with no explanation of the "yet" of 4:4. This clearly establishes a literary connection (cf. Rudolph, 98).

[33]   Wolff, XXV; J. Jeremias, "Hosea 4-7," *passim*, and *Hosea*, 19.

[34]   Cf. Andersen-Freedman, 316: "The continuities in theme and in literary texture ... make it impossible to analyze cc 4-14 into discrete sections." But the situation is not quite this extreme.

[35]   Rudolph, 26.

in 13:1, and the complex so introduced continues through 14:1 (13:16). The final complex, 14:2-9 (1-8), concludes the collection with a call to repentance and the prospect of healing and restoration. When one examines the compositional technique employed in this third collection, a greater affinity with Hos. 4-11 than with Hos. 1-2 can be discerned. Connective particles are largely lacking, the separate complexes are demarcated by the same means, and both collections begin with an oracle (or part thereof in the case of 12:1-2) that serves as a superscript for the entire collection. It is therefore highly probable that both derive from the same hand, so that Hosea is likely to have composed this last collection also.[36]

As regards the date of composition for the two collections, Hos. 12-14 preserves Hosea's oracles spoken during the course of events initiated by Hoshea ben Elah's overture to Egypt in a hopeless attempt to rid himself of his Assyrian overlord (2Kgs 17:4). Hosea refers to this event in 12:2(1)b and thereby establishes the setting of the collection as a whole. In the final complex the deportations have apparently begun (14:3 [2]) and Samaria, if it has not already fallen, is certainly about to (14:2 [1]). The collection may then have been composed shortly after the fall of Samaria in 722, perhaps even during the siege. With respect to Hos. 4-11, the simple fact that they form a collection independent of Hos. 12-14 suggests that the collection was already completed prior to the proclamation of the oracles contained in the latter collection. Otherwise one would expect a single collection encompassing Hosea's entire prophetic activity in the post-Jeroboam II years. A date prior to Hoshea's overture to Egypt is thus indicated. Hosea's literary efforts at this time may be explained by the assumption of a dormancy in his prophetic appearances (cf. Isa. 8:16-22). Feeling that a period of his prophetic ministry was at a close, he was led to commit to writing the content of his proclamation. Alternatively, the desire to preserve his words through the impending disaster may have provided the impetus for Hosea's literary activity. In either case a date sometime during the reign of Hoshea ben Elah (731-723) is indicated, in the first case rather the first half, in the latter case rather the second half.

As previously indicated, the various sources for the book made their way to Judah with the refugees from the northern kingdom. Here they were arranged in their current order and provided with a superscript (1:1) sometime around 710, give or take a decade. Whether the subscript (14:10 [9]) was also added at the same time or was appended later remains uncertain. Both explanations are possible, but positive evidence one way or the other is lacking.

Two models have been proposed for the proper understanding of the nature of the literary complexes within the larger collections. The first was put forward by H. W. Wolff who, at least for Hos. 4-14, spoke of sketches of Hosea's appearances (*Auftrittsskizzen*) which were composed shortly after each appearance by the levitic-prophetic opposition circles with which Hosea identified and in which he was at home.[37] On this view we have (almost) direct access to Hosea's prophecies in the original "kerygmatic units" in which they were first spoken. Each kerygmatic unit actually corresponds to a single situation and/or appearance, and the order of the various sub-units within each unit corresponds to the actual order in which they were delivered. All we need do is identify the situation and

---

[36] Those attributing the redaction of Hos. 4-11 to Hosea's disciples naturally do the same here; see above p. 28 and n. 33.

[37] H. W. Wolff, "Hoseas geistige Heimat," and *Hosea*, XXIV-XXV.

supply the responses or objections of Hosea's audience to illuminate the train of thought within each unit.

A counter-proposal has been submitted by J. Jeremias.[38] Analyzing the sequence of topics touched upon in the units preserved in 4:4-19 and 5:1-7, he notes a definite parallelism in the structural composition. These complexes consist basically of 1) the primary guilt of the leaders (4:4-10; 5:1-2); 2) the resulting misorientation of the people (4:11-14; 5:3-4); and 3) the hopelessness and inalterability of Israel's present condition (4:16-19; 5:5-7).[39] This parallel construction suggests a purposeful redactional ordering of Hosea's prophecies rather than a quasi-stenographic record of his appearances. Jeremias also points out various phenomena which in his opinion speak more for the purposeful literary combination of oracles originally delivered on different occasions than for a series of rhetorical rebuttals within a single situation. In this connection he appeals to the resumption within a complex of central themes by means of words or roots employed in slightly different constructions (e.g. רוח זנונים, 4:12, and רוח, 4:19; זבח as a verb, 4:13, and in the noun מזבח, 4:19) and to shifts in the person(s) addressed and the situation presupposed (e.g. 4:4 addressed to a priest, 4:7f perhaps spoken only to Hosea's disciples and concerned with the priests collectively). Then, drawing upon the study of A. Alt,[40] he refers especially to the various units in 5:8-11 (8-9.10.11) as deriving in all probability from different stages in the course of events connected with the Syro-Ephraimite war. Hence, the current placement of the various oracles within a complex must be seen as redactional and need not imply an original temporal connection among them.

Of the two proposals that of Jeremias enjoys the greater probability, though not all of his arguments are equally forceful. Similar language features might be expected within a single appearance of the prophet, and one will not always be inclined to agree with Jeremias' view of the situation into which a given oracle was spoken. But the similar composition of constituent complexes is difficult to explain in terms of a common argumentative technique employed by Hosea. This is all the more true when one keeps in mind that Hosea is supposedly responding to objections from his audience which would dictate at least to a certain extent the direction of his reply. Moreover, it is in and of itself a weakness of Wolff's model that so much must be read between the lines in order to establish a connection between the rhetorical units within each kerygmatic unit. Thus, for example, Wolff acknowledges that 5:9b clearly marks the end of a speech and that in 5:10 the focus shifts from Ephraim to the military commanders of Judah. To account for both facts within a single appearance of Hosea, Wolff must postulate an interjection from the audience which objected to the threat of v. 8-9 by pointing to Judah's guilt. Hosea then proceeds to deal with the topic so introduced. However, one suspects that in this manner a connection could be established between almost any two units. At any rate this is a highly speculative procedure for which it is difficult to devise any means of even relatively objective control. The model advocated by Jeremias avoids this weakness.

Having thus sketched the growth and development of the book of Hosea, we can now turn to the examination of Hosea's conception of the history of Israel. When treating the

---

[38] "Hosea 4-7. Beobachtungen zur Komposition des Buches Hosea."

[39] ibid., 49-50.

[40] "Hosea 5,8-6,6," KS II, 164-177.

relevant passages, we will now be in a position to begin with the respective complexes identified in the foregoing analysis when seeking to isolate the original oracles.

Chapter 3

HOSEA'S CONCEPTION OF ISRAEL'S HISTORY

We begin our study with Hos. 12:3-15 (2-14), both because of the length of the passage itself and because of the scope of the history it treats. Both factors promise to facilitate an initial and yet extensive insight into Hosea's perception of the history of his people.

A. The Four Periods of Israel's History, Hos. 12:3-15

3   And[a] Yahweh has a contention with 'Israel'[b]

    ' '[c] to visit (it) upon Jacob according to his ways,

      according to his deeds he shall return (it) to him.[d]

4   In the womb he succeeded/deceived[a] his brother,

    and in his might[b] he strove with a divine being.

5   He 'strove'[a] against an angel and prevailed;

    He[b] wept and sought grace from him.

   (In) Bethel[c] he found[d] him,

    and there he spoke with 'him',[e]

6   But Yahweh, God of Hosts,

    Yahweh is his memorial:[a]

7   "And you, with your God you shall return.[a]

    Keep loyalty and justice,

      and wait upon your God continually."

8   Canaan, in his hands are scales of deception;

    he loves to oppress.

9   And Ephraim said, "Indeed, I have become rich!

    I have found might[a] for myself.

   In all my undertakings will not be found[b] against me

    any guilt which is sin."[c]

10 But I am Yahweh your God

     from the land of Egypt.[a]

  I will again make you dwell in tents

     as in the days of the festival/meeting.[b]

11 I will speak[a] to[b] the prophets;

     I will multiply vision(s)[c];

         and through the prophets I will perform symbolic actions.[d]

12 If Gilead was[a] (wicked) might[b],

     surely they were delusion.

  In Gilgal they sacrificed ('to'?) bulls.[c]

     Their altars also have become[a] like stone-heaps

         in the furrows of the field.

13 Jacob fled to the field of Aram;

     Israel served for a wife,

         and for a wife he kept.

14 But by a prophet Yahweh brought up

     Israel from Egypt,

         and by a prophet he was kept.

15 Ephraim has provoked bitterly.[a]

     So he will leave his blood(guilt) on him;

         his Lord will return to him his reproach.

Textual Notes

3a The *waw* is redactional (cf. *Form*). It is not to be appended to יובל (cf. Wellhausen; Marti; Harper; Nowack; Sellin; Wolff), but rather יכרתו is to be emended to יכרת (dittography of *waw*) with 𝔊 as all the verbs of v. 2 are singular (cf. Ehrlich; Duhm, "Anmerkungen," 37; Robinson).

3b That "Judah" is secondary here is indicated by the fact that Ephraim is clearly the focus of the entire passage. The parallelism with Jacob both here and in v. 13 further supports this view (cf. Ginsberg, "Hosea's Ephraim," 341-342).

3c The grammatical construction in 𝔐 is dubious. König §413v interprets it as the result of the need for compact sentence structure. But a third masculine singular imperfect would be equally compact, and of the examples he cites none follows upon a noun-clause. Diedrich (*Anspielungen*, 30-32) proposes a *lamed emphaticum* and third masculine singular perfect connected to the preceding clause by a *waw* and compares Prov. 2:8. He offers no translation, but one may suspect something like "and indeed he visits ..." However, the comparison with Prov. 2:8 is not exact. Alternatively, one could assume an emphatic *waw* (GKC §114p) "even to visit," but again the lack of a finite verbal form is problematic. Perhaps the simplest solution is to delete the *waw* with 𝕲 (so Harper; Robinson; Wolff).

3d   On the continuation of an infinitive plus preposition by a finite verb cf. GKC §114r.

4a   The verb עקב has received varying interpretations. The qal form occurs three time in the OT, Gen. 27:36; Jer. 9:3; Hos. 12:4; the piel occurs only in Job 37:4, but the reading is not certain (BDB suggests יְעַכְּבֵם). 𝕲 renders consistently with a form of the verb πτερνίζω "strike with the heel; trip up, supplant" (Liddell-Scott), whereas S consistently renders with the verb *nkl,* "deceive, defraud" (Payne-Smith). Modern lexica tend to reflect this: BDB lists "follow at the heel, fig. assail insidiously, circumvent, overreach"; KBL "seize at the heel, beguile"; and HAL "betrügen," though the translation of KBL is also repeated. The Arabic cognate *'aqb* has been cited by some scholars as supporting the meaning "to follow" and hence "overtake, supplant" (cf. Ackroyd, "Hosea and Jacob," 249), a meaning supported by later Hebrew usage: "follow; go beyond, supersede" (Jastrow, 1104). Inasmuch as the idea of grasping the heel cannot be demonstrated but merely postulated for the verb (conceded even by Rudolph, 228, and *contra* Neef, *Heilstraditionen,* 37, who holds that this meaning is required because Hosea is interpreting Gen. 25:26; cf. also Gese, "Hosea 12:3-14," 41; McKenzie, "Jacob Tradition," 312-313), this meaning must be abandoned. That leaves "follow; supplant" and "deceive, defraud." Given the paucity of the evidence and the feasibility of both renderings for all three occurrences, it would seem best to admit both meanings for the verb.

4b   און, which means "might, power" in a neutral sense, has been vocalized by the Massoretes in two different manners. When used in a positive sense, it is pointed אוֹן, in a negative sense אָוֶן (cf. Mowinckel, *Psalmenstudien* I, 31, and on the negative usage of the term *idem, The Psalms in Israel's Worship* I, 199-200 and Additional Note XXVIII in *ibid.* II, 250. The difference in vocalization is not likely to have been known to Hosea and his contemporaries.

5a   The verb וישר has been variously analyzed. The pointing of 𝔐 admits of two derivations, either from שור (= סור; cf. Judg. 4:18; 14:8; 16:19) or from שרר (Σ 𝒱). Wolff opts for שרר, which is taken to mean "sich als Herr erweisen." He then feels obliged to repoint אֶל as אֵל (the preposition for שרר is על in Judg. 9:22) and to delete מלאך as a gloss. Ackroyd ("Hosea and Jacob," 248, 250) avoids textual emendation by pointing out that אל and על are frequently interchanged, leading him to translate "he lorded it over the angel and prevailed." Alternatively, שור (= סור) also requires no emendation and occurs in 8:4; 9:12. Rudolph favors this view and translates "aber er (Gott) war ausgewichen auf einen Engel," which he then interprets as meaning that God had turned himself into an angel. The entire sentence thus becomes for Rudolph a gloss on אלהים (v. 4) designed to excuse Jacob's behavior as due to his inability to recognize his true opponent. Aside from the fact that Rudolph merely assumes God to be the subject of the verb without considering the possibility that Jacob could (still) be the subject, the meaning "turn into, become" for סור/שׁור is otherwise unattested. Retaining Jacob as subject yields "he turned aside to (the) angel," the only objection to which would be that it makes no sense in this context (so Jeremias, who follows Wolff). More convincing is the view that, just as in v. 4b, the verb שׂרה is present here. This requires repointing ‮יֹשַׂר‬ either to וַיָּשַׂר (BDB; Duhm, "Anmerkungen," 39; Nyberg; Robinson) or to וַיָּשַׂר (Ehrlich; Mays; Gese, "Hosea 12:3-14," 41 n. 8). Among those favoring this view אֶל is frequently emended to אֶת in accordance with v. 4b, but this is unnecessary. The preposition has the meaning "against" here, cf. Gen. 4:8; Isa. 3:8; and BrSyn §108c. This analysis gains support from the resulting play on the name Israel.

5b   I.e. Jacob, cf. the *Comment*.

5c   Some scholars have taken בֵית אֵל here to be a divine epithet and the subject of the following verbs (Nyberg; Eißfeldt, "Der Gott Bethel," 17-18 = 221; Ginsberg, "Hosea's Ephraim," 343-346; Ward). Evidence of a deity with the name "Bethel" is drawn primarily from the Elephantine papyri where the term appears as a theophoric element in a few personal names (cf. Noth, *Personennamen*, 127-128; Eißfeldt, *op. cit.*). Of the OT passages commonly cited as evidence of a deity Bethel at the sanctuary of the same name (Gen. 31:11, 13; 35:1, 7; 1Sam. 10:3; Jer. 48:13), none must be so interpreted (not even Jer. 48:13; cf. Rudolph, *Jeremia*, 280). For Hos. 12:5 the arguments of Eißfeldt are not convincing since he must either delete שׁם "there" or refer it to Bethel as the conceived, but not expressed location of the events. The argumentation presupposes Bethel to be a divine name and then attempts to alleviate the resulting difficulties rather than first listening to the implications of the text itself. The parallelism with שׁם clearly indicates that Bethel is a place name and as such is used adverbially (cf. GKC §118g). That leaves Yahweh and Jacob as the possible subjects of the verbs. For a discussion of this problem see the *Comment*.

5d   The imperfects here have been variously interpreted. One view is that they are iterative and have the two episodes recounted in Gen. 28:10-22; 35:1-15 in mind (König §157b: Vriezen, "Jacob dans Osée XII," 75; Wolff, 276; Ackroyd, "Hosea and Jacob," 251-252; cf. Neef, *Heilstraditionen*, 41-43). Others interpret them simply as preterits (Coote, "Hosea XII," 396; Gese, "Hosea 12:3-14," 42 n. 13), but this usage would be unique in the current passage. More probable is the view that the imperfects are employed as a *praesens historicum* (König §158; Rudolph, 229). They thus serve to emphasize the present validity of the events referred to and introduced by them. For a discussion of the subject and object of these verbs see the *Comment*.

5e   ‮יֹ‬ is to be vocalized either עִמָּנוּ in analogy with the Ugaritic form of the proposition with affixed -n, i.e. 'mn (cf. Dahood, *Ugaritic-Hebrew Philology*, 32; idem, *Psalms II*, 275; Mays; Kuhnigk, *Nordwestsemitische Studien*, 146; Andersen-Freedman) or עִמָּנוּ in assonance with the suffix on the previous verb (de Boer, "Genesis XXXII 23-33," 162 n. 2; Gertner, "Hosea XII," 279 n. 1; Jeremias). Others emend to עִמּוֹ (Marti; Harper; Ehrlich; Nowack; Sellin; Robinson; Wolff; Rudolph). In light of 4:15, it is highly unlikely that Hosea would straightforwardly maintain that Yahweh had been speaking with contemporary Israel at Bethel.

6a   This verse is probably not part of the divine speech to Jacob, as indicated by the unanimously attested third person suffix of זִכְרוֹ. The reasons behind Robinson's revocalization to זָכְרוּ are unstated. (Did he have 𝕾 in mind? Cf. Nyberg). The term זכר may be used as a synonym for "name" (Ex. 3:15; Isa. 26:8; Ps. 135:13; Job 18:17; Prov. 10:7; cf. Ps. 9:7 and Schottroff, *THAT* I, 512), in which case the possessive suffix refers to the person so named, here Yahweh.

7a   The combination שׁוב ב occurs some 50 times in the OT, if one includes temporal expressions such as בעת ההיא, ביום ה..., which occur 9 times in conjunction with the verb שׁוב. The use of ב in such expressions reflects a common construction for temporal clauses and should not be taken as unique to the verb שׁוב. Of the remaining 41 occurrences, the most common usages describe either state, as in the construction שׁוב בשׁלום ("return in peace," 11 times), or instrumentality, as in שׁוב בכל לבבם ובכל נפשׁם ("return with all their heart and with all their soul," 5 times). A locative meaning may he observed in 1Kgs. 8:48; Neh. 9:17 (emended), in both instances accompanied by the preposition אל(ל) denoting the destination. Similarly, a locative meaning is the most probable in Jer. 8:6 (so Rudolph; Bright; but cf. RSV). The phrase שׁאר ישׁוב בו in Isa. 10:22 may also be mentioned here, although strictly speaking בו refers back to עם and modifies שׁאר, i.e. a remnant in it (= among the people) shall return (cf. Wildberger). An adversative usage may be seen in Jer. 3:10, also in combination with אל denoting the destination: וגם בכל זאת לא שׁבה אלי. But here again the preposition ב is at best loosely connected with the verb שׁוב. For the sake of completeness Ps. 23:6, וְשַׁבְתִּי בבית יהוה, should also be mentioned. However, the text is to be emended either to וְשִׁבְתִּי with 𝕲 (so Briggs) or to וְיָשַׁבְתִּי with 𝕾 (so Gunkel; Kraus). That leaves four instances in which ב specifies the destination, i.e. "return into sacks" Gen. 43:18, and "return onto (someone's) head 1Kgs. 2:33; Obad. 15; Ps. 7:17. On the basis of this survey, the instrumental usage is to be preferred. The imperfect תשׁוב has future sense here; otherwise, the imperative or jussive would have been used (Rudolph; Utzschneider, *Hosea,* 192).

9a   Cf. note 4b.

9b   Impersonal usage of the plural verb, cf. GKC §144f.

9c   𝕲 and 𝕿 end Ephraim's speech at v. 9a and envision the prophet speaking in v. 9b. The question is whether this view is based on a text with third masculine singular suffixes or whether the attempt to interpret a difficult text led to the introduction of these suffixes to clarify the meaning. That Hosea should insert his own response to Ephraim's statement before Yahweh's response seems unlikely. It is therefore probable that the third masculine singular suffixes in the versions reflect a misinterpretation based on the reading of חֲטָא as חָטָא.

10a   𝕲𝕾 and one 𝕿 manuscript attest the reading העליתיך מארץ מצרים (most 𝕿 manuscripts attest הוצאתיך), whereas 𝒟 supports 𝔐. The situation is the same for

13:4 with the exception that here all 𝕿 manuscripts except one support the reading העליתיך. It is possible that the verb has fallen out in both verses as a result of homoioteleuton, but this is asking a bit too much of coincidence. The preference for a verb corresponding to העליתיך over הוצאתיך is due to העלה in 12:14.

10b Cf. the *Comment.*

11a On the continuation of an imperfect by *waw* + perfect cf. BrSyn §41f; Lambdin §98b.

11b על reflects the commanding and/or commissioning of the prophets by Yahweh to speak his word, cf. GKC §119aa.

11c Circumstantial clause of contemporaneous event(s), cf. GKC §142c; BrSyn §41i.

11d The exact meaning of דמה piel in the present context remains uncertain. Some have argued that the meaning must be "destroy" on the grounds that elsewhere in Hosea the root has this meaning (4:5, 6; 10:7, 15; so Wellhausen; Robinson; Weiser; Mays). But this argument overlooks the fact that none of these occurrences is a piel form. Rudolph reads אֶדַּמֶּה (hithpael denominative of דמות) and translates "Gestalt gewinnen, sich darstellen" ("I present myself"). In Isa. 14:14, the only occurrence of this form, the meaning is "make/consider oneself like (someone)" (cf. BDB, KBL, HAL). Though this does not exclude Rudolph's analysis, neither does it corroborate it. The context of the current passage indicates that some form of prophetic activity is intended. Nyberg considered the verb to be a technical term whose exact meaning is unknown. Wolff, comparing דמה I "liken, compare > devise," considers it a technical term for the announcing of God's plan. However, this aspect of the prophetic activity has already been addressed in v. 11aα (cf. note 11b). It therefore seems preferable to see here a technical term for the performing of symbolic action(s) by a prophet, in Hosea's case his marriage with Gomer; cf. Johnson, *Cultic Prophet,* 42-43 (followed by Jeremias), who interprets the term as "'to picture' something in the present which is to happen in the future." Comparing Ps. 48:9, he concludes that the picturing is acted out and not merely mental.

12a The "tenses" of the noun-clauses are problematic. The first clause is usually taken as referring to the past, whereas the second is usually taken as referring to the future and interpreted as a prediction of judgment (e.g. Wolff; Rudolph; Mays; Jeremias). However, v. 12b is completely surrounded by "past-tense" verbal forms, and so it too must be interpreted as referring to past events (so correctly Andersen-Freedman).

12b Cf. note 4b.

12c The fact that cattle were perfectly acceptable animals for sacrifice led Hitzig to propose the reading לַשֵּׁדִים "to the demons," building on 𝔊's ἄρχοντες = שרים and assuming haplography of ל. Sellin adopted the reading of 𝔊, thereby winning a subject for the verbs. But 𝔐's "bulls" is well attested by 𝔖𝕿𝔙. The vocalization of the plural שְׁוָרִים instead of the expected שׁוֹרִים remains unexplained. Should 𝔐's vocalization be erroneous, the reading of 𝔊 may be the result of defective orthography, but cf.

Jastrow, 1541, where this vocalization seems to be substantiated in later literature. It may be, however, that a לֹ has been lost through haplography or that the last לֹ of גלגל at one point did double duty.

15a Adverbial accusative, cf. GKC §118q.

Form

    Hosea 12 is one of the most discussed and yet least understood passages in the entire book. Not even its beginning and conclusion have been agreed upon. It was argued above that Hos. 12:3-15 forms a larger complex following the superscript to the last three chapters in 12:1-2.[1] The transition from v. 2 to v. 3 is syntactically rough, which is best explained by taking the initial *waw* as a redactional connection. The unity of v. 1-2 and v. 3-15, be it kerygmatic,[2] original,[3] or redactional,[4] is defended primarily on the grounds that the common theme of deception runs through the entire chapter. Thus, מרמה "deception" occurs both in v. 1 and v. 8, and תמרורים "very bitter(ly)" sounds similar. But it is quite striking that these are the only formal connections which can be drawn, and the appropriateness of the reference to תמרורים, which in itself has nothing to do with deception, is highly questionable. Moreover, the elevation of the theme of deception to the motivating factor and *sine qua non* of v. 3-15 runs into difficulties as early as v. 5, where Jacob's crying and asking for grace must be transformed into a deceptive ploy by which he achieved victory. On the positive side, the parallel construction of v. 3bß and v. 15bß argues strongly for setting these verses at the boundaries of the unit.[5] The introductory character of v. 3a further supports this view. Wolff considers v. 3ff to be only loosely connected with v. 1-2 and sees a new rhetorical section beginning with v. 3.[6] Mays, too, sees in v. 3 an "opening formulary announcement."[7] Consideration of the vocabulary also strengthens the argument. Jacob is the focus of attention in v. 3-7, 13; the term און "might" occurs in v. 4, 9, 12, מצא "find" in v. 5, 9 (*bis*), and שמר "keep" in v. 7, 13, 14. There is also the reference to prophets in v. 11 (*bis*), 14, and to the Exodus in v. 10, 14. One looks in vain for corresponding vocabulary and references in v. 1-2. The same may be said of 13:1(-4), where the mention of Ephraim as in 12:15 is inadequate to overturn the weightier considerations just listed.[8] Hos. 12:3-15 may therefore be taken as a unit.

    The integrity of v. 3-15 has been variously challenged. At the turn of the century, v. 5-7, 13-14 were considered secondary additions on the grounds that they cast Jacob in a favorable light, which was considered incompatible with the message Hosea intended to convey.[9] Robinson added that Moses was first considered a prophet in Deuteronomy and

---

1   See above p. 28.
2   Wolff.
3   Rudolph. H. Lubsczyk (*Auszug Israels*, 30) cannot decide between a literary or kerygmatic unity.
4   Mays; Jeremias; F. Foresti, "Hos. 12," 180, 185.
5   H. Gese ("Hosea 12:3-14") offers no reason for ending the unit with v. 14.
6   Wolff, 269: "3 wirkt nach 1-2 durchaus wie ein erster rhetorischer Einsatz."
7   Mays, 162.
8   *Contra* Sellin; F. Diedrich, *Anspielungen*, 93-110.
9   Nowack; Marti; Harper.

hence v. 13-14 must be late. A recent proponent of this type of literary-critical reduction
of Hos. 12 is J. Vollmer.[10] He eliminates v. 5-7 for the reasons mentioned above,[11] and
for v. 13-14 adds that Hosea would hardly have repeated himself in such a manner. The
double occurrence of both באשה "for a wife" and בנביא "by a prophet" is incongruous
with Hosea's rich vocabulary.[12] Vollmer also deletes v. 10-11. After v. 9b, which he emends
in accordance with 𝕲 (see textual note 9c), v. 10a is impossible because, even if v. 9b is
not emended, one expects a threat. However, v. 10a can only be the introduction to a
prophecy of salvation (Heilswort). This in turn would have to be followed by further
exposition of this salvation in v. 11. But v. 11 looks back at the effectiveness of the
prophets, which according to Vollmer is difficult to conceive of for Hosea. Moreover, the
use of חזון "vision" as a category of prophetic revelation and the use of ביד "by the hand
of" plus the person through whom Yahweh speaks both reflect usages later than Hosea.[13]
In the distillation of his results Vollmer bemoans the fact that literary criticism has become
"unmodern."[14] This, however, is to be welcomed, if one understands "unmodern," as
Vollmer does not, to mean the attempt to refrain from projecting modern tastes and
predilections upon the text. Statements like "one expects ..." must be supported by form-
critical arguments relating to the structure of the genre, arguments upon which Vollmer
barely touches. Moreover, given the fact that the Old Testament represents in all
probability only a small portion of Israel's literary output, we are in no position to say
when particular words were invested with specialized meanings or when these meanings
came into currency in the population at large except in those rare instances in which the
data are so extensive as to eliminate distortions due to chance.[15] As regards the
elimination of v. 5-7, 13-14 on the grounds that they reflect positively on Jacob, it would
seem methodologically unsound to remove them as incompatible with v. 4, since this verse
need not be interpreted in a negative manner.[16] It may also be noted that there is no lack
of negative interpretations of v. 5-7, 13, though these are largely the result of associating
v. 1-2 too closely with v. 3-15 and are often quite forced.

   Some scholars consider only v. 6 to be secondary, maintaining that it is a "doxological
insertion."[17] Behind this contention lies a two-step argument. First it must be established
that the verse is hymnic. The mere presence of a noun-clause (or two noun-clauses) is not
sufficient to establish the hymnic character of a passage (cf. e.g. 12:1b-2a), and Wolff
offers no arguments in support of the identification. Still, it may be acknowledged that the
verse employs elevated language, so that should the verse indeed be hymnic, then secondly
the possibility must be considered that Hosea borrowed the piece for his own purposes.[18]
Wolff argues that the verse "seems strange" and that the divine title is without parallel in

---

[10]   Geschichtliche Rückblicke, 105-113.

[11]   ibid., 106-108.

[12]   ibid., 110.

[13]   ibid., 109.

[14]   ibid., 111 n. 302. This statement is made specifically with reference to the elimination of v. 5-7, but literary
       criticism in general also seems to be in view.

[15]   This consideration also nullifies Robinson's argument concerning Moses as a prophet, see above p. 39.
       Furthermore, earlier sources also depict Moses as a prophet, see below p. 51.

[16]   Cf. textual note 4a.

[17]   Wolff; cf. Mays; Jeremias.

[18]   Jacob; Andersen-Freedman.

Hosea.[19] The first argument, however, is purely subjective, and the second cannot carry the full burden of proof. For it to do so one would have to presuppose that an idea or phrase must occur twice before it can be authentic, but such a presupposition is arbitrary. Also, the argument in this form can at best establish that Hosea drew upon a set or common phraseology. This in fact appears to be the case. The divine title יהוה (אלהי) צבאות "Yahweh (God) of Hosts" was not confined to Jerusalem, but was also known and cultically cultivated in the northern kingdom,[20] and would therefore have been well known to Hosea.[21] The cultic background also accounts for the elevated language, and hence there are no compelling reasons to deny Hosea the verse.

Turning to structure, the passage opens with the announcement that Yahweh has a contention with Israel and a statement of his purpose in the contention (v. 3). The style here is comparable to that of 4:1-3 where Yahweh's ריב is presented by Hosea. Hosea's speech extends through v. 9 and is dominated by past-tense narration. Within this historical retrospection Hosea cites an earlier oracle of Yahweh (v. 7) and puts words in Ephraim's mouth to communicate his attitude and actions (v. 9). In v. 10, introduced by a strong adversative, Yahweh becomes the speaker. His speech certainly continues through v. 11, as the first person singular verbs clearly show. The clauses of v. 12 are third person, although the verse could still be part of Yahweh's speech. It is not until v. 14 with its reference to Yahweh in the third person that clear evidence of a switch in speaker is present. The close parallelism between v. 13 and v. 14, however, requires that they be taken together. We are thus led to the conclusion that v. 10-12 contain Yahweh's speech, whereas in v. 13-15 Hosea is once again the speaker.

Hosea's initial speech traces Jacob's "ways and deeds" (v. 3) from before his birth down to the present as represented in his descendants (v. 1-9). In his response Yahweh declares how he intends to return these deeds upon his descendants. This declaration begins with a reminiscence of the high-point of Israel's early history and proceeds to a depiction of future salvation with implicit judgment (v. 10-11). Yahweh's speech closes with a look at the sin necessitating his action (v. 12). At this point everything has in essence been said, and it remains only for Hosea to summarize the results. In so doing he picks up and emphasizes the main points of Jacob's and Yahweh's deeds (v. 13-14) and states the point of contention revealed in the exchange and alluded to at the beginning of the passage (v. 15; cf. v. 3). Hosea thus ends the passage where it began, intentionally picking up the formulation of v. 3bß in v. 15bß. But with two significant differences! The "deeds" of v. 3bß have become the "reproach" of v. 15bß, so there can be no doubt that things have turned out negatively. But for whom? The reproach is Ephraim's, not Jacob's! This observation is crucial to a proper understanding of the passage.

---

[19]   We give Wolff the benefit of the doubt here in listing these as two separate arguments. But one suspects that the verse "seems strange" precisely because Hosea does not use this divine title elsewhere.

[20]   Cf. O. Eißfeldt, "Jahwe Zebaoth," KS III, 113-114, 122; *idem*, "Psalm 80," esp. 74-76 = KS III, 228-230; A. S. van der Woude, *THAT* II, 499, 506.

[21]   *Contra* H. Gese, "Hosea 12:3-14," 41 n. 5.

Comment

Hosea begins with the declaration that Yahweh has a ריב "contention" with Israel. The relationship between them has been disturbed; משפט as the proper order of things no longer obtains.[22] The source of the disturbance lies in Jacob/Israel's conduct, and so Yahweh resolves to bring the inherent consequences of his actions upon him. Both פקד "visit" and ישיב "(cause to) return" are in themselves neutral terms.[23] Here they express Yahweh's activity in bringing to completion the effects emanating from Jacob/Israel's behavior. Whether these effects are positive or negative depends on his actions, and in the case of negative effects, Yahweh's purpose is not merely punishment but the removal of the negative repercussions disturbing the relationship, thereby paving the way for restoration.[24]

Within this framework the recitation of Jacob's deeds commences. But here the difficulties begin. Did Jacob supplant or deceive his brother in the womb? It is difficult to conceive how Jacob could have deceived Esau in the womb. Was he born prior to Esau although the latter should have legitimately been the firstborn?[25] This is not likely. Neither is Jacob's grasping his brother's heel a more likely candidate.[26] This interpretation presupposes Gen. 25:26 (or a similar tradition), but there is no mention of deception here and hence reference to the Genesis narrative does not clarify matters. The view that Hosea has combined elements from Gen. 25:26 and Gen. 27:36[27] also presupposes Hosea's familiarity with the Genesis narratives and tacitly admits the difficulty of conceiving of a deception in the womb. However, it is possible to imagine Jacob supplanting Esau in the womb. Not that he was born first when he should have been born second (this has already been rejected as a viable option), but rather he was destined before birth to inherit what should have been Esau's as the first-born. Jacob supplanted Esau as the designated heir. If Jacob was so designated by Isaac, then Hosea would be drawing upon a no longer extant tradition. But what could motivate Isaac to take such a step? It therefore seems more likely that Jacob was destined by God to become the heir. This interpretation is of course compatible with the birth narrative in Gen. 25:21-26 where Rebekah is told that of the twins in her womb and the peoples they represent "the elder shall serve the younger." This is probably how Hosea's audience initially understood him, and it is difficult to avoid the conclusion that Hosea intended it so. But Hosea's use of עקב differs from Genesis where it refers to Esau's heel,[28] and an accompanying undertone of deception in

---

22   On the meaning of ריב and its connection with משפט cf. D. R. Daniels, "Prophetic Lawsuit," 352-353.

23   Cf. W. Schottroff, *THAT* II, 470, where the predominantly negative usage of "visit upon" is interpreted as developing from the neutral idea of "visit in order to check on someone or something."

24   Cf. K. Koch, "Vergeltungsdogma," 10-16, esp. 14-15 = 141-148, 145-146.

25   H. Gunkel, *Genesis*, 296.

26   So H. L. Ginsberg ("Hosea's Ephraim," 342 note i), who must qualify this as an "*attempt* to supplant his brother" (emphasis original). But this is begging the question.

27   E.g. L. Ruppert, "Jakob-Tradition bei Hosea," 495.

28   This is the "Achilles' heel" of H.-D. Neef's argument. He fails to elucidate the context in Hosea, contenting himself instead with presupposing a dependence on the Genesis tradition and then pointing to resulting points of correspondence (*Heilstraditionen*, 36). But under such circumstances his argument is merely a *petitio principii* and proves nothing. Similar criticism must be directed at H. Gese ("Hosea 12:3-14"). His "methodological principle" (p. 38) that in difficult situations the text is to be understood in a manner that

Hosea should not be excluded. Hosea has stated that Yahweh has a contention with Israel (v. 3a), and the audience would be anticipating clarification of the cause. Their increased attentiveness in this direction will no doubt have enabled them to pick up this undertone.[29]

Hosea next recounts the episode of Jacob's struggle with a divine being, v. 4b-5a. In the present context the parallelism of אוֹן "might" with בֶּטֶן "womb" would cause the audience to think primarily in terms of "manhood, virility," but again an accompanying undertone of "his wickedness" may also be present. This is all the more possible in light of the ambiguity of the verb עקב. Yet in the patriarch Jacob these traits are merely latent. Hosea does not dwell on them or develop them - until v. 8-9! The repetition in v. 4b and v. 5aα, besides being based in the dictates of the poetic structure, serves to prevent misunderstanding about the identity of the אלהים in v. 4b. It was not God himself but an angel with whom Jacob struggled. In this struggle Jacob prevailed, wept, and sought grace. Some scholars have seen a contradiction here since if Jacob was victorious he would hardly have wept and sought grace from his defeated opponent. W. L. Holladay has suggested that v. 4-5a are chiastic in structure, with the result that the weeping and seeking grace refer rather to Jacob's reunion with his brother Esau recounted in Gen. 33 since here the terms בכה "cry" and חן "grace" occur.[30] But this suggestion rests more on an analysis of the Hosea text on the basis of the Genesis accounts than on its own internal merits. The same objection must be made to L. M. Eslinger's emendation and syntactical analysis of v. 5a to correlate with a particular analysis of Gen. 32:29.[31] Others interpret Jacob's weeping as a deceptive ploy perpetrated to gain a tainted victory.[32] However, without claiming that Hosea is referring to the narrative of Gen. 32:23-32, it may be pointed out that in this narrative, too, Jacob prevails and asks to be blessed by his opponent. Evidently no insurmountable contradiction was felt. Perhaps יכל "prevail" is used in both instances (Gen. 32:29; Hos. 12:5) more in the sense of "be capable, endure" than of "be victorious." Be that as it may, Jacob's weeping in Hos. 12:5a is best understood as part of his seeking grace from his divine antagonist.[33]

A comparison of v. 4b-5a with Gen. 32:23-32 reveals both similarities and differences. The common conception of Jacob prevailing and requesting a blessing has already been noted. However, whereas prevailing is expressed by the same verb in both accounts, the verbs describing the request for grace differ. This difference, though, can be adequately explained by the transposition from direct speech (Gen. 32:27) to third-person narrative (Hos. 12:5). Hosea is describing what in essence took place. More difficult to account for

---

agrees with the Jacob tradition in Genesis predisposes his results, as do his frequent preliminary considerations of what is to be expected in Hosea's argument before actually examining the text itself.

[29] This does not dictate that everything following v. 3 must necessarily be taken negatively, *contra* C. Jeremias, "Erzväter," 213.

[30] W. L. Holladay, "Chiasmus," 56-58. He is followed by L. M. Eslinger, "Hosea 12:5a," 92.

[31] L. M. Eslinger, "Hosea 12:5a," 93-94, using the analysis of Gen. 32:29 proposed by F. I. Andersen, "Note on Gen. 30:8," 200.

[32] E.g. Sellin; Rudolph.

[33] A. Bentzen, "The Weeping of Jacob, Hos. XII 5A." However, the view that the weeping is a deceptive ploy is misguided. H. Gese ("Hosea 12:3-14," 42) sees a direct reference to Gen. 32:27, whereas E. M. Good ("Jacob Tradition," 144) sees an allusion to a lost tradition which derived the name Allon-bakuth (cf. Gen. 35:8) from Jacob's crying, though why he was crying cannot be said. This interpretation, however, is in the unenviable position of presupposing Genesis and yet not being able to draw any significant support from it!

is Hosea's reference to an angel. The Genesis narrative starts out with Jacob wrestling with a man (v. 25), but he later turns out to be a divine being (אלהים, v. 29, 31). The identification of this divine being as an angel may be Hosea's own interpretation, along with the addition of Jacob's weeping. Alternatively, Hosea may have known a similar, but divergent form of the tradition in which Jacob's opponent was explicitly stated to be an angel (rather than a "man"?) and which contained some mention of Jacob's weeping.[34] A definitive answer to this problem cannot be given at this point since it cannot be shown that Hosea is directly quoting the Genesis narrative, and so the question is best left open until the evidence from Hosea's other allusions to the Jacob traditions has also been examined.

With v. 5b-7 the scene shifts to Bethel. As already hinted at (cf. textual note 5d), the subject of the verbs of v. 5b and the referent of the third person masculine singular suffixes are not immediately clear. However, once it is recognized that v. 7 contains an oracle of Yahweh delivered at Bethel,[35] it becomes probable that Yahweh is the subject of the verb "spoke" in v. 5bβ. The parallelism with v. 5bα further suggests that Yahweh is also the subject here. Jacob would then be the antecedent of the suffixes. Thus, Yahweh found Jacob at Bethel and spoke with him there. The emphasis on Bethel at the beginning of the clause and the use of the verb "find" imply that the initial encounter is intended. It was at Bethel that God first spoke with Jacob and initiated their direct relationship. But before Hosea relates the content of the divine speech, he clarifies in no uncertain terms the identity of the deity that spoke to Jacob. It was Yahweh, the God of Hosts (v. 6). The interpretation of the divine epithet יהוה צבאות is a matter of some dispute. It may be that צבאות is to be taken as an intensive plural abstract approximately meaning "might, power."[36] This reference to the might of Yahweh would then underscore his ability to fulfill what he promises, thereby setting the tone for v. 7.[37] Alternatively, צבאות may refer to the heavenly and earthly armies created and led by Yahweh in battle.[38] The prior mention of an angel (v. 5a) may speak for Hosea's understanding the term in this manner. Certainly the verse establishes that the God who spoke to Jacob is the God of later Israel, as indicated by both the divine title and the reminiscence in v. 6b of the revelation of the divine name Yahweh (cf. Ex. 3:15). This strong emphasis on the identity of the God at Bethel as Yahweh suggests that Hosea is combating the syncretism of Baal with Yahweh. This interpretation is further supported by the adversative beginning of the verse. In the popular conception it was Baal-Yahweh (cf. 2:18 [16]) who had spoken with Jacob. To judge from the early chapters of the book, the identification of the two deities seems to have been limited to the realm of agriculture and fertility in Israel. Hosea therefore counters with a divine epithet which, especially if the connection with (heavenly) armies is correct, derives from and points to a wholly different sphere where the identification had not occurred or at least was not prominent.

---

[34] So F. Foresti, "Hos. 12," 192-194.
[35] The argument of E. Blum (*Komposition*, 162) that v. 7 could be a speech of Jacob transformed into a warning addressed to the people has no foundation in the context.
[36] O. Eißfeldt, "Jahwe Zebaoth," KS III, 110-113, 120; A. S. van der Woude, *THAT* II, 505.
[37] Cf. Rudolph.
[38] Cf. e.g. F. M. Cross, *Canaanite Myth and Hebrew Epic*, 69-70.

In v. 7 Hosea then relates the oracle received by Jacob.[39] It consists of a promise (v. 7a) and two commands (v. 7b). Jacob was promised Yahweh's assistance in returning, presumably to Bethel and the land promised him, unless one assumes that the return was for no particular reason. This implies that Jacob was leaving the land when he received the oracle. Given Hosea's reference to Jacob's flight to Aram (v. 13), it is likely that Hosea conceived of Jacob as on his way to Aram when he received the oracle. Jacob was thus given the assurance that Yahweh would return him to the land. But he was also commanded to observe חסד and משפט and to wait for his God. חסד "loyalty" is the attitude and ensuing conduct emanating from the relationship existing between parties.[40] It is more than action resulting merely from "rights and duties"; it is also conduct motivated by genuine devotion.[41] משפט "justice" signifies the proper order of life in which everyone receives that which is rightfully his due. The realm of משפט is not confined to the judicial aspect of life, but includes all aspects of life.[42] The last clause of v. 7 must be seen in connection with the first. It is "his God" who will bring Jacob back to the land, and so he must patiently wait for his God to act on his behalf. His own independent efforts in this regard will come to naught. Yahweh, and only Yahweh, can return him to the land. The constellation of v. 7 indicates that Hosea saw the gift of the land not as an unconditional promise but as predicated upon human conduct. The implicit allusion to משפט in v. 3 is made explicit in v. 7 and connected with the land. God promised Jacob the land but required him to live in accordance with חסד and משפט and in sole dependence on Yahweh (v. 6!) his God.[43]

The situation presupposed by v. 5b-7, i.e. Jacob's initial encounter with Yahweh as he is fleeing to Aram, is paralleled only in Gen. 28:10-22.[44] However, comparison of the oracles in Gen. 28:13-15 and Hos. 12:7 reveals that they have little in common.[45] Only in the promise of return (Gen. 28:15a; Hos. 12:7a) can a faint echo be postulated. But the Genesis narrative contains no command for Jacob, whereas in Hosea's version this element

---

[39] F. Foresti ("Hos. 12," 184) interprets the verse as Hosea's invitation to "the people, the actual Jacob" to return to their God. But that the singular "you(r)" should refer to the people finds no support in the text. (Foresti also understands עמנו as equivalent to עמו, ibid., 183 n. 24; cf. textual note 5e.).

[40] N. Glueck, Ḥesed in the Bible; cf. the similar view of K. D. Sakenfeld, The Meaning of Ḥesed in the Hebrew Bible.

[41] A. R. Johnson, "Hesed and Hasid." E. Kellenberger (ḥäsäd wä'ä̆mät, 77-81) argues that חסד can denote the willfully helpful action(s) and attitude that actually create a relationship rather than derive from it. In the present context this would have to be stated with a view to the coming relationship with Laban. Though Kellenberger is perhaps correct in asserting that חסד does not necessarily presuppose an existing relationship, he is less convincing when he then contends that even within an existing relationship the exercise of חסד goes beyond that which may legitimately be expected on the basis of that relationship. That חסד can be commanded (Hos. 12:7) or expected (Hos. 4:1; 6:4, 6) speaks decidedly against such a view.

[42] Cf. K. Koch, The Prophets I, 59 = Die Profeten I, 70. Specifically for Hosea cf. Wolff, 121.

[43] This interpretation differs slightly from that offered by K. Koch ("Die Entstehung der sozialen Kritik bei den Profeten," 255), who considers Jacob's occupation of the land as ending with the command to observe חסד and משפט. But this overlooks the future nature of תשוב (cf. textual note 7a). Jacob's return to the land does not end but rather begins with the command to observe חסד and משפט. This does not, however, materially affect the connection between חסד, משפט, and the land worked out by Koch.

[44] A reference to Gen. 35:5-15 is therefore excluded; so also Rudolph.

[45] For E. Blum (Komposition, 161-163) no satisfactory solution to the problems surrounding Hos. 12 has yet been proposed. He therefore excludes the evidence from Hosea when analyzing the current text in Gen. 28:(13-)15.

is extremely important. Is Hosea then dependent on the Genesis tradition in its extant form? The situation is the same, and a marginal similarity in the oracle is perceptible, and yet the marked differences in content are not to be glossed over. If Hosea knew the tradition in the extant form but reformulated it to suit his own purpose, he would be open to the charge of falsification, which would seriously undermine his credibility. Was Hosea then drawing upon a tradition known to himself and his listeners only in an oral and unfixed form? Certainly all that can be assumed for the majority of Hosea's audience is an oral familiarity with the tradition, which might allow Hosea greater scope for reformulation. But v. 7 does not give the impression of being Hosea's free creation. Especially the reference to "loyalty and justice" reflects the well-known phraseology of the liturgies for admittance to the sanctuary[46] and hence will have been a well-known portion of the tradition, both to Hosea and to his audience. It therefore seems most probable that Hosea is drawing upon a variant form of the tradition in Gen. 28:10-22 in which not only divine assistance for the return to the land was promised, but Jacob was also exhorted to practice loyalty and justice in anticipation of and while waiting for the fulfillment of the promise. The question of an oral or a written source is quite difficult to decide. The fact that Hosea employed a variant form of the tradition has been interpreted as speaking more for the former than the latter.[47] But as a citizen of the northern kingdom familiar with the situation at Bethel, Hosea is certainly geographically closer than the Yahwist to the location where the tradition was most cherished. It is therefore quite probable that the Yahwist, generally placed in the south, drew upon an oral form of the tradition which had made its way south. If this reconstruction is accurate, then Hosea could be drawing on a written source, but this is not a necessary conclusion. It is also possible that his knowledge of the tradition derives strictly from its oral presentation. As already indicated, the majority of Hosea's audience almost certainly came to know the tradition in this way, and the same is no doubt to be said for Hosea. Whether he also knew (and had read) a written form of the tradition cannot be said with any degree of confidence. The question is perhaps best left open. In any case v. 7 certainly constitutes the heart of Hosea's survey of Jacob's life to this point. The events related in v. 4-5 (esp. v. 4) have planted the seeds which will germinate and ripen in v. 8-9, 12. But the standard by which the fruit is to be evaluated is set in v. 7.

With v. 8 the focus of attention has again shifted. The verse begins with the exclamation "Canaan," with which Hosea personifies the Canaanites in order to depict their most typical traits. Characteristic of Canaan is his use of deceptive scales and his penchant for oppression. The Canaanites were so indissolubly associated with trade that the word "Canaanite" also came to mean "merchant" (Prov. 31:24; Job 40:30; Ezek. 17:4; Zeph. 1:11; Zech. 11:7; 14:21). This has led some scholars to interpret Hosea as chastising only shifty business practices adopted by Ephraim from the Canaanites but forbidden by Israelite law.[48] However, עשק "oppress" is too broad to be confined only to business practices. Hosea has in view the entire lifestyle of the Canaanites (cf. Isa. 1:10ff.) whose basic essence was the use of deception and oppression to amass wealth. Implicit in the entire verse is the condemnation of the Canaanization of Ephraim.

---

46 Cf. K. Koch, "Tempeleinlassliturgien," 54-56. R. Vuilleumier ("Traditions d'Israël," 492) considers the similarity between Hos. 12:7 and Mic. 6:8 to be "striking"; cf. already E. Beer, "Hosea XII," 287.

47 J. Rieger, Bedeutung der Geschichte, 56.

48 So Rudolph, citing Deut. 25:13; Lev. 19:36: Ezek. 45:10; and Deut. 24:14; Lev. 19:13.

This becomes explicit in Ephraim's response (v. 9), which is calculated to counter this charge. He does not deny that he, too, has become rich and powerful, but claims that he has made his fortune honestly. None of the means he employed to attain his position of power has brought any sin upon him. But the choice of words tells a different tale. Ephraim's achievement is described as finding אוֹן. But whereas for Jacob his father this term was ambiguous, in Ephraim's case it has a definitely negative sense. This is indicated by the close association of v. 8 and v. 9 as charge and response. Ephraim's might has its source in wickedness, in deception and oppression. Ephraim has ignored the command of v. 7. This command applies not only to Jacob but to Ephraim as well since as Jacob's son (descendants) he is conceived of as present in Jacob at the time of the command and Jacob is conceived of as living on in his son (descendants).[49] Ephraim's claim of self-righteousness thus turns out to be self-deception!

In v. 10 Yahweh himself steps in. He identifies himself as Ephraim's God from the land of Egypt.[50] The "self-introductory formula" employed here emphasizes Yahweh's gracious acts, in this particular instance the Exodus from Egypt as eliciting a response of gratitude which motivates conduct in accordance with Yahweh's law.[51] But Ephraim has acted in a manner totally at variance with the relationship established through the Exodus by adopting Canaanite attitudes and practices. The Canaanization of Ephraim necessitates a new beginning. Yahweh will again cause Ephraim to dwell in tents. The phrase כִּימֵי מוֹעֵד is commonly interpreted as the Feast of Booths (= Succoth) on the basis of the mention of tents. However, this feast was celebrated in booths (סֻכּוֹת) constructed from foliage, not in tents. Moreover, this festival seems to have been connected with the Exodus (Lev. 23:43) subsequent to Hosea's day,[52] whereas a connection with the Exodus is strongly implied in the present context. This would suggest a reference to the Passover and the Feast of Unleavened Bread. The OT texts do not specifically associate tents with either of these festivals, but the (semi-)nomadic background of the Passover renders a dwelling in tents for this feast at least possible.[53] The plural "days" would then reflect the integration by Hosea's time of the two originally distinct festivals. Alternatively, מוֹעֵד could refer to the time of the Exodus itself as corresponding to the מוֹעֵד of the Passover.[54] This view is supported by Wolff's observation that the phrase כְּיוֹם/כִּימֵי "as in the day(s) of" is employed by Hosea to introduce analogies from Israel's early history (2:5, 17 [3, 15]; 9:9). In either case Hosea envisions a reprise (עֹד "again") of the conditions following the Exodus from Egypt, and this includes for Hosea prophetic guidance in the form of word, visions, and symbolic actions (v. 11).

---

[49] On the notion of "corporate personality" cf. H. W. Robinson, "The Hebrew Conception of Corporate Personality."

[50] This indicates that Ephraim in v. 9 is conceived of primarily in terms of the personified tribe and/or nation of the same name. On Hosea's use of the term "Ephraim" see below p. 68 n. 128 and L. Rost, *Israel*, 26-27.

[51] Cf. K. Elliger, "Ich bin der Herr - Euer Gott," esp. p. 15; and W. Zimmerli, "Ich bin Yahweh," esp. 189-191 = 22-24, who coined the term "self-introductory formula."

[52] Cf. R. de Vaux, *Ancient Israel* II, 501-502.

[53] On the semi-nomadic background cf. L. Rost, "Weidewechsel und altisraelitischer Festkalender," and J. Pedersen, "Passahfest und Passahlegende." On the association with tents cf. Pedersen, *op. cit.*, 175, and M. Noth, *Pentateuchal Traditions*, 67 = *Überlieferungsgeschichte*, 72.

[54] Cf. G. Sauer, *THAT* I, 744; K. Koch, *ThWAT* IV, 746.

In v. 12 Ephraim's sin is again the focus of attention. Unfortunately, the events referred to cannot be identified with certainty. Is Hosea referring to events of the recent past so that a contemporary's knowledge of prevailing conditions at Gilead and Gilgal would be necessary to understand the verse?[55] Or are events of the more distant past intended? Gilgal was a famous ancient sanctuary closely associated with the crossing of the Jordan and the entry into the land.[56] Gilead could refer to the town of that name (cf. 6:8) or more probably to the region east of the Jordan. As a geographical term it encompassed a wide area,[57] including in the south Shittim and the surrounding area, which according to biblical tradition was the last stop before crossing the Jordan and also the site of the Baal-Peor episode (cf. Num. 25:1; 33:49; Josh. 3:1). Does v. 12aα contain a veiled reference to the sin of Baal-Peor (cf. 9:10)? The preceding reference to the Exodus leads one to think in terms of events from this general period. V. 12aβ then condemns the continued cultivation of the Canaanite cult at Gilgal. Hence, it may be that "to bulls" (לשׁורים) is to be read and interpreted as a reference to the Canaanite cult in which the bull symbolized a deity, usually El or Baal.[58] The ultimate source of Ephraim's אוֹן "might" (v. 9) is thus traced back to the Canaanite cult. They began to draw upon this source at the time of the Baal-Peor episode and continued to do so at Gilgal. Then, as they spread throughout the land, they erected altars (or adopted Canaanite cultic sites) which Hosea sees as in reality dedicated to the Canaanite Baals. The altars thus became as prevalent as "stone-heaps in the furrows of the field." Hosea is here playing upon the assonance between Gilgal (גלגל) and stone-heaps (גלים). These stone-heaps were piled up by the farmer when he ran into stones while plowing the fields.[59] They were therefore practically everywhere to be seen (cf. 8:11; 10:1). Ephraim's attachment to the Canaanite cult spread like an epidemic (cf. 4:17-19; 5:3; 8:4; 9:1; 11:2; 13:1-2). שׁוא "delusion" refers to that which is false and deceptive, and so can be used in connection with idolatry (Jonah 2:9 [10]; Ps. 31:7).[60] It can also stand for the false gods themselves (Jer. 18:15; perhaps also Ps. 24:4), as it probably does here. Consequently, the "might" that Ephraim thought he had acquired (v. 9) is in fact a delusion because the cult from which he ultimately derives it is a delusion.

In the final section, v. 13-15, Hosea recapitulates the thrust of the passage. Attempts at interpreting v. 13 negatively are particularly forced. Perhaps the most common interpretation among modern commentators is that an allusion to the sexual rites of the fertility cults lies concealed in Jacob's uxorious tendencies.[61] This is possible in light of v. 12, but represents a narrowing of the focus of Hosea's critique, which is more fundamental and encompassing. Also, it should be remembered that the wife (wives) Jacob worked for was (were) the ancestress(es) of Israel and hardly a "foreign woman."[62] Neither can the

---

[55]   So Rudolph; Mays; cf. also D. Grimm, "Erwägungen zu Hos 12:12."

[56]   Cf. Josh. 3-5 and R. de Vaux, *Early History*, 598-608, esp. 603-606, with further literature.

[57]   Cf. R. de Vaux, *Early History*, 571-572; Y. Aharoni, *Land of the Bible*, 38-39.

[58]   Cf. D. Grimm, "Erwägungen zu Hos 12:12," 342-343, and A. Mazar, "Bull Site," 30-32, with further literature. The overall interpretation of the verse offered here, however, is viable even without this emendation.

[59]   Dalman, AuS II, 16-17.

[60]   Cf. J. F. A. Sawyer, *THAT* II, 882.

[61]   Initially proposed by Wolff.

[62]   So correctly Rudolph *contra* Wolff.

flight to Aram be impugned. Hosea merely states the fact of the flight in a matter-of-fact, non-judgmental manner, and Yahweh's promise of aid for the return presupposes consent.[63] That leaves a contrast between two types of שמר (keeping). Rudolph maintains that Jacob's keeping was inappropriate because, rather than keeping loyalty and justice, he kept sheep. Rudolph ends up at the same point as Wolff in that he also sees Jacob's fault in his desire for women, which he interprets as a sideswipe at the fertility cult.

But must v. 13-14 he understood as a contrast in the sense of an antithesis? Could it not be that v. 14 represents an enhancement over against v. 13? There can be no doubt that according to Genesis Jacob kept Laban's flocks in order to earn his wives, but this is not what *Hosea* says. He does not explicitly mention what Jacob kept; the emphasis lies on the fact of the keeping. The implication is that Jacob obeyed the oracle he had received (v. 7). In his dealings with Laban he kept not only sheep but also חסד and משפט,[64] and was blessed with a wife (or wives). Jacob's keeping is then paralleled by Yahweh's keeping Israel through prophetic agency. That Moses is meant here is universally admitted, though some see a reference to Samuel in the second mention of a prophet. The two prophets would then correspond to Jacob's two wives.[65] This interpretation is plausible, though uncertain. The fact that Hosea speaks generally of a prophet(s) rather than specifically of Moses (and Samuel) indicates that the emphasis is on the prophetic office as such.[66] Combined with v. 11, this verse demonstrates the extreme importance of the prophetic office in Hosea's thinking. The prophets are the only true and faithful agents of Yahweh's protective guidance for his people.[67] This care began with Moses as the prophet *par excellence* and, whether Hosea also referred to Samuel or not, he certainly viewed the office as continuing down to his own day (6:5).[68] So crucial are the prophets that Hosea cannot conceive of a future renewal without them (v. 11).

In stark contrast to Jacob and Yahweh, Ephraim has kept nothing; rather, he has "provoked bitterly" (v. 15). The Hiphil of כעס "provoke" is employed especially to denote apostasy from Yahweh and the worship of foreign gods,[69] and picks up the thought of v. 8-9, 12. The phrase ישיב לו "return to him" refers back to v. 3, and the substitution of "his reproach" for "his deeds" leaves no doubt that Ephraim has fared poorly in the contention. But it is specifically Ephraim and not Jacob who has fared poorly. Ephraim and not Jacob has provoked bitterly. By his actions he has effectively severed his relationship with Yahweh and incurred death-bringing sin (דם "blood[-guilt]"). Yahweh will see to it that the effects of Ephraim's actions are brought to completion. His days as an independent nation are numbered.

---

[63] Cf. Rudolph.

[64] Similarly E. Beer, "Hosea XII," 291.

[65] W. F. Albright, *Samuel*, 9; *idem, Yahweh and the Gods of Canaan*, 23; cf. also Andersen-Freedman.

[66] Cf. R. B. Coote, "Hosea XII," 401 n. 2.

[67] This interpretation is rejected by L. Perlitt ("Mose als Prophet," 603-605) on the grounds that Hosea saw the prophets as wielders of the divine word (6:5) and not as keepers of Israel. But this sets up a false alternative. The activities are complimentary, and indeed no doubt overlap to a certain extent.

[68] E. Jacob ("La Femme et le Prophète," 85) writes: "Osée emploie déjà ... le terme (viz. נביא) pour désigner la succession ininterrompue des prophétes nécessaire au fonctionnment de l'alliance." Cf. also Rudolph, 231-232; F. Foresti, "Hos. 12," 187-188 n. 37.

[69] F. Stolz, *THAT* I, 840-842; N. Lohfink, *ThWAT* IV, 298, 300-302.

Results

What conception underlies and informs Hosea's survey of Israel's history?

1. At first glance it might appear that Hosea viewed the patriarchal period, or perhaps more reservedly Jacob's era since he is silent on Abraham and Isaac, as the age of the pristine God-man relationship. Jacob is privileged with a direct revelation from Yahweh and is assured divine assistance. He has no need of an intermediary to request and communicate divine oracles to learn Yahweh's will. This he experiences himself. But the appearance is deceiving. Hosea's attitude towards Jacob is rather ambiguous. At no point does Hosea condemn him outright, and yet at no point can one speak of unqualified approval. Jacob supplanted Esau as heir, but with undertones of deception. Jacob struggled with an angel, but with undertones of wickedness. Even in his most positive statement concerning Jacob, Hosea confines himself to saying that Jacob kept, without specifying what he kept. Thus, even Jacob's obedience to the oracle he had received is only "by implication."

With Ephraim, however, the traits which were latent in Jacob become the prominent characteristics. That Jacob passed these traits on to his son and descendants is to be expected. But it is first the association with Canaan that brings them to the fore. Ephraim's might is associated with deception and oppression. This fact finds external expression in Ephraim's adoption of general Canaanite practices, but has its underlying cause in his participation in the Canaanite cult. The cult imparts to its participants certain powers and qualities seen as necessary for a prosperous existence and which therefore express themselves in everyday life. Hosea sees the Yahweh cult as connected with loyalty and justice, both of which Jacob is accordingly called upon to preserve through their expression in his conduct (v. 7). The Canaanite cult, however, imparts a wicked power which expresses itself in deception and oppression (v. 8, 12). As Ephraim spread throughout the land, Canaanite cultic forms incompatible with the worship of Yahweh were nevertheless incorporated into Ephraim's cultic worship. The result was the Canaanization of Ephraim stemming from the Canaanized cult. Consequently, Hosea sees the cultic sites in the land as a predominantly negative factor in Israel's history, a factor bringing about Israel's fall.

2. Juxtaposed to this line of development stands the Exodus from Egypt. Yahweh brought Israel up from Egypt, delivering them from slavery and making a truly meaningful existence possible. This he accomplished through a prophet, Moses. Although the divine will, the knowledge of which is vital to a life of peace and prosperity, must now be mediated, it can be regularly experienced. It may be that in this connection Hosea has the tent of meeting in mind (cf. v. 10b) as the point of contrast to the cultic sites of the land. The tent of meeting was Israel's cultic sanctuary in the wilderness period according to Old Testament tradition. It was here that Yahweh met with Moses and made known to him his will, and it was here that Moses mediated for anyone who sought Yahweh (Ex. 33:7-11). With the Exodus Jacob's continually waiting for his God is replaced by Yahweh's continual care for his people through the prophets and with a pure cult.

3. What do Hosea's statements concerning Jacob and the Exodus-wilderness period reveal about his relationship to the corresponding traditions in Genesis, Exodus, and Numbers? With respect to Jacob we have repeatedly encountered features in Hosea's references which impede a direct identification of Hosea's source with the forms of the

traditions preserved in Genesis. In his allusion to the birth narrative he employs the root עקב in a different manner and suggests a hint of deception latent in Jacob. As for the Jabbok episode, Hosea speaks of an angel where Genesis speaks of a man, and there is no express point of correspondence in the Genesis account to Hosea's mention of Jacob's weeping. We have also seen that Hosea probably knew the tradition of Jacob's initial encounter with Yahweh at Bethel in a variant form of the account in Gen. 28. He also recounts the encounter at Bethel subsequent to the Jabbok episode, contrary to the arrangement found in Genesis. This may indicate that, although the individual traditions were known to Hosea, he was not aware of a fixed chronological ordering of these traditions. But this is not likely. Hosea connected the Bethel experience with Jacob's flight to Aram, that is, with a particular historical moment in the life of the patriarch. Also, Hosea's arrangement appears to be schematic and the choice of episodes in v. 4-5a dictated by the play on the names Jacob and Israel. Once the decision was made to employ these names, Hosea was committed to draw upon the traditions in which they were "explained," irrespective of their chronological relationship to the other traditions employed. Hence, it seems likely that Hosea knew these traditions in a form in which the individual traditions had been ordered into a presentation of the life of Jacob.

Hosea's allusions to Jacob's flight to Aram also shows both points of similarity and dissimilarity. Both Hosea and Genesis refer to a flight (ברח, Hos. 12:13 [12]; Gen. 27:43). In Genesis Jacob flees to Haran (27:43; 29:4), though he is sent by Isaac to Paddan-aram to seek a wife (28:2, 5-7; cf. 31:18). Hosea, however, has Jacob flee to the field of Aram. Once there, it is then Israel who, according to Hosea, serves for a wife, whereas in Genesis the name Jacob is consistently used in this context. Hosea's use of Israel may simply be due to the result of poetic variation in parallel to Jacob, perhaps also in preparation for the mention of Israel in the next verse, so that too much weight should perhaps not be placed on this difference. The careful examination of the evidence strongly suggests that Hosea did not draw upon the forms of the traditions preserved in Genesis, but rather upon variant forms of these traditions. In almost every instance there are both points of contact and points of divergence between Hosea and Genesis, and this fact is best explained by the hypothesis just offered. Since the forms of these traditions in Genesis are for the most part attributed to J (the references to Paddan-aram are usually ascribed to P, and portions of 28:11-22 are often assigned to E),[70] Hosea would thus not be drawing upon this source. Whether Hosea's knowledge derived only from oral recitation or also included a familiarity with a written source could not be determined.

As for the Exodus-wilderness period, Hosea displays not only a knowledge of Yahweh as the one who brought Israel up from Egypt but also of Moses as Yahweh's prophet in this period. This, of course, agrees with the Exodus-Numbers depiction of Moses, where he uses the messenger formula common in prophetic speech (e.g. Ex. 7:17, 26; 8:16; 9:1, 13; 10:3). Upon Moses also rested the spirit which caused the seventy elders to prophesy when they received a portion of it (Num. 11:25). This same spirit rested upon Eldad and Medad, and also caused them to prophesy (Num. 11:26-30). But unlike the other elders, they failed to go out to the tent of meeting and so were prophesying in the camp. When Joshua complained to Moses, the latter replied, "Are you jealous for my sake? Would that

---

[70] Besides the commentaries see e.g. E. Otto, "Jakob in Bethel," 167-182, esp. 167-170, but cf. E. Blum, *Komposition*, 7-35, esp. 19-25.

all the Lord's people were prophets, that the Lord would put his spirit upon them" (v. 29). Clearly Moses is understood here as a prophet. The prophetic activity of the seventy elders, by contrast, is viewed as a temporary condition connected with the initial reception of the spirit (cf. 1Sam. 10:10). On the other hand, Num. 12:6, part of a tradition recounting the questioning of Moses' authority by Aaron and Miriam, may be taken as implying that prophets other than Moses, who in this tradition is seen as more than a prophet, were present at this time. But the premise remains hypothetical since no other prophet was active in this period according to the Exodus-Numbers account.[71] Whether Hosea knew of prophets other than Moses in the wilderness period is not immediately clear. This may be implied in v. 11, but the repeated reference to the one prophet through whom Yahweh brought Israel up from Egypt and through whom he cared for Israel rather suggests that Hosea knew only of Moses. On this point, too, then, there is basic agreement between Hosea and the account in Exodus and Numbers. Whether Hosea was dependent on a written or an oral source for his knowledge could not be ascertained owing to the general nature of his statements.

4. From the foregoing discussion it becomes apparent that Hosea conceived of the history of Israel as falling into four periods: 1) the (non-prophetic) patriarchal period; 2) the Exodus-wilderness period; 3) the period of Canaanization in the land; and 4) the period of renewal. It is striking, however, that he does not present them chronologically. The development from Jacob to Ephraim is followed as if the Exodus had never occurred! It is therefore inaccurate to say that Hosea referred to the Exodus-wilderness period to demonstrate or illustrate the sin of Israel. This occurs without reference to this period. When Hosea does refer to the Exodus, it is in contradistinction to the development which he has already indicated. The Exodus-wilderness period thus retains its salvific character despite its (chrono)logical position within the development from Jacob to Ephraim. However, the effects of the salvific beginning have been negated by the subsequent Canaanization, and so the reprise of the salvific period becomes the means of the redemption of Israel. But the period of renewal represents an enhancement over against the initial salvific period. The latter was marked by Yahweh's care and guidance of his people through one prophet; in the future salvific period several prophets will be active and Yahweh will greatly increase the number of visions.

The boundary between the patriarchal period and the Exodus-wilderness period is naturally marked by the appearance of Moses as Yahweh's prophet sent to bring Israel up from Egypt. More precisely, it may perhaps be associated with the Passover in Egypt as initiating the liberation from Egypt.[72] Since Hosea nowhere else treats the patriarchal period, we must be content with what we have gleaned from this passage. The boundary between the Exodus-wilderness period and the period of Canaanization can only be set provisionally on the basis of Hos. 12. In this regard v. 8-9 presuppose only contact with Canaanite customs without specifically identifying the initial point of contact, and the interpretation of the difficult v. 12 offered above should be considered nothing more than a suggested solution. Hence, it is desirable to define this boundary more precisely and certainly, and so we turn to an examination of Hos. 9:10-13.

---

[71] Balaam may be an exception. However, he appears to have been considered a diviner (Num. 22:7), and in any case did not exercise his office in Israel.

[72] See above on v. 10, p. 47.

B. The Period of Canaanization

1. The Fall at Baal-Peor, Hos. 9:10-13

10   Like grapes in the wilderness
     I found Israel.
Like an early-fig on a fig tree ' '[a]
     I saw your[b] fathers.
They came to Baal-Peor
     and devoted themselves to shame.
They became abominations
     like their 'lover'[c].

11   Ephraim,[a] like a bird their glory flies away:
     no[b] birth, no[b] pregnancy, no[b] conception.

12   Even if they raise their children
     I shall make them childless among[a] men.
For woe to them[b] also
     when I 'depart'[c] from them.[b]

13   Ephraim, when I saw[a] (him),
     was 'like a palm planted in a meadow'[b].
But Ephraim (now) must bring forth[c]
     to the slayer his children.

Textual Notes

10a בראשיתה overloads the colon and is to be deleted with S. It is hardly a gloss on בכורה, the infrequency of which in the OT is purely accidental. It was no doubt a quite common word (cf. *Comment*). Inasmuch as "fig tree" and "wilderness" do not form a particularly close synonymous pair, it is more probable that בראשיתה was added as a closer parallel to "wilderness." The same consideration probably led Duhm to delete כבכורה and to make the minor emendation to כתאנה בראשיתה. Hence, it is properly translated "in its beginning" or "in its first season," i.e. when the fig tree was young and began bearing fruit. Rudolph argues that in this case the phrase is "inessential for the comparison." In his view the phrase can only mean "as its firstfruit" (so also Robinson; Wolff; Jeremias) or "at its beginning" in the sense of the beginning of the current season. He then deletes the phrase because in either case "nothing new is stated." But wherein lies the difference between "inessential" and "nothing new" in this case?

10b 𝕲𝕾𝕯 attest "their fathers." 𝔐 is to be retained as the *lectio difficilior* with the versions altering the suffix in accordance with the context (so also Wolff; Rudolph). The reverse process, original "their" becoming "your," would be inexplicable.

10c The form כְּאָהֲבָם can only be derived from the infinitive construct אֱהֹב, elsewhere attested only in Eccl. 3:8. But the comparison with the plural noun שִׁקּוּצִים makes it more probable that a nominal form is to be read. Hence point כְּאֹהֲבָם from the active participle (so also Wolff, whose "friend," however, is too weak; Mays). A derivation from *אֹהַב "loved object" (Rudolph; Jeremias) also requires revocalization to כְּאָהֳבָם, cf. Prov. 7:18.

11a *Casus pendens* (cf. Harper; Mays; Andersen-Freedman) with anacrusis. This provides a more balanced bicolon than the alternative translation "Ephraim is like the birds, their glory flies away" in which "glory" must refer either to the flock or (more likely) to the brood of young which flies away upon reaching maturity. Connecting "Ephraim" with the previous line to read "like Ephraim's lover" (Sellin; Mauchline; Ward) entails the arbitrary removal of the suffix from "their lover."

11b מִן *privativum*, GKC §119w.

12a מִן *privativum* in the sense of "from among," cf. 1Sam. 15:33.

12b גַם "also" indicates that an additional group is in view here. Since in v. 11-12a the parents are the focus, the reference here must be to the children. With מֵהֶם "from them" Ephraim as a whole is again in view.

12c Reading בְּשׁוּרִי from שׁוּר "travel, journey," cf. Isa. 57:9; Cant. 4:8. That שׁוּר is a variant of סוּר cannot be demonstrated with certainty.

13a There are no grounds for altering כַּאֲשֶׁר רָאִיתִי which is supported by 𝕲𝕾𝕯 (though vocalized as a second singular). רָאֹה picks up the same verb in v. 10.

13b This segment of text is one of the most opaque in the entire book, text-critically speaking. 𝔐's "to Tyre planted in a meadow" makes little sense in the context, and Tyre was situated on an island, not in a meadow. Consequently, it has become common to emend the text on the basis of 𝕲 to לְצַיִד שָׂתוּ (שָׂתֹה לָה) בָּנָיו "he has (they have) made his sons into prey (for him)" (Wellhausen; Marti; Harper; Sellin; Wolff; Ward; Mays; cf. also Ehrlich; Robinson). But this produces a rather cumbersome grammatical construction when connected with v. 13a, and the imagery of prey (and predators) is otherwise absent in the passage. Since the passage contains botanical imagery (v. 10; cf. v. 16), it is best to follow Hitzig's suggestion (himself following Arnoldi in Justi, *Blumen althebräischer Dichtkunst*, 536ff) and connect צוֹר with Arabic ṣawr "(small/young) palm." The feminine form of the participle שְׁתוּלָה "planted" most likely resulted from the misunderstanding of צור as Tyre (cf. GKC §122h). Alternatively, though less likely, צור = "small palm" could be feminine despite its masculine form (so Rudolph).

13c On this meaning of (הוה +) the infinitive construct + ל, cf. GKC §114hk; BrSyn §§25eß, 47.

Form

As indicated above,[73] Hos. 9:10-17 form a single literary complex. But is this complex redactional in nature or does it constitute an original unity? Earlier in this century it was common to take v. 10-17 as a single unit on the basis of a common theme, yet this often entailed deletions or transpositions.[74] Although this view still has its proponents,[75] most commentators are now of the opinion that v. 10-17 are composite in nature.[76] A look at the structure confirms this view. The passage begins with divine speech which continues through v. 13. Yahweh's speech is interrupted by an interjection of Hosea, v. 14, directed at Yahweh, whereupon the divine speech resumes in v. 15 and continues through v. 16. The passage is then concluded by v. 17 where Hosea is again the speaker. The parallel construction of v. 10-14 and v. 15-17, in which a divine speech (v. 10-13; 15-16) is commented upon by Hosea (v. 14, 17), strongly suggests that at least two independent units have been preserved and combined here. Wolff, who also perceives this parallelism in structure, attempts nonetheless to rescue its unity by interpreting it as the report of an audition experienced by Hosea. Rudolph has aptly countered that one would then expect the possessive suffix in "your fathers" to be singular (it is plural in the Hebrew), to which it may be added that the second person address to Yahweh in v. 14 contrasted with the third person reference to him in v. 17 suggests two separate occasions. That the third masculine singular suffixes of v. 15 continue those in v. 14 must consequently be attributed to the redactional composition.[77]

Turning to v. 10-14, the shift from divine speech to prophetic response points to the composite nature of these verses as well. In v. 14 Hosea speaks directly to Yahweh, imploring him to bring about the mildest form of the fate announced in the preceding oracle. But it does not form part of the oracle itself,[78] which spans v. 10-13. To limit the pericope to v. 10 as a self-contained *Scheltwort*[79] rests on the form-critically untenable view that a *Scheltwort* (= diatribe or indication of the situation) represents an independent

---

[73] See above p. 28.

[74] Thus Marti and Nowack delete v. 14, 16aß-17; J. Lindblom, (*Hosea*, 85-97) only v. 14; and Harper transposes v. 16 to follow v. 11.

[75] Wolff; M. J. Buss, *Prophetic Word*, 36, 88; Andersen-Freedman; H.-D. Neef, *Heilstraditionen*, 68-70.

[76] Sellin (with transposition of v. 13 to follow v. 10); Rudolph (with transposition of v. 16a to follow v. 10, v. 16b to follow v. 11): Mays; Deissler; Jeremias.

[77] So also Rudolph; Jeremias.

[78] Emphasized also by Rudolph.

[79] R. Bach, *Erwählung Israels*, 15; J. Vollmer, *Geschichtliche Rückblicke*, 78; R. Kümpel, *Berufung Israels*, though without stating a genre.

prophetic genre.[80] Robinson thus considered v. 10 a fragment having "no real connection" with v. 11a, which he also considered an isolated fragment. However, a connection between the fertility cult and children, the result of human fertility, is quite comprehensible. There are thus no grounds for disassociating any part of v. 10-13 from the whole, and these verses may consequently be taken as an originally independent oracle. There is no reason to doubt that the intercessory prayer in v. 14 is genuine and was Hosea's response to the oracle, but it is not likely to have accompanied the oracle in the public proclamation.

Analyzing the structure of v. 10-13, the passage begins in v. 10 with "past tense" verbal forms (perfect and consecutive imperfects) narrating Yahweh's initial delight in Israel's ancestors and their subsequent apostasy to Baal-Peor. This is followed by a shift to "future" forms (imperfect and consecutive perfect) in v. 11-12 which announce Ephraim's coming childlessness. The perfect in the relative clause of v. 13a returns the focus to the timeframe of v. 10a, though v. 13a as a whole is a noun-clause. This is also true of v. 13b, but here the use of the infinitive to express purpose (cf. note 13c) implies either a present or, more probably, a future frame of reference. This structure can be readily understood as conforming to that of a prophecy. The initial v. 10 forms the indication of the situation and v. 11-12 the prediction, with v. 13 functioning as the concluding characterization.

Comment

The prophecy begins by comparing Israel with "grapes in the wilderness," a phrase often interpreted as expressing Yahweh's unexpected pleasure at discovering an extremely rare but refreshing phenomenon.[81] However, there is no evidence that grapes ever grew in the wilderness.[82] To locate these grapes at an oasis (Rudolph) may give them a degree of plausibility, but goes beyond the text itself which knows nothing of an oasis. Furthermore the point of the comparisons in v. 10a is not the rareness and unexpectedness of the fruits. Early figs are produced in sufficient quantities to be brought to market for sale and are a regular part of the fruit production of the fig tree.[83] It is consequently far more probable that the "grapes in the wilderness" are normal grapes which have been "transplanted" into the wilderness by Hosea because that is where Israel was when "found" by Yahweh.[84]

In what sense then are the verbs "found" and "saw" to be taken? R. Bach, followed by Wolff, argues that these are election terms deriving from a special "discovery tradition," which in contrast to the Exodus tradition located the beginning of the relationship between

---

[80]   C. Westermann, *Basic Forms*, 142-161, 169-189 = *Grundformen*, 102-115, 120-136; K. Koch, *Biblical Tradition*, 191-194 = *Formgeschichte*, 233-237.

[81]   So R. Bach, *Erwählung Israels*, 18; Wolff; Rudolph; J. Vollmer, *Geschichtliche Rückblicke*, 79; Jeremias; cf. also Mays.

[82]   According to M. Zohary (*Plants of the Bible*, 55) grapevines are indigenous to regions with temperate climates, and Dalman (AuS IV, 319-320) states, "Wenn es regenlos, also Wüste wird (Jerem 4,26), hört der Weinbau auf. Trauben in der Wüste sind anomal."

[83]   Dalman, AuS I/2, 379. The word בכורה "early fig" would therefore have been quite common.

[84]   So also J. Lindblom, *Hosea*, 95 n. 1: "Die Bildersprache ist durch die geschichtliche Wirklichkeit beeinflusst."

Yahweh and Israel in the desert.[85] But elsewhere Hosea clearly traces the Yahweh-Israel relationship back at least as far as the period of slavery in Egypt (12:10 [9]; 13:4), so that it is unlikely that he would express a contrary view here. This has led H. Gese to interpret the wilderness period in Hosea as commencing with and encompassing the Exodus, so that, although the verbs "find" and "see" are election terms here, Hosea is not dependent upon a tradition locating Israel's election in the wilderness *as opposed to* the Exodus.[86] Indeed, this interpretation harmonizes with Hosea's view of Israel's history as expressed in Hos. 12, where no distinction between the Exodus and the ensuing wilderness period was apparent.[87] These considerations alone render Bach's interpretation improbable.[88] But that "find" and "see" are election terms here is debatable. The language of v. 10a is unquestionably metaphorical, which argues against pressing these verbs too literally. In fact they are used figuratively in the sense of "consider, experience."[89] Such a usage of ראה "see" is attested in Judg. 9:36 and a similar, though somewhat different usage of מצא "find" in Isa. 10:14. Thus, in the wilderness Yahweh experienced as much delight in Israel as one experiences when eating grapes or early figs. Early figs grow on the branches of the previous year and are especially prized for their juiciness. They were in fact the very best that the fig tree had to offer (Jer. 24:1ff; cf. Judg. 9:10f). Hence, it is said of the early fig: "when a man sees it, he eats it up as soon as it is in his hand" (Isa. 28:4). The vine and the fig tree together form a proverbial picture of the ideal condition. He who is prosperous and lives in peace with his neighbors and his God dwells "under his vine and under his fig tree" (1Kgs. 5:5 [4:25]; 2Kgs. 18:31 = Isa. 36:16), a phrase also used to depict the restored fortunes of Israel (Mic. 4:4; Joel 2:22; Zech. 3:10). Such was Yahweh's joy during the wilderness period.

But with Israel's arrival at Beth-Peor the idyll was shattered. According to the account preserved in Num. 25, the Israelites, at the invitation of the Moabite women, engaged in the cultic sacrifices and ritual dedicated to Baal-Peor. The cultic practices were no doubt sexual in nature, since it was the Moabite women who invited the Israelites to take part. The description "play the harlot" (25:1) may also point in this direction. It is therefore quite probable that it was a fertility ritual in which the Israelites participated. That Hosea is referring to this incident is probable, but whether he knew the tradition in the same form in which it has come down to us cannot be determined given the brevity of his allusion. However, the characterization of Baal as "their lover" suggests that Hosea also connected this episode with fertility rituals.[90] Through their participation in this cult, the

---

[85]   R. Bach, *Erwählung Israels,* 17.

[86]   H. Gese, "Bemerkungen zur Sinaitradition," 146-148 = 40-42; cf. also Jeremias; H.-D. Neef, *Heilstradition,* 113-119; M. Köckert, "Hoseabuch," 22 n. 64.

[87]   See above pp. 50, 52.

[88]   The same holds for the view of R. Kümpel (*Berufung Israels,* 18-32), who argues on the basis of Gen. 16 that the "מצא-tradition" was originally an Ishmaelitic tribal and cult tradition which was taken up by Israel. To account for Hosea's usage of the formula (*sic*), מדבר must be transformed into a chiffre for the dire situation of a person prior to his encounter with God. As a result, Kümpel then claims that "Hosea never speaks of a historical 'wilderness period' that ended with the entry into Canaan" (p. 31). This patently contradicts Hosea's view.

[89]   So also Ehrlich; Sellin; Rudolph.

[90]   This statement depends more on the presence of the root אהב "love" than on the specific analysis of the form כאהבם, so that a reading other than that adopted above (textual note 10c) would not effect this interpretation.

Israelites "devoted themselves to shame." The verbal forms of the root נזר indicate separation (abstention) from something, often for the purpose of separation (devotion) to something.[91] Hence, the Nazirite may be called a "Nazirite to/of God" (נזיר אלהים, Judg. 13:5, 7; 16:17). In contrast to the view expressed in Num. 6, where the Nazirite takes a temporary vow of ritual devotion, the Nazirite retained his status for a lifetime in Hosea's day and before.[92] Thus, Hosea did not view the fall to Baal-Peor as an isolated event of limited duration and with no further repercussions. On the contrary, Israel, represented by the fathers, had devoted himself to Baal for the duration of his life. This devotion to Baal entailed as a consequence that the participating Israelites became "abominations like their lover." Devotion to Yahweh meant that the Nazirite became holy (Num. 6:5). His special relationship to Yahweh caused him to take on the characteristic most typical of Yahweh's nature. Yahweh's holiness consecrated the Nazirite, making him holy. But Baal was not holy; he was an abomination, at least from Yahweh's and Hosea's point of view. And so Israel, as a consequence of their entering into relationship with Baal, took on the nature of Baal, becoming abominations.

With v. 11-12 the prophecy moves into the predictive phase. כבוד, traditionally rendered "glory," denotes that which makes a person "weighty." It endows him with significance and importance, which he then expresses in a manner perceptible to others. This may take the form of wisdom, wealth, (political) power, and/or family, to list a few prominent possibilities. The more abundant these are, the greater a person's כבוד.[93] When this is kept in mind, the word "glory" receives two possible connotations. The first is that the children as the glory of their parents "fly away." Ephraim will no longer be blessed with children. Yahweh is the true God of fertility! Without him there is neither birth, nor pregnancy, nor conception - only sterility. And even if they were to bear and raise children (or are the already existing children intended?), these, too, would be slain, because they have been profaned by their (indirect) association with the Baal cults brought about by the participation of their parents in them. The second nuance is that Yahweh himself is seen as abandoning Ephraim because of the latter's contaminated nature. This is supported by the statement in v. 12b that Yahweh will depart from them.[94] This results from Yahweh's holiness, which is incompatible with the profane or unclean, and such is Ephraim. When Yahweh departs, withdrawing his glory, Israel's glory naturally vanishes because it has been cut off at the source. Israel's glory derives ultimately from Yahweh's glory.

The entire oracle is summarized in v. 13. It picks up the verb ראה "see" from v. 10a and resumes the botanical imagery. The first half of the verse thus refers to the pre-Baal-Peor era. When Yahweh gazed upon Ephraim, he possessed all the beauty and attraction of a thriving young palm planted in a meadow and promising to bear sweet fruit. But in bitter disappointment of his promising beginning Ephraim now brings forth children (fruit) only to be slain.

---

91   Cf. Lev. 15:31; 22:2; Ezek. 14:7; Zech. 7:3; and the lengthy treatment in Num. 6.
92   Cf. Amos 2:11-12 and the Samson story, Judg. 13-16.
93   Cf. C. Westermann, *THAT* I, 798-801; M. Weinfeld, *ThWAT* IV, 25-27.
94   So Andersen-Freedman.

Results

On the basis of Hos. 9:10-13 the boundary between the Mosaic period and the period of Canaanization can now be set definitively. It is marked by the episode with Baal-Peor in which Israel first fell to the enticements of the Baal cults. Here lies the germ of all subsequent apostasy, the point where Canaanite practices first infected Israel. The passage also sheds a certain light on Hosea's conception of the wilderness period. It is a period characterized by Yahweh's joy and delight in Israel. He was pleased with what he found and saw in Israel This observation immediately raises the question of Hosea's awareness of wilderness traditions containing the so-called murmuring motif, in which Israel's discontent calls forth Yahweh's wrath. The problem has been approached in various ways. Mention has already been made of Bach's attempt to trace the passage back to a special "discovery tradition." But since this passage is the only passage in Hosea that can be adduced for a special wilderness tradition[95] and need not be interpreted in this way, there is little foundation for Bach's view.

H. Gese, part of whose position was also touched upon above, interprets the passages cited in support of the "discovery tradition" as a reinterpretation of the Sinai tradition. In his opinion three characteristics point in this direction: 1) location in the wilderness; 2) the event of a meeting between Yahweh and Israel; and 3) an ideal relationship between Israel and Yahweh expressed in terms of personal relationships, e.g. husband-wife, father-son. The Sinai event is now expressed in terms of the personal self-revelation of Yahweh.[96] Gese must admit[97] that the reinterpretation lacks a clear reference to the theophany and covenant, so that the objection of J. Vollmer[98] that on this view the Sinai tradition has been "reinterpreted" by omitting its decisive elements, is not without a certain justification. Furthermore, in Hos. 9:10 it is a question not of Israel's experience of (the self-revelation of) Yahweh, but of Yahweh's experience of Israel.[99] One could consequently speak at most of a veiled allusion to Sinai in which one particular aspect of the tradition, namely Israel's agreement to enter into the covenant, forms the focus and is seen as bringing joy and delight to Yahweh. Such an interpretation could claim 2:17b as support.[100] And yet it is difficult to rid oneself of the suspicion that the allusion is too well veiled to be understood. And even if it be admitted, it fails to address the entire issue, since the

---

[95] Besides 9:10, the primary passages in Bach's treatment are 9:15; 10:11-13a; 11:1-3; 13:5. But the argumentation on 9:15 and 11:1-3 is strictly *e silentio* and in neither case convincing. On 11:1-3 see below p. 67. As for 9:15, Bach hesitates to identify the events referred to, which is understandable, but leaves a gaping hole in the argument since, if the reference is to the beginning of the monarchy in Israel, as many scholars believe, then it cannot be said that merely the wilderness period is by implication pure. By this reasoning the entire pre-monarchic period would be pure, in blatant contradiction of 9:10! Hos. 13:5 is dependent on the Exodus tradition (see below pp. 75-76), and 10:11-13a deals with Ephraim subsequent to the settlement in the land (see p. 68 n. 128).

[96] H. Gese, "Bemerkungen zur Sinaitradition," 147-149 = 41-43.

[97] *ibid.*, 148 = 42.

[98] *Geschichtliche Rückblicke*, 126 n. 347.

[99] It is also for this reason inaccurate when C. Barth ("Wüstentradition," 19) claims that the interpretation of Hosea as having a positive view of Israel in the wilderness period is based solely on an argument from silence.

[100] See below pp. 100-101.

wilderness period was not limited to Sinai in Hosea's thinking but extended from the Exodus to the episode with Baal-Peor.

Vollmer explains the discrepancy between the negative depiction of the wilderness period in Exodus-Numbers and Hosea's positive estimation of the same on the basis of the prophet's "magnificent freedom over against tradition."[101] Hosea's perception of Israel's sin is that Israel has adopted Canaanite cultic practices which in turn facilitated adherence to Canaanite customs in other areas. The core of the problem is devotion to Baal. But this could not occur as long as Israel was wandering in the wilderness where there were no Baals. In contradiction to the tradition known to him from the E source, Hosea interprets the wilderness period as a period of harmony because the danger of apostasy to Baal was not yet a real threat. The harmony could not be intruded upon by a foreign god; Yahweh was alone with Israel in the desert.[102]

We are in agreement with Vollmer's interpretation of Hosea's perception of the root cause of Israel's sin. But the very nature of Hosea's perception renders it inconceivable that he knew of the tradition of the golden calf now preserved in Ex. 32. Admittedly, the identification of the calf with Baal is not to be found in the tradition, but how else would Hosea have understood it if he had known it? For Hosea the "calf of Samaria" is a foreign, indeed false god.[103] Given Hosea's vehement polemic against the veneration of the calf image in Bethel, it is quite unbelievable that he should have known of a tradition relating Israel's worship of a golden calf in the wilderness but nevertheless considered that period to be one of undisturbed harmony between Yahweh and Israel.[104] Vollmer does not treat this issue, so we do not know whether he sees elements of E in Ex. 32 or not. Some scholars do,[105] but it is more probable that the entire chapter belongs to J, with the possible exception of v. 7-14 which are generally held to be a deuteronomistic addition.[106] On the other hand, Vollmer is explicit in his affirmation of the presence of the murmuring motif in E.[107] However, E can nowhere be identified with certainty in these traditions, and in the passages cited by Vollmer, more speaks for an identification with J than with E.[108] Consequently, the grounds for Vollmer's assertion that Hosea's positive view of the wilderness period contradicts the tradition known to him vanish, since it cannot be demonstrated that Hosea's source depicted the wilderness period negatively.

In light of the foregoing discussion, the simplest explanation of Hosea's positive attitude toward the wilderness period is that the traditions known to him depicted it positively, or at least not negatively. Whether we possess variant forms of the traditions

---

[101] *Geschichtliche Rückblicke,* 82.

[102] *ibid.,* 81-82, 125-126.

[103] 8:4-6; 10:5-6; 13:1-3. Both 8:4-6 and 13:1-3 suggest that Hosea identified the calf with Baal; cf. also 2:10 (8).

[104] Similarly O. Procksch, *Geschichtsbetrachtung,* 132.

[105] Whereas it was formerly common to find E in greater or lesser portions of Ex. 32, the number of scholars accepting this view has diminished considerably. Among more recent treatments advocating such a position cf. W. Beyerlin, *Sinaitraditionen,* 24-28, 144-153; J. P. Hyatt, *Exodus,* 300-304.

[106] Similarly M. Noth, *Das zweite Buch Mose,* 200-202; B. S. Childs, *Exodus,* 558-559; cf. also S. Lehming, "Versuch zu Ex. XXXII."

[107] Vollmer assigns Ex. 17:1-7 (combined with J) and Num. 21:4-9 to E (*Geschichtliche Rückblicke,* 82 n. 135).

[108] The same conclusion has been reached independently of one another by G. W. Coats, *Rebellion in the Wilderness,* and V. Fritz, *Israel in der Wüste.* On the passages cited by Vollmer (see previous note), cf. Coats, *op. cit.,* 53-55, 115-117; Fritz, *op. cit.,* 10-11, 29-30, 95-96.

known to Hosea cannot be determined with certainty, but the possibility cannot be excluded. It is generally recognized that the so-called murmuring motif is a tradition-historically secondary development within the wilderness traditions.[109] Opinions differ as to the origin of this motif and as to the motivating factors behind its expansion into the various traditions in which it is now found,[110] and it lies beyond the scope of this study to pursue the question further. What is important for our purposes is the general agreement on two points: 1) the conclusion that these traditions once existed in a form that did not contain the murmuring motif, and 2) the conviction that, however explained, the development of the murmuring motif in the extant traditions is a southern production. It is therefore quite possible that at an earlier date a form of these traditions lacking the murmuring motif found its way into the north and was still current in Hosea's day. Hosea then would have derived his positive view of the wilderness period from a form of the traditions which emphasized Yahweh's care and provision for his people and in which the period was not tainted by Israel's rebellion. This reconstruction has the advantage of not relying on dubious literary-critical decisions. It also meshes well with the results of studies reached in other contexts and does not necessitate the postulation of traditions which are otherwise unknown and consequently beyond even a semblance of objective control. It also agrees well with the results reached for Hosea's knowledge of the Jacob traditions.[111] Whether he knew these traditions in oral or written form could not be determined. The variant forms of the wilderness traditions appear to be present in distinct geographical regions, and hence nothing stands in the way of the assumption of a written source, but neither of an oral source. Specific positive evidence is at this point lacking, and the question is therefore best left open.

2. A Son Goes Astray, Hos. 11:1-7

1   When Israel was a child I loved him,

    and out of Egypt I called my son.[a]

2   (Yet when) they called[a] to them,

    then they went 'away from me'[b];

   'they'[b] (repeatedly)[c] sacrificed to the Baals,

    and burned incense to the idols.

---

[109] M. Noth, *Pentateuchal Traditions*, 58-59 = *Überlieferungsgeschichte*, 62-63; G. W. Coats, *Rebellion in the Wilderness*, 249-250; S. J. de Vries, "The Origin of the Murmuring Tradition," 51-58; V. Fritz, *Israel in der Wüste*, 136.

[110] M. Noth (*Pentateuchal Traditions*, 124-125 = *Überlieferungsgeschichte*, 136-137) sees the origin in Num. 11:4-35*. Both Coats and Fritz consider the motif to be the work of the Yahwist, Coats (*Rebellion in the Wilderness*, 251) interpreting it as polemic directed against the northern cult, Fritz (*Israel in der Wüste*, 134) interpreting it as the Yahwist's means of explaining the failure of the conquest from the south and preparing the way for the conquest from Transjordan. De Vries ("The Origin of the Murmuring Tradition," 56-58) arrived at the same conclusion as Fritz.

[111] See above pp. 50-51.

3   But I guided[a] Ephraim;

'I took them'[b] in 'my'[c] arms.

But they didn't realize that I cared for them.

4   With human cords I led[a] them,

with bonds of love.

I was to them as 'one'[b]

who lifts (the) yoke[c] over their jaws.

I bent[d] down to him

to feed 'him'[e].

5   ' '[a] He shall return to the land of Egypt,

and Assyria, he shall be his king,

because they refused to return (to me).

6   The sword shall whirl in his cities

and consume his oracle-priests[a]

and devour because of their counsels.[b]

7   Then[a] my people are hung on (their) turning away from me.[b]

To 'Baal'[c] they call,

'but'[c] he can't raise them[d] up at all.[e]

Textual Notes

1a   The emendation of לִבְנִי to לוֹ כְּדִי, connecting כדי with the following clause (Wellhausen; Harper; Robinson), finds no support in the textual transmission. The emendation to לוֹ בני, translating "and from Egypt on I called him my son" (Ehrlich; Lindblom, *Hosea*, 100 n. 2; cf. $\mathfrak{SC}$), has against it that קרא would then have somewhat different meanings in v. 1 and v. 2. However, the context is better served by identical usages (cf. Rudolph).

2a   Retaining 𝔐. The popular emendation to כקראי "the more/as often as I called them" or "when I called them" creates unwarranted tension with v. 1 where Israel is pictured as answering Yahweh's call positively (Vollmer, *Geschichtliche Rückblicke*, 57-58 note a). Andersen-Freedman also retain 𝔐 but see here a reference to the Baal-Peor episode analogous to 9:10. Thus the subject of קראו is understood to be the Moabite women who enticed the Israelites to participate in their cult. But the text is far too vague to sustain so specific an identification. (How would the audience have been able to make the connection?) Also, the frequentative verbs of v. 2b (cf. note 2c) are difficult to reconcile with this view. Better is Bach's interpretation of the verb as having an (initially) impersonal subject (*Erwählung Israels*, 65 n. 76; Vollmer, *loc. cit.*).

"They" are the Baals and idols of v. 2b which remain unspecified in v. 2a to create suspense, thereby generating increased attention among the listeners/readers, but also avoiding repetition of בעלים in both halves of the verse.

2b For 𝔐's מפניהם "from them" read with 𝔊 הֵם מִפְּנֵי, and connect הם with the following clause. 𝔐 was induced by the preceding plural forms. Bach's objection (*Erwählung Israels*, 65 n. 76) that the resulting הם becomes problematic ("Aber mit dem הם ist dann doch nichts Rechtes anzufangen"; he reads simply מפני and deletes הם) is refuted by 9:10b (cf. also 4:14; 6:7; 7:13; 8:4, 9).

2c If the imperfects of v. 2b are taken as referring to past action, which is the generally accepted view (but cf. Wellhausen; Marti; Nowack), then these verbs must he frequentative (so also Harper; Rudolph). A desiderative usage (so Jeremias: "they wanted to sacrifice ...") is all too weak here.

3a The form תִּרְגַּלְתִּי (on tiphel cf. GKC §55h) is a hapax legomenon commonly rendered "to teach to walk." This rendering, however, has no support in the versions and is not unproblematic in the context. Andersen-Freedman note that a נער (v. 1) "is not an infant that must be taught to walk," and indeed in v. 2 Israel possesses this capability to their detriment. Moreover, this translation conflicts with the continuation since, as Rudolph remarks, one does not teach children to walk by picking them up. (Rudolph's solution does not overcome this problem, though, cf. note 3b). Both 𝔖 and 𝔗 translate "lead, guide, drive," which suits the context well and receives some support from the piel usage of the root רגל "spy, reconnoiter."

3b The grammatically impossible form קָחָם is obviously corrupt. 𝔖𝔗𝒱 support the reading אֶקָּחֵם (𝔊 אֶקָּחֶנּוּ), which is adopted here. This is either a circumstantial clause (guided ... by taking) or more probably a frequentative imperfect. Rudolph's objection that the perfects of v. 3aα and v. 3b render this unlikely fails to note that the frequentatives in v. 2b are also sandwiched between two perfects (cf. also אמשכם v. 4 between a perfect and a consecutive imperfect). His alternative, first proposed by Nyberg, is to read מִקָּחָם from the noun מִקָּח "taking," assuming haplography of *mem*. The resulting construction is analogous to Gen. 30:37 and is translated "taking them by his arms." The discordance of the suffixes presents a problem, though, which cannot be eased by reference to the shift from v. 4a to v. 4b where each clause is internally consistent in contrast to the proposed reading for v. 3a. It is also questionable whether the preposition על may be rendered "by" rather that "on, up into" in combination with מקח.

3c Assuming dittography of *waw* and reading זְרוֹעֹתָי with 𝔊𝔖𝒱; cf. also 𝔗.

4a Literally "drew, pulled." The picture is that of a farmer leading his yoke of oxen from the field, which necessitated that he "pull" them along.

4b Pointing כמרימי and interpreting the ending as a *ḥiriq compaginis*, GKC §90k-m (so also Vollmer, *Geschichtliche Rückblicke*, 58 note e).

4c   The repointing of עֹל "yoke" as עֻל "suckling" (Sellin; Wolff; Ward; Mays) is questionable on several grounds. It rests in part on the erroneous interpretation of תרגלתי as "teach to walk" (cf. note 3a), and continues the parent-child imagery through v. 4. But the verb "pull, draw" of v. 4a is ill-suited for such imagery. Neither does the alteration of אדם to חסד, which has no support in the textual transmission, change the situation. Wolff's objection that for the lifting off of a yoke one would expect the compound preposition מעל rather that simple עֹל is factually false. The yoke does not rest on the jaws (rather on the neck, cf. 10:11) so that it would not have to be lifted off of them but rather over them. (Dalman's "von den Kinnbacken" [AuS II, 99] most likely means "away from" and not "off of.")

4d   Reading וַאַט, qal consecutive imperfect of נטה. The absence of the final *he* indicates a consecutive imperfect rather than an imperfect. Also, since an intransitive usage of the hiphil of נטה is dubious, the form has been pointed as a qal (with Rudolph).

4e   In all other occurrences the hiphil of אכל is not constructed with *lamed* but rather takes a (double) accusative; hence, for אוכיל לא read אוכילו and not אוכיל לו (so also Rudolph). On the use of the imperfect to express a complimentary verbal idea cf. GKC §120c.

5a   Cf. note 4e.

6a   The meaning "oracle-priest" for בד is indicated by Isa. 44:25; Jer. 50:36 (so already Elhorst, "Das Ephod," 266) and may receive limited confirmation from the Akkadian *baddum* attested in a Mari letter (cf. ARM II 30, (1')9' and Driver, "Babylonian and Hebrew Notes," 19-20). However, *baddum* has also been interpreted (probably correctly) as referring to a military officer (CAD II, 27; cf. AHw, 95), rendering it precarious to place too much weight on this evidence. It has recently been suggested that the בדים in Jer. 50:36 are in fact military functionaries (Andersen-Freedman, building on Rabin, "Hebrew *BADDIM* 'Power,'" 57-58) on the grounds that they stand in parallelism with the warriors (גּבּוֹרֶיהָ). But this is unlikely. The verbs of Jer. 50:36 (יאל, חתת) are not synonymous and the verse probably forms a chiasm with the end of v. 35: princes - wise men - בדים - warriors. Hence the בדים are again grouped with the wise men as in Isa. 44:25. Oracle-priests fit admirably in the present context, *contra* Rudolph. The alternative derivation from בד = "empty, idle talk" (Wolff; Willi-Plein, *Schriftexegese*, 201; Köckert, "Hoseabuch," 6 n. 16) is in light of the divergent suffixes in this and the following colon less likely, and Wolff felt it necessary to translate the term as "prattlers" rather than "prattle."

6b   The textual tradition lends no support to an emendation of the consonantal text of 𝔐. Even 𝔙 *(capita eorum)* can be taken as supporting 𝔐 indirectly if understood as referring to the leaders of the people. Neither do the plural verbs of 𝔊𝔖 reflect a variant consonantal text but rather a variant consonantal division, namely וְאָכְל הֶם מֵעֲצוֹתֵיהֶם "and they (= the people) will eat of their counsels." This would provide a nice transition to v. 7, but entails the difficulty of the third masculine plural suffix finding its antecedent not in the nearby subject of the clause (הם = the people) but rather in the previous clause (בדיו).

7a A causal clause, cf. GKC §158a; BrSyn §135b.

7b Elsewhere the suffix attached to מְשׁוּבָה is subjective, but the context here requires an objective sense. Alternatively, in light of the frequentatives in v. 2 (cf. note 2c), one could read מְשׁוּבֹתָיו "his apostasies," taking the *waw* from וְאֶל or assuming haplography. But the discordance of the plural participle and the singular suffix remains troublesome (cf. note 3b). Another possibility is to take the suffix to be a genitive case ending following the preposition (Kuhnigk, *Nordwestsemitische Studien*, 136-137).

7c Reading וְאֶל בַּעַל יִקְרָאוּ וְיַחַד for וְאֶל עַל יִקְרָאֻהוּ יַחַד on the basis of the rest of the verse and also 11:2 (cf. Sellin; Wolff; Mays). The introduction of הוּא (from יִקְרָאֻהוּ) as the subject of v. 7b destroys the balance of v. 7b. Interpreting עַל as an alternative name for Baal (Jeremias; cf. Nyberg) yields the same meaning.

7d The form יְרֹומֵם is probably contracted from *יְרֹומְמֶם (cf. GKC §72cc and Nyberg); hence, emendation to יְרִימֵם is unnecessary.

7e Literally "altogether, wholly, completely," cf. v. 8; Isa. 27:4; and perhaps Ps. 33:15. Here יַחַד seems to modify primarily the negation: he is altogether unable to raise them up, i.e. he can't raise them up at all.

Form

In its present form Hos. 11 constitutes a literary unit. This is demonstrated by v. 11 which pictures a return from Egypt and Assyria and thus presupposes an exile to these lands. Such an exile is announced in v. 5. The crucial motivating factor for the return from exile is explained in v. 8-9. Yahweh will return his people to their homes solely because of his holiness and love, not because of any merit accrued by Israel. Whether this literary unity has its roots in the oral stage or reflects the redactional unification of originally separate units is difficult to decide. Israel is referred to in the third person in v. 1-7, directly addressed in v. 8-9, and then returns to the third person in v. 10-11. The chapter is composed as divine speech, but this is apparently interrupted in v. 10 which is frequently deleted as a later addition.[112] E. Rohland sought to defend the unity of the chapter by interpreting it as having the form of legal proceedings against a rebellious son. The disobedience is recounted (v. 1-4) and the punishment proposed (v. 6-7). But the father can't bring himself to carry out the punishment (v. 8-9), as indicated by the continuation (v. 11, v. 10 being secondary).[113] However, this view founders on v. 11 which, as already pointed out, presupposes that the banishment to Egypt and Assyria has in fact occurred. Also, the different imagery employed in v. 10-11 over against v. 1-7 argues against the

---

[112] E. Rohland, *Erwählungstraditionen*, 52 n. 2; Wolff; Mays; Deissler; Jeremias. Marti; Nowack; J. Lindblom (*Hosea*, 101) all delete v. 11 as well, whereas Rudolph retains v. 10aα and connects it with v. 9.

[113] E. Rohland, *Erwählungstraditionen*, 52-53; similarly Wolff.

original unity of these verses. It may also be questioned whether v. 8-9 were ever publicly proclaimed.[114] If they were, it is quite unlikely that they formed an independent oracle since they would then be highly susceptible to misinterpretation as a declaration that no harm would come to Ephraim. It is therefore possible that v. 8-11 represent an original unit spoken at a time when Ephraim's demise was painfully apparent to all. Certain is that the logic of v. 1-7 is self-contained. The following v. 8-9 constitute a reaction to these verses and are followed by a depiction of subsequent events in v. 10-11 without, however, negating the message of v. 1-7. Consequently, the latter may in any case be considered separately.

The first four verses of the passage certainly relate to actions in the past, some of which may continue on into the present. The timeframe of v. 5, however, and in dependence on it v. 6, has been variously interpreted. Wolff (followed by Mays) argues that the transition from perfect or consecutive imperfect to imperfect occurs twice in v. 1-4 and hence that the transition from v. 4 to v. 5 is to be understood similarly. H. Donner also connects v. 5 with v. 1-4 on the grounds that the noun-clause of v. 5aß must be interpreted as referring to the present.[115] However, the "tense" of a noun-clause is determined by that of the surrounding verbal clauses and not vice versa.[116] Against Wolff it may be pointed out that the imperfects of v. 1-4 are frequentative, which is made unlikely for v. 5 by the continuation in v. 6, which would also have to be understood frequentatively. Moreover, when Hosea speaks of a return (שוב) to Egypt (8:13; 9:3) it is always a future event, whereas current excursions to Egypt are expressed differently (7:11 "calling"; 12:2 [1] "carrying oil to"). The best interpretation, then, is to see a shift to a future frame of reference in v. 5-6.[117]

The foregoing analysis indicates that the structure of v. 1-6 is that of a prophecy. The indication of the situation is found in v. 1-4, the prediction in v. 5-6. It is from the standpoint of this result that an analysis of v. 7 may best be attempted. If it originally belonged with v. 1-6, then it must either continue the prediction of v. 5-6 or form the concluding characterization of the prophecy. Now the language of v. 7 speaks for connecting it with v. 1-6.[118] "Turning away" (משובה) recalls Israel's return (שוב) to Egypt and especially his refusal to return (שוב) to Yahweh in v. 5. Also, "call to Baal" brings to mind the calling and the Baals of v. 2. Is v. 7 then part of the prediction or the concluding characterization? In the first case the idea would be that the people will remain unfaithful even in judgment. This may be true of the early stage, but Hosea elsewhere envisions the process as dissolving Israel's attachment to Baal (2:9 [7], 16-25 [14-23]). This consideration, coupled with the connections with v. 2, 5b which depict present conditions, suggests that v. 7 summarizes Ephraim's current situation and practice and hence may best be taken as a concluding characterization.

---

114   Jeremias sees v. 7-11* as spoken only to the inner circle of Hosea's followers; cf. also M. J. Buss, *Prophetic Word*, 36.

115   H. Donner, *Israel unter den Völkern*, 89-90.

116   Cf. GKC §141e; similarly J. Vollmer, *Geschichtliche Rückblicke*, 61-62.

117   Cf. Rudolph; J. Jeremias, "Eschatologie," 226-228.

118   J. Jeremias ("Eschatologie," 229) fails to take this evidence into account and further goes awry in assuming the beginning of v. 7 to be adversative without considering other possibilities (cf. textual note 7a).

Comment

The prophecy begins with the Exodus from Egypt. At the beginning of Yahweh's history with Israel as a people stands the liberation from slavery. The father-son imagery implies Israel's "helpless dependence"[119] on Yahweh, a point that will be picked up and developed in v. 3-4. But v. 1 penetrates even deeper. Israel owes its very existence as a free people to Yahweh's gracious act of deliverance. Because he loved him, he called Israel to himself.

The continuation is harsh, both with respect to grammar (asyndetic) and content. Not a word is lost on Israel's response to Yahweh's call. Instead the recitation moves quickly to the call of the Baals, juxtaposing the two. When the Baals called, then Israel responded by departing from Yahweh's countenance (פנים). The term may have cultic connotations here,[120] especially in light of the continuation: they sacrificed to the Baals and burned incense to their images. The heart of the problem lies in Israel's participation in the Baal cults. This infidelity is all the more incomprehensible in that Yahweh had been constant in his care for his people. The adversative beginning of v. 3 underscores this incomprehensibility as well as the fact that it was Yahweh and not the Baals who cared for Israel. Wolff understands רפא "heal, care for" as referring strictly to the Exodus from Egypt on the grounds that Hosea uses the verb for deliverance from political distress (5:13; 6:1; 7:1). But Hosea can also use it of Yahweh's healing Israel's apostasy (14:5). Moreover, the verb רפא is not limited to healing already contracted illnesses but may also include "preventive medicine" (Ex. 15:26; 2Chr. 30:20). It is therefore better to interpret the entire verse as emphasizing the continued care which Yahweh showered on his people. He guided their steps and protected them in his arms.

This theme is continued in v. 4 where, however, the imagery shifts to that of a farmer and his cattle. The חבלי אדם "human cords" are usually interpreted on the basis of the parallelism with "bonds of love" as "humane cords." However, the expressions most closely parallel to חבלי אדם point to a different meaning. In 2Sam. 7:14 Yahweh promises David concerning his descendant, "I will be his father and he shall be my son. When he commits iniquity, I will chasten him with the rod of men (בשבט אנשים), with the stripes of the sons of men (בנגעי בני אדם). Here the phrases "the rod of men" and "the stripes of the sons of men" clearly convey the idea that Yahweh will correct his "son" through human agency. This will also be the meaning of the "human cords" in the current passage. Yahweh pulled Israel along, i.e. guided him, through human agency.[121] Given Hosea's conception of Israel's history, only the prophets can be intended.[122] This view has been challenged on two grounds. H. Donner argues that the context makes perfectly clear that Yahweh operates through human agency, so that the emphasis of this point is superfluous. He consequently emends to בחבלי אהבה "cords of love," deletes "bonds of love" as a gloss, and transposes v. 4b (emended) to take the place of the now removed gloss.[123] The

---

[119] Mays, 153; cf. Wolff; Rudolph.

[120] For the use of פנים in cultic language cf. A. S. van der Woude, *THAT* II, 454-457.

[121] Cf. H. Donner, *Israel unter den Völkern*, 85: "'Mit Menschenseilen' bedeutet schwerlich etwas anderes als daß Jahwe sein Liebeswerk an Israel auf menschliche Weise vollbrachte."

[122] See above pp. 47, 49 on 12:11, 14, and cf. 6:5; 9:8. This view is also advocated by E. Zenger, "Durch Menschen zog ich sie," 193-194.

[123] *Israel unter den Völkern*, 85.

complexity of Donner's reconstruction does not exactly instill great confidence in his proposal. Also, his premise that the phrase is superfluous, even if it be admitted (though this is quite debatable), is a stylistic judgment and not a text-critical argument. H.-D. Neef in fact argues in precisely the opposite direction. He maintains that Yahweh's inner affection for his people, which dominates the passage, renders the mention of human agents inappropriate.[124] But this underestimates the role of the prophets in Hosea's thinking. For Hosea the prophets constitute one of the deepest and clearest expressions of Yahweh's love and care, so that their mention here cannot be considered inappropriate. Still, the prophets do not form the focus of the verse, which falls rather on Yahweh's activity. Yahweh's guidance of Israel was not harsh and unrelenting, but an expression of his love (v. 1). And just as a good farmer tends to his livestock, so too Yahweh removed the yoke and fed Israel. He provided the means of livelihood for the people he had called out of slavery to be his own. But Israel did not comprehend that all this came from Yahweh (2:10 [8]). The verb ידע (v. 3b) has the sense of "internalize, take to heart." When something is internalized, it is truly known and becomes a motivating and determining factor in one's behavior. But Israel failed to take to heart all that Yahweh had done for him and hence failed to act accordingly. Instead, he went to the Baals (v. 2).

Can the references in v. 3-4 be more precisely defined? Does Hosea have concrete historical events in mind, particular historical periods, or Israel's history in general? Some scholars localize the events of v. 3-4 in the period prior to Israel's entry into the cultivated land and so see here a combination of the Exodus (v. 1) and wilderness (v. 3-4) traditions.[125] H. Donner even sees in v. 4 a specific reference to the miraculous feeding of the Israelites in the wilderness.[126] J. Vollmer also applies v. 3-4 primarily to the period prior to the apostasy of v. 2, but questions whether Yahweh's love and care can be confined to this period.[127] However, the shift from Israel (v. 1) to Ephraim (v. 3) indicates that v. 3-4 refer to the period subsequent to the settlement in the land since Hosea never uses "Ephraim" for the people prior to this event.[128] The arrangement is thus "chronological." Has Hosea then omitted the wilderness period?[129] This is possible, though not necessary. In the passages so far examined, Hosea has made no perceptible distinction between the Exodus and the wilderness as two discreet historical periods, and it is quite possible that he has compressed both into v. 1. The evidence to this point is not conclusive, but the further course of the investigation will confirm that this latter interpretation is the more probable.[130]

In v. 5-6 the consequences of Ephraim's apostasy are drawn. Because Ephraim has abandoned Yahweh, Yahweh will abandon Ephraim to his fate. He relies on his oracle-priests who, at least to Hosea's mind (so the context would seem to imply, cf. v. 2, 7),

---

124   *Heilstraditionen*, 92 n. 119. Neef adopts the common interpretation "humane cords."

125   E. Rohland, *Erwählungstraditionen*, 54-55; Wolff; Mays; H.-W. Jüngling, "Reden von Gott," 348-349.

126   *Israel unter den Völkern*, 88.

127   *Geschichtliche Rückblicke*, 64.

128   Of the 35 occurrences in Hosea only 3 can possibly be understood in this way: 10:11; 12:9; 13:1. We have already seen that 12:9 refers to the post-settlement period (see above pp. 46-47, 50). Of the other two neither must be so taken, and the overwhelming evidence of Hosea's usage elsewhere argues compellingly against taking them so. They, too, will refer to the post-settlement period.

129   So Jeremias.

130   See below pp. 70-77 on 13:4-8 and pp. 92-110 on 2:16-25 (14-23), esp. pp. 100-101 on 2:17 (15).

seek their oracles from Baal. Ephraim's orientation is away from Yahweh (v. 2), and he refuses to change course (v. 5b). His pursuance of this misguided course will lead him back to Egypt and make Assyria his king (v. 5a). The oracle-priests who lead Ephraim astray shall fall by the sword, and their counsels shall be brought to naught (v. 6). Only in Yahweh is salvation to be found, but Ephraim has obstinately refused to return to him (v. 5b; cf. 6:11b-7:1) and is entangled in his turning away towards Baal (v. 7a). He is so corrupt that he cannot do differently (5:4; 7:10). But Baal will both be robbed of his spokesmen and prove to be powerless to respond. He will be wholly incapable of sustaining Ephraim in the coming disaster (v. 7b), just as he is incapable of preventing it.

Results

The view of Israel's history expressed in this passage harmonizes fully with the conception already worked out for Hosea. Indeed, certain aspects are more clearly depicted here. From this passage it is manifest that for Hosea the primary datum of Israel's history is the Exodus. Israel's election is founded on this event. Also, it becomes apparent that the period in the arable land was understood by Hosea as a period of struggle for Israel's loyalty. Despite Ephraim's repeated apostasy, Yahweh strives to regain the loyalty of his people by repeatedly attempting to show them the way back to him. If the interpretation of v. 4a advocated above is correct, then the prophets appear again as Yahweh's preferred means of guiding his people. But how is the future conceived? Hosea describes it as a return to Egypt and vassalage under Assyria, or perhaps full incorporation into the Assyrian empire as a province with the total loss of all semblance of sovereignty. The key question at this point is whether Hosea employs Egypt as a theological code word for the revocation of salvation history and Israel's election.[131] Most conducive to this view is 8:13, but the passage need not be understood in this manner. Elsewhere Egypt appears in conjunction with Assyria (7:11; 9:3; 11:5, 11; 12:2 [1]), and even in 7:16; 9:6 Egypt appears as the destination of those fleeing from destruction at the hands of the Assyrians. The presence of Assyria in these contexts is problematic for this view. Is it at all probable that, when he said Assyria, Hosea meant concretely Assyria, but when he said Egypt, he also meant concretely Assyria but theologically Egypt? The evidence suggests rather that Hosea anticipated the actual flight of portions of Israel to Egypt and that this is all that he has in mind when referring to these events. He intends neither the cessation of salvation history nor the annulment of Israel's election.

Looking back upon the historical retrospections in Hos. 9:10; 11:1ff, it is significant to note that just as in Hos. 12 the references to the Exodus-wilderness period prior to the episode with Baal-Peor do not directly illustrate Israel's sin, which in both cases is the worship of (the) Baal(s). This idolatry is juxtaposed to and contrasted with the harmonious and salvific earlier period. It does not have its roots in the wilderness. But the retrospections do not make Israel's sin more comprehensible. On the contrary, it becomes all the more incomprehensible when held up against the background of the salvation and blessings of the earlier period. The implicit understanding of the corresponding traditions underlying Hosea's usage must therefore be that these traditions recount the events

---

131   So Rudolph; Jeremias; cf. also Wolff and Mays on Hos. 9:3, and M. Köckert, "Hoseabuch," 12-14.

establishing Yahweh's claim upon Israel and Israel's responsibility towards Yahweh. If Yahweh had no claim upon Israel, and if Israel had no responsibility towards Yahweh, then there would be no grounds for condemning Israel's turning away from Yahweh. These traditions hence possess for Hosea a binding character. Inherent to their meaning is at the very least the obligation of fidelity to Yahweh.

C. The Mosaic Wilderness Period

The investigation to this point has dealt primarily with the cleft between the Mosaic wilderness period and the subsequent period of life in the arable land and the cause of this cleft. Hosea sees this in the Canaanization of Israel which he traces back to the episode with Baal-Peor. Here the process which continued down to his own day began. Although the focus has so far been on this aspect of Hosea's conception of Israel's history, the inherent nature of the subject matter nevertheless required that attention also be devoted to the statements made concerning the previous Mosaic period. We now turn to other texts which treat the wilderness period more fully or permit inferences pertaining to events of this period.

1. The Relationship in the Wilderness, Hos. 13:4-8

4   But[a] I am Yahweh your God
         [b]from the land of Egypt.
     And a god besides me you do not know[c],
         and there is no savior except me.

5   I knew[a] you in the wilderness,
         in a land of afflictions.[b]

6   When I brought them to pasture[a],
         they became satisfied;
     Satisfied, their heart became proud;
         Therefore, they forgot me.

7   I have become[a] to them like a lion;
         like a leopard I will lurk[b] along the way.

8   I will attack them like a bear robbed of her cubs;
         I will tear open their heart-chamber.
     There[a] [b]lions[c] will devour them[b];
         The beasts[c] of the field will rend them asunder.

Textual Notes

4a The *waw* here is adversative (and redactional, cf. *Form*), emphasizing the fundamental
    distinction between Ephraim's molten images (v. 2) and Yahweh.

4b The expanded text of 𝕲 is definitely secondary as shown by the shorter texts of
    𝕾𝕮𝕯. On the verb העליתי "I brought you up," attested by 𝕲𝕾𝕮, cf. the discussion
    of Hos. 12:10, note a.

4c Baumann ("ידע und seine Derivate," 177) proposed reading תדע as a jussive, but the
    following colon renders it far more likely that the form is indicative (cf. Wolff).

5a It has become common to emend 𝔐 to רעיתיך "I pastured you" on the basis of 𝕲𝕾
    (also implied by 𝕮, "I supplied all your needs") and מרעיתם in v. 6. Baumann (*op.
    cit.*, 35), however, maintained that 𝕲 didn't read differently but rather interpreted
    𝔐 correctly. Huffmon ("Treaty Background," 35 n. 23) argues that the obvious
    expansion in v. 4 (see note 4b) diminishes the reliability of 𝕲 which as a consequence
    need not be followed here. Andersen-Freedman are of the opinion that מרעיתם (v. 6),
    rather than supporting the emendation of 𝔐, influenced the versions and intruded
    itself into v. 5. In fact the proposed emendation poses extreme interpretational
    difficulties. If emended, there would be no alternative to identifying the pasture of
    v. 6 with the wilderness mentioned in v. 5, which would then locate Israel's pride and
    forgetfulness in the wilderness. But this is difficult to reconcile with Hosea's view as
    expressed elsewhere. The episode with Baal-Peor marked the beginning of Israel's fall
    from Yahweh (9:10) with the implication that Israel had been faithful until then (see
    above, pp. 56-60). Moreover, the wilderness figures positively in Hosea's view of the
    early period of Israel's history in 2:16-17 (14-15). 𝔐 is therefore to be retained
    (similarly, Bach, *Erwählung Israels,* 37). 𝕲𝕾 would then reflect texts in which a *yodh*
    had fallen out by haplography and the resulting דעתיך, a grammatically improper
    form, was read as רעתיך because of the proximity of מרעיתם.

5b The exact meaning of the hapax legomenon תלאבות is unclear. The Akkadian cognate
    la'ābu means "afflict, infect," in certain contexts specifically "infect with *li'bu*-disease."
    li'bu-disease is frequently paired in the texts with "high fever," but can also occur in
    more extensive lists of symptoms. Other texts point to a skin disease (cf. the remarks
    in CAD 9, pp. 35 and 182). Wolff, in rejecting KBL's "Fieberschauer; fevers," argues
    that v. 6 suggests rather the lack of food than the presence of disease. This is true,
    but overlooks v. 4 (esp. v. 4bß), which suggests also political distress, so that KBL's
    concentration on the (uncertain) meaning "fever" for the Akkadian is perhaps too
    narrow. Our rendering is based on the more general meaning "afflict" (cf. also AHw:
    "etwa 'strapazieren'").

6a According to Nyberg an abstract noun that functions here as an infinitive and, since
    only one suffix is morphologically feasible, the third plural was selected because the
    first singular is clear from the context. The construction is thus equivalent to כִּרְעוֹתִי
    אֹתָם. Alternatively, the text may be repointed כְּמוֹ(וֹ) רְעִיתָ(י)ם (Halévy [according to

Harper]; Andersen-Freedman). On the continuation of a temporal clause by a consecutive imperfect, cf. GKC §111g.

7a 𝔊𝒱 support וְאֶהְיֶה, a reading frequently adopted (Wellhausen; Marti; Harper; Nowack; Sellin; Mauchline; Vollmer, *Geschichtliche Rückblicke,* 67). But the emendation is "not exactly necessary" (Duhm; cf. the *Comment*) and 𝔊𝒱 probably represent assimilation to the following imperfects (Wolff).

7b 𝔊𝒮𝒱 support the pointing אַשּׁוּר "(on the way to) Assyria." The translation "lurk" retains 𝔐 and adapts the common meaning "look, regard, watch" for שׁוּר to the current context (cf. Vollmer, *Geschichtliche Rückblicke,* 67-68). Against the suggestion of Eitan ("Biblical Studies," 5; followed by Rudolph), who compares the Aramaic שְׁוַר "jump up, leap" and the Syriac and Arabic *s'r* "assault, assail," it may be pointed out that 𝒯 did not translate with this verb but rather opted for כמן "be hidden, lie in wait," which supports the analysis adopted above.

8a That שָׁם can have temporal meaning is dubious. KBL lists only Ps. 36:13 and 132:17 as evidencing this sense. But in the latter passage שָׁם is undoubtedly locative and refers to Zion, whereas in the former it is questionable whether a temporal interpretation provides better sense. BDB lists a usage "in poetry, pointing to a spot in which a scene is localized vividly in the imagination" and cites Ps. 14:5; 36:13. This may be the usage here or, perhaps more likely, שָׁם refers back to דֶּרֶךְ ("way") in v. 7.

8b Ever since Duhm first made the suggestion it has become common to read כלבים "dogs" for כלביא "like a lion." But, popular though this emendation may be, it has no support in the textual transmission:

𝔊 = וַאֲכָלֵם שָׁם לְבִיאִם

𝒮 = וַאֲכָלָם שָׁם לָבִיא

𝒯 = וְאֹכְלֵם שָׁם כְּלָבִיאִם

𝒱 = וְאֹכְלֵם שָׁם כְּלָבִיא

The parallel colon v. 8bß makes it most probable that 𝒮 has preserved the best reading and has therefore been adopted. The main argument advanced for reading "dogs" is that a return to lion imagery, already used in v. 7, is repetitious and stylistically disruptive (Duhm; Wolff: Rudolph); however, this argument belongs in the realm of stylistic analysis and critique, not that of textual criticism. It is methodologically improper to alter an otherwise viable text to suit modern literary sensibilities. This is all the more true when the text in question receives corroboration from the versions.

8c Singular nouns used collectively.

Form

The extent of the literary complex 13:1-14:1 (13:16) is demarcated by the beginning of another historical retrospection following 12:3-15 in 13:1 and the imperative of 14:2 (1) which opens the subsequent literary complex.[132] The complex begins by recalling Ephraim's prominent position within Israel in the pre-monarchic era, v. 1a. But he incurred guilt through Baal and initiated the process of decline which would (will) ultimately issue in his death, v. 1b. In v. 2 the focus shifts abruptly but unmistakably to the present (ועתה "even now"), in which the idolatry begun in the earlier age flourishes uninterrupted. V. 3 then announces that the cultic objects of Ephraim's idolatrous worship of Baal shall be blown away. The "therefore" introducing v. 3 signals the transition from the indication of the situation (v. 1-2) to the prediction (v. 3),[133] so that v. 1-3 form a self-contained prophecy. In contrast to v. 1-3 where Ephraim appears in the third person, in v. 4-5 he is directly addressed. This is necessitated by the self-introductory formula, v. 4a, but is dropped in favor of the third person in v. 6, which is then sustained through v. 8. V. 4-5 further contrast with v. 3 in that they return to historical retrospection, this time going back behind the pre-monarchic period in the arable land (v. 1) to the Exodus and wilderness period (v. 4-5). With v. 6 the retrospection reaches the entry into the land, linking up with v. 1. This may explain the shift to the third person. The wilderness period is the period of the more direct relationship between Yahweh and Israel, whereas with the entry into the land the period of alienation begins. In v. 7-8 the focus again shifts, this time to the future. The consecutive imperfect ואהי "I have become" of v. 7a might seem to contradict this statement, but in fact it denotes the completion of a change in Yahweh which will have future consequences. It is on these future consequences that the emphasis is laid in v. 7-8, as indicated by the five imperfects in these verses. The structure of v. 4-8 thus also conforms to that of a prophecy. V. 4-6 form the indication of the situation, v. 7-8 the prediction. The adversative *waw* linking v. 4-8 with v. 1-3 must accordingly be understood as a redactional connection intended to contrast the impotence of Ephraim's idols (= Baal) with the power of Yahweh as demonstrated in the Exodus.

It is unlikely that v. 9-11 represent the original continuation of v. 4-8. The shift to the direct address of Israel in v. 9-11 speaks against this, as does the transition from the imperfects of v. 7-8 to the perfect introducing v. 9.[134] Also, the perspective is different in the two units. Whereas the prophecy of v. 4-8 looks forward to the coming disaster, v. 9-11 presuppose that the destruction has already begun.[135] Within the context of Assyria's march into Israel and the siege of the latter's cities (v. 10), the foolishness of Israel's desire for a king is laid bare. He is wholly unable to save Israel from the progressing

---

[132] See above pp. 28-29.

[133] C. Westermann, *Basic Forms*, 149 = *Grundformen*, 107; K. Koch, *Biblical Tradition*, 212 = *Formgeschichte*, 260.

[134] זה is to be repointed שְׁחֶתְךָ with S; so also Marti; Nowack (with a question mark); Ehrlich; Sellin; Robinson; Wolff; Rudolph; Mays; I. Willi-Plein, *Schriftexegese*, 225; Andersen-Freedman; Jeremias.

[135] The narrative form in v. 7a may also reflect this. Nevertheless, the fundamental vantage point with respect to the disaster differs from that of v. 9-11.

onslaught.[136] Thus, v. 9-11 also have a different theme than v. 4-8 and hence are to be taken as a distinct unit.

The analysis of v. 4-8 as an originally independent prophecy has been questioned by Jeremias, who considers v. 3, as well as v. 2aδ-bα, secondary and so takes v. 1-8* as an original unit. He argues that later Judean's took up Hosea's words in 6:4 and expanded them to underscore the non-existence of handmade gods. In this they show themselves dependent on Deutero-Isaiah. Furthermore, לכן "therefore" (v. 3) is restricted in Hosea to chapter 2, and that is not accidental. Indeed, the removal of v. 3 allows the adversative introduction of v. 4 to follow directly upon the references to the molten calf images in v. 2. But, attractive though this may be, Jeremias' arguments are not convincing. The primary intent of v. 3 is not to expound the ontological essence of idols but to announce their fate. Yet even the argument from the history of Israelite religion is dubious. Such a history must be written on the basis of the texts and not the texts rewritten on the basis of a supposed history of religion. At several points Hosea's thinking runs in the direction of exposing the ridiculousness of venerating man-made idols.[137] Given the extent of the evidence no other conclusion is possible than that Hosea was a precursor of Deutero-Isaiah on this score.[138] That v. 3a is paralleled verbatim in 6:4b is at best a two-edged sword since, the authenticity of 6:4b not being questioned, this establishes the formulations as Hoseanic. Why couldn't Hosea have used them more than once? And lastly, although Jeremias claims that לכן has been purposely confined to chapter 2, he fails to explain what this purpose was, so that in effect this claim remains unsupported.

In a similar vein J. Vollmer has argued that v. 4 is secondary.[139] He maintains that v. 4a is a promise that has no place between the threats *(Drohworte)* contained in v. 1-3 and v. 5-8, and that the language of v. 4b is reminiscent of Deutero-Isaiah, in particular זולתי "except me" (Isa. 45:5, 21) and מושיע "savior" (Isa. 45:11, 21). However, זולה must have been a common word,[140] and its use in conjunction with Yahweh is also attested prior to Deutero-Isaiah.[141] The same can be said of מושיע.[142] It may also be noted that the characterization of v. 4a as a promise is hardly appropriate. The verse looks to the past, not to the future. There are thus no grounds for denying that v. 4-8 originally formed an independent prophecy deriving from Hosea.

---

[136] Hos. 13:10b is also aimed at the monarchy, though indirectly. In a bygone era Israel sought to meet the challenge of an enemy threat by selecting a king (cf. 1Sam. 8). In the face of the Assyrian threat Israel might he tempted to do the same, but now there are no judges who could give them a king.

[137] Cf. esp. 8:6a; 14:4. Their authenticity is denied by Jeremias but defended by Harper (only 8:6a); Sellin; Robinson; Wolff; Rudolph; Mays; Andersen-Freedman; Deissler. See also 4:12, 17; 8:4; 10:5-6; 11:2; 14:9.

[138] Cf. the similar thought expressed by Isaiah, Isa. 2:8, 20 (Wolff).

[139] *Geschichtliche Rückblicke*, 68-69.

[140] Deut. 1:36; 4:12; Josh. 11:13 (as a conjunction); 1Sam. 21:10; 1Kgs. 3:18; 12:20; 2Kgs. 24:14; Ruth 4:4.

[141] Ps. 18:32 (31) = 2Sam. 22:32; 2Sam. 7:22 = 1Chr. 17:20; cf. also Isa. 26:13; 64:3.

[142] In application to Yahweh cf. 1Sam. 10:19; 2Sam. 22:3; Jer. 14:8; Ps. 7:11 (10); 17:7; and perhaps 2Sam. 22:42 = Ps. 18:41; cf. also Ps. 106:21. In application to a human deliverer cf. Deut. 22:27; 28:29, 21: Judg. 3:9, 15; 12:3; 2Kgs. 13:5; Isa. 19:20.

Comment

The oracle begins with the self-introductory formula in which Yahweh presents himself as the God who liberated Israel from slavery in Egypt. Because of the formula's association with legal material and proclamation, it implicitly reminds Israel of his debt of obedience owed to Yahweh as the appropriate response to his gracious act of liberation.[143] This point is driven home by emphasizing the fact that Yahweh is the only deliverer Israel has ever known (v. 4b) and conversely that Yahweh already knew Israel in the wilderness before Israel had any contact with the Baal's of Canaan. The meaning of the Hebrew ידע "know," although also encompassing the cognitive, is not exhausted by the intellectual aspect. It denotes a knowledge deriving from experience and issuing in the proper practical conduct with respect to the object known.[144] Thus it can be used to denote technical "know-how,"[145] as well as sexual intercourse between a man and a woman as an experience imparting knowledge of one another.[146] The verb can also express the idea of "taking care of" as an action deriving from a knowledge of the needs of a situation,[147] and also the act of divine choice.[148] The contextual framework established by v. 4a indicates that the verb ידע in v. 4b, 5a refers not to the intellectual awareness of the existence of other gods, but rather to the historical experience of the Exodus. Israel came to know only Yahweh because it was he alone and no other deity that liberated the Hebrew slaves in Egypt. Here Hosea shows himself dependent on the Exodus tradition, which in both the Yahwistic and Priestly versions is perceived as imparting the knowledge of Yahweh.[149] The statement that Yahweh knew Israel in the wilderness (v. 5) may be understood in two ways. It may refer to Yahweh's taking care of Israel in a parched and inhospitable land.[150] But this interpretation is subject to the same reservations mentioned in connection with the possible reading "I pastured them."[151] Alternatively "know" may here refer to Israel's election.[152] H. B. Huffmon has argued that the term is used here in a technical sense relating to the covenant. It expresses Yahweh's election and recognition of Israel as his covenant people, a usage which he also sees in Amos 3:2.[153] However, neither Amos 3:2 nor Hos. 13:5, nor their immediate contexts speak *expressis verbis* of a covenant. Also, it is striking that within the Old Testament covenant tradition, be it Sinai or Shechem, the verb ידע is not attested. On the other hand, it is very prevalent within the Exodus

---

143   Cf. on 12:10 and the works by K. Elliger and W. Zimmerli cited on p. 47 n. 51.

144   See E. Baumann, "ידע und seine Derivate"; G. J. Botterweck, "*Gott Erkennen" im Sprachgebrauch des Alten Testamentes;* J. Bergman and G. J. Botterweck, *ThWAT* III, 479-512; W. Schottroff, *THAT* I, 682-701.

145   E.g. Ex. 36:1; 1Sam. 16:16-18; 1Kgs. 5:20; Isa. 29:11; Jer. 1:6; Amos 5:16.

146   E.g. Gen. 4:1, 17, 25; 24:16; 38:26.

147   E.g. Gen. 39:6, 8; Ps. 31:8-9.

148   E.g. Gen. 18:19 of Abraham; Ex. 33:12, 17; Deut. 34:10 of Moses; Jer. 1:5 of Jeremiah; 1Chr. 17:17 of David.

149   In J: Ex. 5:2; 7:17; 8:6, 18 (10, 22); 9:14, 29; 10:2; 11:7. In P: Ex. 6:7; 7:5; 14:4, 18; cf. 29:46. P also knows of events in the wilderness that imparted the knowledge of Yahweh, Ex. 16:6, 12, 15. See also W. Zimmerli, *Erkenntnis Gottes,* 22-27, 54 = 61-66, 96.

150   See n. 147.

151   See textual note 5a.

152   See n. 148.

153   H. B. Huffmon, "Treaty Background," 31-37, esp. p. 35.

tradition, so that the cited texts are better understood as referring to the Exodus as the beginning of the relationship between Yahweh and his people Israel.[154] Hosea thus sees the Exodus and the wilderness wanderings as a single period.[155] Whether this was a period of complete harmony between Yahweh and Israel is not the concern of the text. Rather the emphasis is upon Yahweh as the sole God of Israel in this period.

With v. 6 the wilderness is left behind and Israel enters the land. Yahweh has brought his people to pasture. But with what disastrous results! Overwhelmed by the bounty of the land and the prosperity which flowed from it, Israel became prideful. He failed to internalize the underlying realities which together created and sustained his existence. The terse statement "they forgot me" stands in stark contrast to the double occurrence of "know" in v. 4-5. The statement that Israel knew no other gods in the wilderness period indicates that Israel later forgot Yahweh in favor of other gods. Israel's pride led to idolatry. Israel forgot that Yahweh had ended his slavery in Egypt; that Yahweh had chosen Israel to be his own people, obedient and loyal to him alone; that Yahweh had given him the land and caused it to yield its produce (cf. 2:10-11 [8-9]). By his actions Israel has *de facto* ceased to be Yahweh's people (1:9).

The consequences of Israel's severance of the bond with Yahweh are depicted in v. 7-8 with illustrations taken from the animal world. That this wild animal imagery actually derives from covenant/treaty curses[156] is for Israel problematic since such imagery is not a pronounced feature of Israel's covenant traditions (only Lev. 26:22; Deut. 28:26, 38-39, 42). The verses themselves fall neatly into three parts: 1) preparation for the attack, v. 7; 2) the attack itself, v. 8a; and 3) the after-effects, v. 8b. The savior who had delivered Israel, the shepherd who had grazed and protected his flock now becomes himself the predator bringing destruction. He will himself bring about Israel's violent end. This is not arbitrary vengeance on Yahweh's part, but develops organically from the seed planted by Israel in his actions. In forgetting Yahweh and severing his bond to him, Israel has cut himself off from the source of his existence. His death as a nation is thus the inevitable consequence.

Results

The conception of Israel's history informing this passage is in all essentials that which has already been encountered in the previous texts. Here, as in 11:1 (cf. 12:10, 14 [9, 13]), the Exodus marks the beginning of the Yahweh-Israel relationship. The wilderness, though not a period devoid of hardships, was the period in which the relationship between Yahweh and Israel was undisturbed. Once again the possibility that Hosea knew the tradition of the golden calf is excluded.[157] In the wilderness Israel knew Yahweh and only Yahweh, and Yahweh knew Israel and made them his people. With the entry into the land Israel forgot Yahweh. New in this passage is the idea that Israel's pride is the cause of

---

154 Similarly K. Galling, *Erwählungstraditionen*, 9-12.

155 Even R. Bach (*Erwählung Israels*, 41), who is otherwise at pains to emphasize the distinctiveness of his proposed "discovery tradition," must admit that this was Hosea's view.

156 So D. R. Hillers, *Treaty-Curses*, 55-56, followed by Mays. For examples of such treaty curses see Hillers, *op. cit.*, 12-29.

157 See above p. 60.

his idolatry. In contrast to 9:10 where Hosea has the first concrete instance of Baal worship in view, here he has the continued and widespread idolatry throughout the land in mind.

Also in evidence in this passage is the particular nature of Hosea's understanding of the various periods of Israel's history. It allows him to view events which appear to us to represent distinct eras as belonging together as a cohesive whole. This is true of the Exodus and wilderness, and also of the monarchic and pre-monarchic periods. That Hosea is able to see these last two periods as belonging fundamentally to a single period of history is all the more astonishing in light of his opposition to the monarchy in Israel. Some scholars maintain that Hosea does not reject kingship as such but only the particular kings who by their actions prove themselves unworthy of the office.[158] But if our view that Hosea himself is responsible for the redaction of Hos. 12-14 is correct,[159] then it would seem that his arrangement of 13:1-11 in the present order speaks rather for his rejection of kingship itself. Beyond the considerations mentioned,[160] the contrast between Yahweh as Israel's sole deliverer (מושׁיע, v. 4) and Israel's search for deliverance from its king (יושׁיעך, v. 10) also points in this direction. Hosea rejects the kingship in Israel because it represents an attempt to find security in a source other than Yahweh. Hosea's scrutiny of his people's history penetrates to the fundamental character of each period, and the period beginning with the entry into the land has as its basic feature apostasy and rejection of Yahweh. The establishment of the monarchy is just one, albeit an extremely grievous manifestation of the underlying disposition within Israel.

As for the presentation of the pre-settlement period in 13:4-8, it should be noted that no mention is made of Sinai. This indicates at the very least that Hosea did not consider Israel's special relationship to Yahweh to be grounded in the covenant at Sinai but rather in the Exodus from Egypt. But it may also imply that Hosea did not know of a covenant between Yahweh and Israel. It is to this question that we now turn.

2. Hosea and the Covenant

The nature and significance of the covenant idea for the understanding of Israelite religion constitutes one of the most disputed issues in Old Testament research, and the literature treating the subject either directly or indirectly is accordingly legion. It is not our intention here to enter into an exhaustive discussion of this topic but rather to provide a brief sketch of the various positions which have been adopted in the discussion and the major issues involved with an eye to seeing what light an examination of Hosea's prophecies can shed on the problem.[161]

The view that the covenant was central to Israelite religion and hence to a proper understanding of the Old Testament has been classically advocated by W. Eichrodt, who

---

[158] So A. Caquot, "Osée et la Royauté"; E. Jacob, "Der Prophet Hosea und die Geschichte," 283; A. Gelston, "Kingship in the Book of Hosea."

[159] See above p. 29.

[160] See n. 136.

[161] For a more detailed presentation cf. D. J. McCarthy, *Old Testament Covenant. A Survey of Current Opinions,* an expanded version of *Der Gottesbund im Alten Testament. Ein Bericht über die Forschung der letzten Jahre,* and E. W. Nicholson, *God and His People. Covenant and Theology in the Old Testament.*

accordingly organized his presentation of the theology of the Old Testament around the covenant concept.[162] From the Mosaic period onwards, Israel ordered its knowledge of Yahweh and perception of its own unique status within a covenant framework. The covenant relationship was "founded on a primal act in history, maintained on definite conditions and protected by a powerful divine Guardian."[163] So understood, the covenant is "essentially two-sided" and emphasizes the "factual nature of the divine revelation." It also creates "an atmosphere of trust and security" because it gives clear formulation to a divine will free from arbitrariness and caprice.[164]

The basic position advocated by Eichrodt, questioned even prior to his day,[165] subsequently came under renewed fire. J. Begrich argued that ברית originally denoted a relationship between unequal partners in which the superior party extends the ברית-relationship to the inferior. The recipient, however, undertakes no obligations, only the more powerful initiator does. ברית as entailing mutual rights and obligations is a secondary development.[166] A. Jepsen concurred with Begrich's view that ברית referred to an obligation undertaken or a promise given, but contested the view that this occurred one-sidedly on the part of the superior party. In Jepsen's view the obligations undertaken could be unilateral or bilateral, and the ברית could be initiated by either party irrespective of relative strength.[167]

E. Kutsch revised the understanding of ברית even further by insisting that it could also denote the obligation imposed on one party by another. All combinations thus become possible.[168] But only in instances of mutual obligation in the establishment of a completely new relationship between parties who have not previously stood in any direct relationship to one another[169] is it appropriate to speak of a covenant. The validity of this second restriction is highly questionable, but Kutsch also maintains that in all cases involving Yahweh, ברית refers either to his promise given or to an obligation imposed but never to a mutual obligation. There was therefore never a "covenant" between Yahweh and Israel.[170] L. Perlitt has recently taken the argument a step further. He argues that covenant theology (formally he retains the term, though with regard to content he rather favors Kutsch's position) is a deuteronomistic creation. Where it appears in earlier sources, it is

---

[162]   W. Eichrodt, *Theology of the Old Testament* = *Theologie des Alten Testaments.*

[163]   *ibid.*, 36 = 9.

[164]   *ibid.*, 37-38 = 9-10.

[165]   Cf. J. J. P. Valeton, "Bedeutung und Stellung des Wortes ברית im Priestercodex"; *idem*, "Das Wort ברית in den jehovistischen und deuteronomischen Stücken des Hexateuch sowie in den verwandten historischen Büchern"; *idem*, "Das Wort ברית bei den Propheten und in den Ketubim - Resultat"; and R. Kraetzschmar, *Die Bundesvorstellung im Alten Testament in ihrer geschichtlichen Entwicklung.*

[166]   J. Begrich, "Berît," 2-5 = 56-59.

[167]   A. Jepsen, "Berith," esp. 162-165.

[168]   E. Kutsch, "Gesetz und Gnade," 20-26; *idem*, "Der Begriff ברית," 135-137.

[169]   This latter restriction becomes apparent in Kutsch's treatment of various passages. With regard to Gen. 15:8 he states, "Ebensowenig wie die Zusage und der Eid stellt dabei ברית ein neues Verhältnis zwischen Jahwe und den Patriarchen her, so daß sie als 'Bund' verstanden werden könnte," and with reference to the pre-deuteronomic portions of the Sinai pericope, "*berit* bezeichnet nicht ein neues Verhältnis zwischen Jahwe und Israel, das am Sinai zustande gekommen wäre" ("Der Begriff ברית," 137 and 140, respectively).

[170]   E. Kutsch, "Der Begriff ברית," 137-143; *idem*, "Gesetz und Gnade," 27-34.

actually a case of deuteronomistic additions designed to bring these texts into line with deuteronomistic theology.[171]

When examining the works propounding this line of argumentation, one may at times observe a tendency to demand too much of texts that were not composed as an exposition of ברית and are therefore interested in only one aspect of the total phenomenon. This then results in the failure to consider implications inherent in, but not explicitly stated by the context or implications which become apparent only beyond the immediate context. Thus, Kutsch maintains that Josh. 24:25 refers to a unilateral obligation to worship Yahweh undertaken by Joshua and the people. There is no express mention of a reciprocal commitment by Yahweh.[172] But Joshua's recital of Yahweh's past actions on Israel's behalf surely is intended to motivate the people to choose Yahweh as the God they will serve, and it can perform this function only if the underlying conception is that Yahweh will continue to act on behalf of his people. The overall context consequently presupposes a mutual character in the event. The situation with the ברית between Israel and the Gibeonites is even clearer. Kutsch interprets this ברית as the self-obligation undertaken by the Israelite leaders to let the Gibeonites live (Josh. 9:15).[173] But v. 21 presupposes that when the ברית was made the Gibeonites agreed to become "hewers of wood and drawers of water for Israel." In the final subordinate clause להם "to them" picks up the subject of the verb ויהו "they became" and refers to the Gibeonites. The clause itself refers to a previous occasion, which can only be when the ברית was concluded. Josh. 10:1 also reveals the mutual character of the event when it relates that "the inhabitants of Gibeon had made peace (השלימו) with Israel." Josh. 9:15 formulates the matter from the other perspective: "And Joshua made peace (ויעש ... שלום) with them (= the Gibeonites)." What is apparently unilateral according to the grammatical construction turns out in actuality to be functionally bilateral. Israel agreed to let the Gibeonites live, and the Gibeonites agreed to serve Israel.[174]

Another area of research has concerned itself with the question of the role of the covenant in Israel's cultic worship, in particular with the question of a festival or ceremony of covenant renewal. S. Mowinckel was the first to advance the thesis that the structure of the Sinai pericope evidenced in the various sources indicates that these accounts have been patterned after a cultic festival of covenant renewal. This formed part of the New Year's festival as celebrated in Jerusalem.[175] G. von Rad accepted the cultic background for the Sinai tradition proposed by Mowinckel and found confirmation of this view in the similar structure evidenced by Deuteronomy. But unlike Mowinckel he located the festival at Shechem in accordance with Deut. 27 and Josh. 24.[176] Von Rad also argued that the Sinai tradition was to be distinguished from the (Exodus-)Conquest tradition, which he connected with the Feast of Weeks celebrated at Gilgal.[177] A. Weiser rejected von Rad's assignment of the two traditions to separate festivals. He noted that in Josh. 24 historical recitation and the conclusion of a covenant are both part of a larger whole. He further

---

[171]   L. Perlitt, *Bundestheologie im AT.*

[172]   E. Kutsch, "Der Begriff ברית," 140-141; *idem*, "'Bund' und Fest," 317-320.

[173]   E.Kutsch, "Der Begriff ברית," 135; *idem*, "Gesetz und Gnade," 25.

[174]   Cf. D. J. McCarthy, "*Berît* and Covenant," 67-68.

[175]   S. Mowinckel, *Le Décalogue*, 114-129.

[176]   G. von Rad, "Form-Critical Problem," 20-40 = *Das formgeschichtliche Problem*, 18-37 = 28-48.

[177]   *ibid.*, 3-8, 41-48 = 3-7, 37-44 = 11-16, 48-55.

emphasized the fundamentally different nature of the two traditions. The historical traditions represent the revelation of Yahweh's being, whereas the traditions associated with Sinai reveal his will. The seeming independence of the two traditions is due solely to the inherent differences in their content. Weiser therefore concluded that the two traditions do not reflect separate festivals but distinct portions of a single festival. This he identified as a covenant festival celebrated by all Israel at the central sanctuary of the tribal league, the ark, at the beginning of the year in autumn.[178]

Naturally enough, those denying that there ever was a covenant between Yahweh and Israel or who maintain that the idea is a late creation of the deuteronomistic school also deny that there was a festival or ceremony of covenant renewal. What did not exist could not be celebrated or renewed.[179] But even scholars less unfavorably disposed towards the covenant concept object that there is no proof that the autumn festival commemorated the covenant and that in later times the covenant was connected with the Feast of Weeks, which would be difficult to explain if it had earlier been celebrated at the New Year's festival.[180]

Lastly, the use of international treaties as a means of illuminating the covenant in Israel should be mentioned. G. Mendenhall was the first to suggest that Israel's covenant traditions were patterned after an adapted form of the Hittite suzerain-vassal treaties.[181] These consisted of 1) a preamble identifying the suzerain; 2) a historical prologue describing the past relationship with emphasis on the benevolent acts of the suzerain; 3) the stipulations imposed on the vassal; 4) provisions for deposit in a temple and for period public reading of the treaty; 5) a list of gods and natural phenomena as witnesses; 6) curses and blessings. The treaty was enacted by an oath taken by the vassal in an accompanying ceremony.[182] Of these elements only the list of divine witnesses had to be omitted in Israel, but all other aspects are present in Israel's covenant traditions beginning with Sinai.[183] More recent studies, however, have tended to reject the appropriateness of the analogy for the Sinai covenant. D. J. McCarthy thoroughly analyzed the treaty form and the Old Testament texts and came to the conclusion that Proto-Deuteronomy is the first instance of the formulation of the covenant according to the treaty genre.[184] He has received a good following,[185] but here, too, dissenting voices question the validity and usefulness even of this more limited comparison.[186]

These then are the major issues in the current discussion of the covenant in Israel. When examining Hosea's conception of the covenant, it cannot reasonably be expected that the exact form of the covenant known to him can be reconstructed, that is, whether

---

[178]   A. Weiser, *Einleitung,* 72-82; cf. *idem, Die Psalmen,* 14-35.

[179]   Cf. E. Kutsch, "'Bund' und Fest"; L. Perlitt, *Bundestheologie,* 115-128.

[180]   See e.g. R. de Vaux, *Ancient Israel* II, 502.

[181]   G. E. Mendenhall, *Law and Covenant in Israel and the Ancient Near East = Recht und Bund in Israel und dem Vordern Orient.*

[182]   *Law and Covenant,* 31-35 = 57-61 = *Recht und Bund,* 33-38.

[183]   Mendenhall has been followed in his basic analysis by K. Baltzer, *Das Bundesformular,* and W. Beyerlin, *Herkunft und Geschichte der ältesten Sinai-Traditionen.*

[184]   D. J. McCarthy, *Treaty and Covenant.*

[185]   Cf. e.g. R. Frankena, "The Vassal-Treaties of Esarhaddon and the Dating of Deuteronomy"; R. de Vaux, *Early History,* 439-443.

[186]   Cf. e.g. F. Nötscher, "Bundesformular und 'Amtsschimmel'"; and G. Fohrer, "Altes Testament - 'Amphictyonie' und 'Bund'?," 895-897 = 107-110.

or not it was formulated according to the treaty pattern. Hosea's concern was not to give his audience a lecture on the formal structure of the covenant but to point out Israel's transgression. As regards the remaining issues, one may be guardedly hopeful, though here too the same *a priori* consideration does not foster a great deal of optimism. Nevertheless, careful evaluation of the evidence will permit certain inferences concerning these issues. The term בְּרִית occurs five times in the book of Hosea: 2:20 (18); 6:7; 8:1; 10:4; 12:2 (1). Of these 10:4 and 12:2 (1) refer to political alliances and so are not relevant to the current concern. As for 2:20 (18), this is a future בְּרִית and hence will be treated below in connection with Hosea's conception of the period of renewal. That leaves 6:7 and 8:1 as possible candidates in which explicit mention is made of a covenant between Yahweh and Israel.

a. Hos. 6:7-10

7   But they transgressed (the) covenant 'in'[a] Adam;

      there they dealt faithlessly against me.

8   Gilead[a] is a town of evildoers,

      tracked with blood.[b]

9   Like lurking[a] robbers[b]

      is (the) band of priests.

    On the way they murder, (on the way) to Shechem;

      yea, they have performed lewdness.

10 In the house of Israel[a] I have seen repulsiveness;[b]

    There is Ephraim's harlotry;

      Israel is defiled.

Textual Notes

7a   As has been repeatedly noted, שָׁם "there" in v. 7b requires an antecedent, which can only be found in אָדָם "Adam," and hence בְּאָדָם is to be read for כְּאָדָם. That שָׁם may have the meaning "see, lo" proposed by Dahood (*Psalms III*, 40; followed by McCarthy, "*bᵉrît* in OT History and Theology," 113, and Kuhnigk, *Nordwestsemitische Studien*, 82) is more than questionable. Kuhnigk's reference (*op. cit.*, 83 n. 286) to Ps. 48:5-7 fails to convince as שָׁם has a natural geographic antecedent in Mount Zion v. 2-4. Adam, also mentioned in Josh. 3:16, has been identified with *tell ed-Damiyeh* in the vicinity of the confluence of the Jordan and Jabbok rivers (cf. Glueck, *Explorations*, 329-334).

8a   Identified with *Kh. Jel'ad*, cf. the *Oxford Bible Atlas*, 63, 130.

8b   The emendation of 𝔐's עקבה מדם to עקביהם דם "their footprints are blood(y)" (Sellin; Wolff; Mays) has no support in the textual transmission (𝔐 is supported by 𝔖 'Α Σ Θ 𝔙) and is unnecessary.

9a   Taking חכי as an irregular form of the infinitive construct of חכה "wait" (GKC §231, 75aa; Nyberg also finds this ending for the infinitive construct in the לשׂתי of 10:10) and adapting the sense to the context (cf. Harper; Rudolph; Mays; Andersen-Freedman; Jeremias). Wolff's emendation to כ ומחכה "Es lauert wie" yields the same sense, whereas Robinson's ונביאים "and the prophets (are a gang/horde)" is without foundation.

9b   On איש גדודים as a possible plural of איש גדוד, cf. GKC §124r.

10a The reading בבית אל "in Bethel" for 𝔐's בבית ישראל "in the house of Israel" (Wellhausen; Marti; Harper; Nowack; Sellin; Robinson) has no basis in the textual transmission (save for one 𝔗 manuscript) and is hence to be rejected.

10b Reading שׁערוריה with Qre.

Form

     The current passage has been included in the larger redactional composition to he found in 5:8-7:16. As has generally been recognized since A. Alt's definitive essay, 5:8-6:6 contain various oracles pronounced by Hosea during the Syro-Ephraimite war.[187] In the present form of the text 6:7-10 is clearly associated with the foregoing by means of the adversative והמה. The connection, however, is not original but redactional, as indicated by two major factors. Whereas both Judah and Ephraim are addressed in 6:4-6 (cf. also 5:10, 12, 13, 14), attention focuses exclusively on the northern kingdom in 6:7-10.[188] Moreover, the geographical setting has shifted. The events referred to in 5:8, 10 took place near the Judah-Benjamin border and then moved northwards through the territory of Benjamin. The events of 6:7-10 on the other hand are located farther to the north and east in Transjordan and perhaps the hill country of Ephraim. Both of these factors are best explained by the supposition that 6:7-10 were independent of the preceding verses at the oral stage.

     There is some disagreement on the extent of the oracle, some seeing its conclusion in v. 10, others extending it through 7:2. The crux of the matter hinges upon the interpretation of v. 6:11-7aα. All exegetes are agreed that 6:11a is a Judean interpolation. Rudolph argues that because elsewhere in the prophetic corpus שוב שבות always refers

---

187 A. Alt, "Hosea 5,8-6,6. Ein Krieg und seine Folgen in prophetischer Beleuchtung." E. M. Good ("Hosea 5:8-6:6: An Alternative to Alt") constitutes an exception. He attempts to show that the passage is a unity to be understood as a covenant lawsuit. But there is insufficient evidence to support the determination of a covenant lawsuit genre; cf. D. R. Daniels, "Is There a 'Prophetic Lawsuit' Genre?"

188 In Hosea בית ישראל always refers to the northern kingdom (1:4, 6; 5:1; 12:1 [11:12]), and this view is substantiated for the present passage by the parallelism Ephraim-Israel (v. 10).

to the eschatological restoration of Israel this must also be the case here.[189] Also, the positive content and eschatological character of the phrase, and by implication of its parallel in 7:1aα, prohibits their being connected with what follows. This also requires that 6:11a, with which these lines must then be associated, be understood as being favorable towards Judah. However, the coordinating particle גַם "also" introducing 6:11 includes Judah in Ephraim's fate, which is painted in completely negative tones, all positive elements belonging to the addition. Nothing remains in the text which could have motivated the interpolation. Rudolph realizes this and consequently follows Lindblom[190] in considering the addition originally to have been a gloss on 6:1-3 which then entered the text at the wrong point.

The complexity of Rudolph's interpretation and especially the need to transpose the verses to a more suitable context are decided weaknesses. Jeremias seeks to shore up the argumentation on the one hand by extending the interpolation to include 6:10 (though not 7:1aα) and on the other hand by seeing two successive additions - 6:10-11a and 6:11b - within the interpolation. This allows him to retain the verses at their present location, to interpret 6:11a in its natural negative sense, and provides a basis in the original text ("when I heal Israel") for the positive addition in 6:11b intended to include Judah in the future salvation.

As regards Jeremias' interpretation, one can scarcely maintain that it is any less complex than Rudolph's. It is also more than doubtful that 6:11b is viable as an independent gloss and that it fulfills the task Jeremias assigns it. Moreover, the grounds given for the non-Hoseanic authorship of 6:10 are wholly unsatisfactory. According to Jeremias שַׁעֲרוּרִיָה "repulsiveness," which occurs elsewhere only in Jeremiah,[191] indicates an origin no earlier than Jeremiah's generation, as does the use of the abstract זְנוּת "harlotry" which occurs elsewhere in Jeremiah (3:2, 9; 13:27) and Ezekiel (23:27; 43:7, 9) and in passages dependent on them (Hos. 4:11a; Num. 14:33, respectively). Similarly, Hosea is said to have used the term "my people" only at the beginning of his ministry (4:6, 8, 12) and as an exception in 11:7. This last argument confuses description with prescription, and the references given, taken in conjunction with the present passage, demonstrate that Hosea was capable of using the term "my people" throughout his ministry. That Hosea knew and used words deriving from the root זנה is incontestable.[192] Why should he not have used the form זְנוּת? Do the three occurrences in the book of Jeremiah really weigh so much more heavily than the two in the book of Hosea as to justify labelling the word "a typical term of Jeremiah's generation"?[193] If one adjusts the raw numerical count to compensate for the differences in the amount of material preserved, then one comes to the conclusion that percentially Hosea used the term more frequently than Jeremiah or Ezekiel. The same may be said of שַׁעֲרוּר(י)ה where the ratio 1:3 is hardly more supportive of the weight placed upon it. The term refers in all four occurrences to Israel's apostasy from

---

[189] Rudolph, 143-144.

[190] *Hosea*, 86-87.

[191] 18:13; also שַׁעֲרוּרָה 5:30; 23:14; and שַׁעַר 29:17.

[192] As a verb, qal: 1:2; 2:7 (5); 3:3; 4:12, 13, 14, 15; 9:1; hiphil: 4:10, 18; 5:3; the noun זְנוּנִים 1:2; 2:4, 6 (2, 4); 4:12; 5:4.

[193] Jeremias, 94. See also Wolff's equally unjustified contention that the noun was "common" following Jeremiah on the basis of four (!) certain post-Jeremianic occurrences (*Hosea*, 135, note 6:10b).

Yahweh, a theme which, like Israel's "harlotry" and on a par with it, lies at the heart of
Hosea's message. There are thus no plausible grounds for denying Hosea these terms.

That leaves the term שוב שבות (RSV "restore the fortunes"). The phrase is a favorite
of Jeremiah's. It can be used to refer to return from exile,[194] but more frequently envisions
a restoration of peaceful and prosperous conditions following the return,[195] though a clear
distinction between these two aspects is not always possible.[196] It can even be used with
reference to the future of foreign nations.[197] In Ps. 14:7; 53:7 it is used of Yahweh's
deliverance of Israel from evildoers (פעלי און), and in Ps. 85:2; 126:1 (both Ktiv) it seems
to refer to agricultural bounty. Job 42:10 employs the phrase in conjunction with the
double restoration of Job's wealth. Quite interesting is the usage in Lam. 2:14 where the
view is expressed that, had the prophets exposed Jerusalem's sin rather than speaking false
and misleading oracles, her destruction could have been prevented! This last passage is
particularly significant because it attests the presence shortly after 587 BC[198] of a non-
eschatological understanding of שוב שבות which has nothing to do with return from
captivity and is associated with the cultic prophets. This latter point makes it certain that
this understanding reached back into the monarchic period, a conclusion confirmed by the
Psalms cited above.[199] The phrase שוב שבות will thus not have been coined by the
classical prophets but rather adopted by them and pressed into the service of their
message. It originally connoted the restoration of fortunes following some catastrophe, and
this is quite probably the sense of the term in Hos. 6:11b.

On the basis of the foregoing discussion it may be concluded that the Judean addition
encompasses only 6:11a. This being the case, there can be little doubt that the temporal
clauses of 6:11b-7:1aα form the protasis of 7:1aβ.[200] Such a look at the past is more
suitable as the beginning of a new unit than as the continuation of the previous one.[201]

---

194   Jer. 29:14; 30:3; cf. Ezek. 29:14; Deut. 30:3.

195   Jer. 30:18; 31:23; 32:44; 33:7, 11, 26; cf. Ezek. 16:53; Amos 9:14.

196   Ezek. 39:25; Zeph. 3:20.

197   Moab: Jer. 48:47; Ammonites: Jer. 49:6; Elam: Jer. 49:39; Egypt: Ezek. 29:14; Sodom and Samaria: Ezek.
      16:53.

198   On the date of Lam. 2 cf. O. Eißfeldt, Introduction, 503-504 = Einleitung, 682-683; H.-J. Kraus,
      Klagelieder, 40; W. Rudolph, Die Klagelieder, 193; O. Plöger, Die Klagelieder, 129-130.

199   The conventional dating of Ps. 85 and 126 to the post-exilic period rests in large part, if not exclusively,
      on the view that שוב שבות must refer to the return from exile, which is then looked back upon at the
      beginning of both Psalms (R. Kittel, Die Psalmen, 281-282, 396; B. Duhm, Die Psalmen, 325, 436-437; H.
      Schmidt, Die Psalmen, 161, 226-227; H.-J. Kraus, Psalmen, 755, 1032-1033) or the term is held to be
      derived from, and therefore subsequent to, prophetic eschatology (H. Gunkel, Die Psalmen, 373, 551). But
      the matter is not so simple. The subsequent plea for restoration in both Psalms (85:5-7; 126:4-6) remains
      problematic. This is usually explained by pointing to the difference between the expectations of the
      post-exilic community for restoration and their actual situation. Perhaps, but the argument is in danger of
      begging the question. It cannot be shown that שוב שבות refers to the return from exile; this must be
      assumed. When one does not make this assumption, a pre-exilic date becomes quite plausible. Recollection
      of past restorations certainly has its place in motivating Yahweh to act again on behalf of his people. A.
      Weiser (Die Psalmen, 389, 524) favors a pre-exilic date, and A. A. Andersen (Psalms, 607, 864) discusses
      both options but leaves the question open.

200   So also Harper; Mays; Andersen-Freedman; cf. also Sellin; Wolff. Robinson and Jeremias retain only 7:1aα
      but interpret it temporally.

201   Similarly Harper; Wolff. Even Mays, who considers 6:7-7:2 (save 6:11a) to be a single unit, feels this
      intermission when he interprets the oracle as consisting of "two movements," 6:7-10 and 6:11b-7:2.

This elucidation may receive a certain confirmation in the resulting trilogy of sections beginning with *beth* (6:7 [emended text following redactional והמה]; 6:11b; 7:3).

The genre of 6:7-10 is not completely clear. There is no clear pattern in the use of verbal forms and noun-clauses, and the focus of the piece is directed at past deeds (v. 7, 9b) and current conditions (v. 8-9a, 10b). Indeed, the primary concern of the larger complex 6:7-7:16 is to illuminate various sins committed by Israel/Ephraim in exposition of the transitory character of his חסד, a charge leveled in 6:4-6.[202] It would thus appear likely, and nothing stands in the way of the view, that these verses formed the indication of the situation of a prophecy whose continuation has been sacrificed to the broader purpose of the larger complex.

Comment

The question of primary concern in the present context deals with the nature of the covenant mentioned in v. 7. Here opinion is divided into two camps. Some argue that the lack of the first person singular suffix on the noun, i.e. that the text reads "covenant" and not "my covenant," indicates that it is not a covenant between Yahweh and Israel which is referred to here but rather a covenant or contract between king and people[203] or a treaty between Israel and some other nation.[204] Others point to the "against me" of the parallel colon as a sign that it is Israel's covenant with Yahweh that is intended.[205] The methodological weakness of both approaches lies in the narrowness of the foundation upon which they build. A position with regard to v. 7 is adopted, into which the subsequent verses (insofar as they are treated at all[206]) are then pressed. It would seem advisable to examine the remainder of the passage first to see in which direction this leads before coming to a decision regarding the nature of the covenant in v. 7.

Verses 8-9a deal with the lethal escapades of a band of priests. These priests apparently were inhabitants of the town Gilead to which they returned following their raid(s). The town thus became "tracked with blood." The crime itself, however, seems to have taken place a good ten miles away in the vicinity of Adam on the road leading to Shechem. Unfortunately, the motive which drove the priests to act as they did is not specified. Here it is important to observe what the text does not say. It does not say that the priests were seeking to overthrow, let alone assassinate the king.[207] Neither does it

---

[202] Cf. Rudolph, 141.

[203] G. Fohrer, "Vertrag zwischen König und Volk," 16-17 = 345-346; A. Alt, "Hosea 5,8-6,6," KS II, 186 n. 1; Rudolph, 145.

[204] L. Perlitt, *Bundestheologie*, 142-143; Jeremias.

[205] Sellin; Wolff; F. C. Fensham, "Covenant-idea," 37, 47 n. 20; Mays; D. J. McCarthy, "bᵉrît in OT History and Theology," 113; Andersen-Freedman.

[206] This is a particular weakness in Perlitt's treatment of the verse. In this connection he pens the curious statement: "v. 7 kann nicht von v. 7-10a getrennt werden und bildet darum, isoliert genommen, weder zu v. 6 noch zu v. 8ff. ein Gegenüber" (*Bundestheologie*, 142). He then proceeds to treat the verse "isoliert genommen."

[207] This view is based upon the redactional context of the passage, which follows a collection of prophecies dealing with the Syro-Ephraimite war (cf. p. 82, n. 187). The problem lies in finding a suitable revolution. The coups of Shallum (2Kgs. 15:10), Menahem (2Kgs. 15:14), and Pekah (2Kgs. 15:25) have all been proposed, but none of these took place in Adam. G. Fohrer ("Vertrag zwischen König und Volk," 16

even hint at cultic rivalries between antagonistic priestly guilds. The crime as Hosea sees it lies in the fact that murder was committed, though the crime must have aroused particularly forceful indignation in that it was perpetrated by priests. Hence, so far as we are able to discern, for Hosea murder constituted a transgression against the covenant he refers to in v. 7.

Turning to Hosea's evaluation of the nature and consequences of the crime as expressed in v. 9b-10, four main concepts are used. In v. 9b murder is equated with זמה "lewdness."[208] The term generally refers to inappropriate conduct of a sexual nature. In Leviticus, having sexual relations with a mother and her daughter is a זמה (18:17; 20:14), and prostituting one's daughter fills the land with זמה (19:29). In Jeremiah (13:27) and Ezekiel (13 occurrences) the word is always used in connection with Israel's unfaithfulness to Yahweh, and in Ezek. 22:11 it constitutes an action which defiles (טמא). As demonstrated by the story of the rape and murder of a Levite's concubine in Gibeah (Judg. 20:6), the action connoted by זמה is on a par with נבלה "folly," a term which may be used in parallel to "transgress against Yahweh's covenant" (Josh. 7:15). As regards this latter expression, it has recently been pointed out that עבר ברית never refers to a political alliance but always to the covenant with Yahweh.[209]

With respect to שערוריה, it has already been pointed out that all four occurrences (including the present one) are in contexts dealing with apostasy from Yahweh. Similarly, the root זנה in both its nominal and verbal constructions constitutes the term *par excellence* in Hosea's preaching for describing Israel's infidelity to Yahweh and her chasing after the Baals.[210] That Israel is "defiled" (טמא) represents the consequence of her actions. A person or object that is defiled is excluded from participation in the cultic worship of Yahweh and as a result is incapable of (full) communion with him.

Results

When one carefully weighs the evidence provided by v. 8-10, both in terms of what the text does and does not say, then the conclusion appears inescapable that Hosea's primary concern here is with the direct relationship between Yahweh and Israel. Murder is not (merely) a crime against humanity, but a sin against Yahweh. The focus of the passage is on the implications of the actions for the direct relationship between Yahweh and Israel. There is no mention of foreign nations or native kings.[211] Yahweh considers Israel as having "dealt faithlessly against me" (v. 7b). In light of the entire context it is difficult to see how the covenant mentioned in v. 7a should refer to anything other than

n. 30) also considered Hoshea's coup a possibility (2Kgs. 15:30), which has the advantage - and disadvantage - of not being associated with a particular location. J. Day ("Covenant in Hosea," 5) and E. W. Nicholson (*God and His People,* 185-186) also think in terms of political turmoil and revolution in Hosea's day without further specification. Yet even if one adopts the view that the events referred to in 6:7-10 are somehow connected with a *coup d'état,* the passage condemns not the killing of kings or revolution, but rather murder in and of itself.

208 Cf. S. Steingrimsson, *TDOT* IV, 89-90.
209 J. Day, "Covenant in Hosea," 4.
210 See the references listed in n. 192.
211 Similarly, E. W. Nicholson, *God and His People,* 183.

a covenant between Yahweh and Israel. This is again supported by the observation already noted that in the expression עבר ברית the reference is always to the covenant with Yahweh. It has also been noted that this expression "refers to offences which threaten the continuation of the covenant and which, if not purged, will result in its termination ... but not to the nullification of the covenant as such."[212] The expression for nullification is rather הפר ברית.[213] For these reasons, when L. Perlitt objects that בגד "deal faithlessly" as an expression for infidelity to Yahweh never requires specification by the covenant with Yahweh,[214] he places the cart before the horse. The nature of the covenant is defined by the context and not the other way around. And everything in the context points to a covenant between Yahweh and Israel. Also, that בגד does not require specification by the covenant with Yahweh does not exclude the possibility that it may be so specified.

It is possible to go a step further by posing the question as to the manner in which Hosea conceives the covenant. The exposition above indicated that, as far as the events to which Hosea refers are concerned, all that can be said with any degree of confidence is that murder was committed. Anything beyond this is speculation. This would imply that the act of murder itself constituted to Hosea's mind a breach of the covenant. It is therefore probable that Hosea knew of a covenant between Yahweh and Israel, the parameters of which were defined by legal material which included ordinances of a moral character.[215]

b. Hos. 8:1-3

1   To your mouth[a] the shofar![b]

    One like the eagle[c] is over the house of Yahweh,

because they have transgressed my covenant,

    and against my instruction they have rebelled.

2   To me they cry,[a]

    "My God, we know you ' '[b] !"

3   Israel has spurned good;

    the enemy shall pursue him.[a]

---

212 E. W. Nicholson, *God and His People,* 184.

213 W. Thiel, *"HĒFĒR BᴱRÎT,"* 214-215.

214 *Bundestheologie,* 143.

215 Cf. the statement of E. W. Nicholson, *God and His People,* 185, that "as employed in Hosea 6:7 the word *bᵉrît* also refers to Yahweh's *tōrāh.*"

Textual Notes

1a   That חֵךְ "regularly denotes *palate, gums,* etc., always referring to the interior of the mouth, never to the lips" (Harper; similarly Wellhausen; Marti; Nowack; Robinson) is improbable in light of Cant. 5:16; 7:10 where the lips would seem to be primarily intended. In any event the word can envision the mouth as a whole, Job 20:13; 31:30; Prov. 5:3; 8:7 (Sellin; Wolff; Rudolph), a point also acknowledged by Harper.

1b   An implicit imperative (jussive) construction, cf. König §355m, who cites as further examples Ex. 17:16; 2Sam. 20:1b; 1Kgs. 12:16; 22:36b; 2Chr. 10:16; Isa. 8:20.

1c   Torczyner ("Dunkle Bibelstellen," 277-278) proposed repointing נֶשֶׁר "eagle, vulture" as נָשַׁר which, on the basis of the Arabic *našara* "proclaim publicly, promulgate," he rendered "crier, herald." This suggestion has recently been taken up by Emmerson ("Hosea VIII 1-3," 703-704) on the grounds that נֶשֶׁר is inappropriate as a self-explanatory description of an enemy. The reading has much to commend it, but is not necessary. Although the shofar was used by heralds (Lev. 25:9; 1Sam. 13:3; Isa. 18:3), it was also used in military contexts (Josh. 6; Judg. 3:27; 6:34; 7:18-22; 2Sam. 2:28; 18:16; 20:22; Jer. 4:5, 19, 21; 6:1, 17; 42:14; 51:27; Ezek. 33:3-6; Hos. 5:8; Amos 3:6; Zeph. 1:16; Job 39:24-25; Neh. 4:12, 14 (18, 20). Hence the combination of shofar and eagle would be fully adequate to communicate military imagery. The prior mention of the shofar evokes specific associational expectations which naturally form the matrix within which the reference to the eagle is then interpreted by the audience. Also, "herald" must be connected with what precedes it, with the result that the verse is thrown somewhat out of balance, though perhaps not intolerably. The same may be said of the emendations to נצר "watchman" or שמר "guard" (Duhm; Sellin).

2a   Frequentative imperfect for present action, GKC §107f.

2b   "Israel" was not read by 𝕲𝕾 and is most likely a gloss identifying the subject of the verbs "they cry" and "we know" (Robinson; Wolff; Mays; Willi-Plein, *Schriftexegese,* 164) or a copyist's error caused by the proximity of "Israel" in v. 3 (Marti; Nowack). Taking "Israel" as appositional to the "we" of the preceding verb (Harper; Rudolph; Jeremias; Neef, *Heilstraditionen,* 157 note e) is grammatically questionable, as is the supposition that 𝕲𝕾 disapproved of the construction and hence omitted "Israel" (Rudolph). It is also difficult to see how a construction as clear and common as אלהי ישראל "God of Israel," whether preceding (Schmidt, "Hosea 6:1-6," 117 n. 1) or following (Sellin) the verb, should have become disjointed. Buss explains the combination of first person singular suffix and first person plural verb as reflecting the style of laments and prayers of a collective group spoken by a leader where the phrase "my God" is typical (*Prophetic Word,* 91 and n. 68, citing Ps. 83:14; Ezra 9:6; 2Chr. 6:40; Dan. 9:18f).

3a   The form of the third person masculine singular suffix is unusual, cf. GKC §60d and Ex. 22:29; Josh. 2:4; 1Sam. 21:14; 2Sam. 14:6; Ps. 35:8; Eccl. 4:12. König §29,2c explains the form as due to the influence of the shorter perfect suffix, Bauer-Leander §48u of the nominal suffix.

Form

That Hos. 8:1-3 form an originally independent unit is a matter of general consensus among interpreters. Only R. Gnuse has sought to argue for the original unity of 8:1-13, v. 14 being a later addition.[216] He first points to vocabulary links connecting v. 4-11 (repetition of כי), v. 1-3 with v. 4-11 (זנח in v. 3, 5) and v. 12-13 with v. 4-11 (טמא in v. 11, 13). He then pursues the "thematic and theological unity" in which v. 4-13 provide specific examples of Israel's transgression of Yahweh's covenant and laws referred to in v. 1-3. but such arguments alone cannot establish the *original* unity of the passage. They may rather indicate that the secondary arrangement of originally independent oracles was no haphazard affair but was effected to convey a definite theological message. Form-critical considerations are neglected by Gnuse, and so his argumentation lacks the necessary foundation to sustain his position.

As has been noted,[217] the imperative character of 8:1 marks the beginning of a new section within Hos. 4-11. Similarly, the shift to a new topic in v. 4, namely the unauthorized making of kings and idols, marks the beginning of a new unit. These observations are confirmed by the form-critical analysis of the pericope. V. 1-3a depict the current circumstances and past causes which brought them about, whereas v. 3b announces future events. This structure corresponds to that of a prophecy and requires no continuation.

The question of the authorship of the current passage is today[218] regularly decided in favor of Hosea, with the exception (naturally) of the verse of particular interest for our purposes, v. 1b. The modern assault has been championed particularly by L. Perlitt.[219] He advances two arguments in this connection. First, the language and meaning of v. 1b are at home not in Hosea but in the deuteronom(ist)ic literature. But this is the thesis that Perlitt seeks to prove, so the argumentation becomes circular. One cannot merely assume what is to be proved.[220] Yet even so, it has been pointed out that the phrase פשע תורה "is nowhere attested in the Deuteronomic corpus ... but is peculiar to Hosea 8:1,"[221] so that

---

216 R. Gnuse, "Calf, Cult and King: The Unity of Hosea 8:1-13."

217 See above p. 28.

218 Marti and Nowack both considered v. 1-2 in their entirety to be an interpolation. Both followed Cheyne in emending v. 1a to read הרם קול בכח כשפר על בית יהוה "lift (your) voice mightily like the shofar against Yahweh's house," which they then held to be influenced by and derived in part from Isa. 58:1-2. But to make such a far-reaching alteration of the text which has so little basis in the textual transmission and then to brand the resulting conjecture (!) an interpolation is methodologically highly suspect, to say the least. And to assert that Hos. 8:2 has been influenced by Isa. 58:2 requires a healthy imagination as far as the formulation is concerned. To bridge the gap both Marti and Nowack felt compelled to appeal to additional influence from Hos. 7:14, which merely demonstrates the Hoseanic character of 8:2 and the inadequacy of the derivation from Isa. 58:2.

219 *Bundestheologie*, 146-149; followed by W. Thiel, "'Bund' in den Prophetenbüchern," 12, and Jeremias.

220 Cf. the similar criticism expressed by D. J. McCarthy, "*bᵉrît* in OT History and Theology," 114, and J. Day, "Covenant in Hosea," 7.

221 E. W. Nicholson, *God and His People*, 186; also noted by J. Day, "Covenant in Hosea," 7.

the language is not strictly deuteronom(ist)ic. Perlitt's second point is methodologically sounder. He argues that the language and meaning of v. 1b are foreign to Hosea. Hosea knew of no covenant between Yahweh and Israel and conceived of תורה as a series of individual instructions entrusted to the priests. But our examination of the relevant passages has shown or will show that Hosea knew of a (broken) current covenant (6:7) and a (renewed) future covenant (2:20 [18]) between Yahweh and Israel. Moreover, all three occurrences of תורה in Hosea (4:6; 8:1, 12) have been transmitted in the singular, and there is no need to alter any of them to the plural.[222] The phrase תורת אלהיך "the instruction of your God" (4:6) demonstrates beyond a reasonable shadow of a doubt that Hosea could subsume the multitude of laws entrusted to the priests under the singular תורה. Thus, the arguments advanced in support of the non-Hoseanic origin of v. 1b prove to be unfounded.[223]

Comment

The passage begins with a call to sound the alarm in the face of an impending enemy attack. But who is called upon to sound the alarm? How one answers this question depends on the original context which one assumes for the oracle (or vice versa). If one views Yahweh, who is certainly the speaker (cf. v. 1b-2), as speaking to Hosea, then the passage is a private oracle in which Hosea receives the command to announce to Israel the coming downfall and its cause.[224] Equally conceivable is the view that the oracle was delivered publicly, in which case the addressee may be a military look-out.[225] The plausibility of both suggestions has led recent interpreters to exercise caution and leave the question open.[226] Although the question cannot be decided definitively, a certain preference for Wolff's view must be confessed. A public setting for the oracle seems to be indicated by the cultic terminology contained in it. The "house of Yahweh" most probably refers to the sanctuary at Bethel rather than to the land.[227] Further, the verb זעק "cry" (v. 2) is here used of a communal lament, as indicated by the content of the cry: "My God, *we* know you!"[228] Israel anticipates an enemy assault and so has posted a lookout. Meanwhile, the people assemble in a communal lament to seek deliverance from Yahweh. But Hosea rejects their plea as insincere (cf. 7:14; 6:4), because their actions speak too

---

[222] Although the text is difficult, this is also true for 8:12; cf. Wolff, who refers to רב עונך in 9:7, but nevertheless repoints as a plural. Andersen-Freedman and H.-D. Neef (*Heilstraditionen,* 160 n. 144) retain the singular.

[223] L. Perlitt (*Bundestheologie,* 148) also argues that the passage would be improved by removing v. 1b in that a simple alarm without an anticipatory reason for its being sounded would command greater attention. This, however, is a purely subjective opinion, and even if it were to be granted, it does not constitute legitimate grounds for excising the verse. It merely expresses the opinion that Hosea's communicative talents still had room for improvement.

[224] So Harper; Sellin; Rudolph; H. Utzschneider, *Hosea,* 107-108; H.-D. Neef, *Heilstraditionen,* 157. J. Lindblom (*Hosea,* 91) interprets 8:1-7 as Hosea's initial prophetic call.

[225] So Wolff.

[226] G. I. Emmerson, "Hosea VIII I-3," 701; Jeremias; and Mays, who also considers the possibility that "the nation as a corporate person" is intended.

[227] See the excellent discussion of G. I. Emmerson, "Hosea VIII I-3," 706-709.

[228] Cf. textual note 2b and R. Albertz, *THAT* II, 573-575; G. Hasel, *TDOT* IV, 119-122.

clearly against them. They have "transgressed my covenant and rebelled against my instruction" (v. 1b) and have "spurned good" (v. 3a). D. J. McCarthy explains the term טוב "good" as "characteristic of treaty contexts, where it refers to something like comity or good relations between the parties."[229] If this is in fact Hosea's meaning, then we have here an indication that the covenant known to him was connected with treaty concepts. But the explanation rather assumes a treaty context than demonstrates one. Hosea's usage in 2:9 (7); 10:1 suggests a connection with the land and its benefits, and in 3:5 he applies the root to Yahweh (or is the land also in view here?). But to spurn the gift is to spurn the giver, so that Israel has in effect spurned Yahweh himself.

Results

With regard to the issue of particular interest at this stage of the investigation, i.e. Hosea's conception of the covenant, three points are to be made. First, the inference drawn from 6:7-10 finds explicit confirmation in 8:1b. Here "covenant" and "instruction" (תורה) occur in parallelism, so that the conclusion is unavoidable that Hosea knew of a covenant between Yahweh and Israel which was defined at least in part in terms of legal material. The term תורה in Hosea need not be confined to regulations pertaining to ritual purity and holiness, but in all probability encompasses "secular moral law" as well (4:6; cf. also 6:7-10; Deut. 17:8-13).[230] However, since decisions concerning ritual purity and holiness were the unique prerogative of the priests and were called individually תורה, this became the preferred term for the entirety of the legal material preserved, transmitted, and administered by these circles (cf. e.g. Deut. 4:44).

Secondly, Hosea sees the root cause of Israel's impending collapse in her infidelity to Yahweh as expressed in her breaking the covenant. In effect she crossed over (עבר) the bounds set by the covenant and destroyed the foundation of her relationship with Yahweh. The blessings of the intact relationship, a life of peace and prosperity in the land, had consequently been forfeited by her (2:10-15 [8-13]; 3:4-5; 4:3; 8:8, 13; 9:3, 6, 15; 11:5). Hosea's adoption of the marriage imagery for his own proclamation (Hos. 1-3) despite the widespread associations with the Baal cults against which he polemicized is comprehensible only against the background of the covenant.[231] The covenant thus lies at the heart of Hosea's perception of the state and the fate of the Israel of his day.

Lastly, the (fictitious?) setting presupposed by the passage provides a clue to the source of Hosea's knowledge of the covenant. Israel is in a state of distress. Enemy troops have invaded the land and are making their way towards the state sanctuary. The disaster is seen as the result of Israel's failure to uphold the covenant, and the people gather for a communal lament. There is hence a connection between communal laments in the face of disaster and the transgression of the covenant. This in turn suggests that the renewal of the covenant occurred within the context of the cultic rituals performed on occasions of national, and perhaps local, disaster. The ceremony of covenant renewal would thus not

---

229   D. J. McCarthy, "*bᵉrît* in OT History and Theology," 114; cf. W. L. Moran, "Treaty Terminology," 173-176; D. R. Hillers, "Treaty Terminology," 46-47; R. Gnuse, "Hosea 8:1-13," 87, 90.

230   Cf. A. Alt, "Heimat des Deuteronomiums," KS II, 255 n.3.

231   See Mal. 2:14, where ברית is used for the marriage relationship; cf. also Ezek. 16:8, and K. Koch, *The Prophets* I, 88-90 = *Die Profeten* I, 100-102.

have been a regular feature of the Israelite festival calendar but would have taken place only after the (impending) occurrence of a catastrophe had been interpreted as indicating that the covenant had been broken.[232]

D. THE PERIOD OF RENEWAL, HOS. 2:16-25

Having examined Hosea's view of Israel's past history, we now turn to the future renewal which he envisioned.

16 Therefore, behold, I will win her over,

and lead her into the wilderness,

and speak to her heart.

17 And I will give her her vineyards from there,[a]

the valley of Achor as a door of hope.

And she will respond[b] there[c] as in the days of her youth.

even as on the day of her coming up from the land of Egypt.

18 And it shall be on that day,

utterance of Yahweh,

You will call (me)[a] "my husband,"

and no longer will you call me "my lord (Baal)."

19 And I will remove the names of the Baals from her mouth.

And they shall no longer be remembered by their name.

20 And I will make a covenant with them

on that day

along with the beasts of the field,

and with the birds of the air,

and the creeping things of the ground.

And bow and sword and war

I will abolish[a] from the land,

and I will cause them to live in safety.

---

[232] This inference agrees with the conclusions reached by K. Baltzer (*Das Bundesformular*, 59-70) concerning the renewal of the covenant. For more on the ceremony of covenant renewal see below pp. 105-108.

21 And I will betroth you to me forever.

    And I will betroth you to me

        with righteousness and with justice,

            and with (covenant-)loyalty and with compassion.

22 And I will betroth you to me with faithfulness,

        and you shall know Yahweh.[a]

23 And it shall be on that day,

        (that) I will respond,[a] utterance of Yahweh,

    I will respond to the heavens,

        and they will respond to the earth.

24 And the earth will respond to the grain

        and the new wine and the fresh oil,

            and they will respond to Jezreel.

25 And I will plant her for me in the land.

    And I will have pity on Not-Pitied,

    And I will say to Not-my-people, "You are my people,"

        and he will say, "My God."[a]

Textual Notes

17a There are no grounds for emending the text. V. 17a, though probably zeugmatic, is quite intelligible and is furthermore supported by 𝕲𝕾𝕿𝖁. The reading of 𝕲 τὰ κτήματα αὐτῆς "her possessions" has correctly been interpreted as an updating generalization (Wolff; Rudolph).

17b Deriving from ענה I "answer, respond." 𝕲𝕾 derive from ענה III "be bowed down, afflicted," but this is ill-suited to the present context (Rudolph). Frey ("Gedichte Hoseas," 29) connects the verb with ענה IV "sing" understood as "praise," but then interprets this praise as the answer of the congregation. Against the idea of a wedding song here (Audet, "Cantique des Cantiques," 211-214) Rudolph has pointed out that the bride does not sing this song alone. Deem ("The Goddess Anath," 26-27) suggests translating ענה here and in v. 23-24 with "love." However, this is misleading since the meaning being argued for is actually "sexual intercourse by mutual consent" and hence the translation "copulate" would be more appropriate. But this interpretation commands little confidence and is especially difficult to sustain for v. 23-24, which Deem tellingly leaves untranslated.

17c שמה is interpreted as a *constructio praegnans* by Wolff, but this is unlikely (see the *Comment*).

18a 𝕲𝕾 both imply the presence of לִי "to me" in their Vorlage. This could have fallen out due to homoioteleuton (Robinson) or have been influenced by v. 18b (Wolff). In any event it is certainly Yahweh who is being called.

20a Literally "break."

22a There are no grounds for emending to וּבְדַעַת יהוה "and with the knowledge of Yahweh" (*contra* Marti; Nowack; Robinson). Both 𝕲 and 𝕾 support 𝔐.

23a See note 17b.

25a 𝕲𝕯 attest "you are the Lord my God," an expansion unknown to 𝕾.

Form

        The present passage forms part of the larger compositional complex 2:4-25. Most scholars are agreed that this complex is composite in nature,[233] but differences obtain as to what constitute the original units that make up the redactional composition. P. Humbert argued that 2:4-22 possesses a logical progression and cohesion in which "every episode is organically tied to the context."[234] But the logical progression first had to be restored by transposing v. 8-9 to follow v. 15. Moreover, logical progression is of itself not a conclusive argument for the *original* unity of a passage. It may indicate nothing more than that the redactional plan underlying the passage was well-conceived and no haphazard affair. Some commentators interpret v. 4-17 in terms of formal legal proceedings in a court of law. According to Wolff this is indicated by the consistent reference to the defendant in the third person, the verb רִיב, and the introduction of the legal sentence with לָכֵן "therefore" (v. 8, 11, 16). However, this interpretation is beset with insurmountable problems. The root רִיב cannot be limited to the legal sphere as is often done. It means more generally "contend, quarrel, dispute,"[235] so that a legal setting must be demonstrated on other grounds before the term can be taken as referring to a lawsuit or indictment. The particle לָכֵן cannot be adduced for this purpose since it is nowhere attested as introducing the pronouncement of a legal sentence.[236] These difficulties are felt by Mays, who also considers v. 4-17 to be cast in legal style, but then must qualify this view with the statement: "Along the way the style is used as clothing for indictments of guilt and announcements of punishments *in the more usual prophetic fashion*."[237] Moreover, a careful

---

[233] H. Lubsczyk (*Auszug Israels,* 19-26) appears to be an exception, but his arguments are directed at the literary unity, which he seems to understand as primary over against the kerygmatic unity of the passage. Does he mean to imply that Hosea committed these verses to writing prior to their oral proclamation?

[234] "L'unité d'Osée 2,4-22," 166.

[235] Gen. 13:8; 26:20ff; Deut. 25:1ff; Prov. 25:7ff; cf. also M. de Roche, "Yahweh's *rîb,*" and D. R. Daniels, "Prophetic Lawsuit," 352-353.

[236] Cf. D. R. Daniels, "Prophetic Lawsuit," 346.

[237] Mays, 36 (emphasis added).

reading of v. 5 indicates that the matter has not yet reached the point of formal legal action.[238] It is still a family matter.

H. Krszyna has also argued that v. 4-17 should be taken as a unified whole.[239] He takes exception to Wolff's interpretation of these verses as a kerygmatic unit composed of a collection of individual sayings, giving the impression that he considers the unity of v. 4-17 to go back to the oral stage, though Krszyna is not specific on this point. Indeed, as one might expect from the title of his article, Krszyna concerns himself with the *literary* unity of the passage and does not pose the question of the original or redactional nature of the unity.[240]

Despite these efforts, the unity of Hos. 2:4ff is redactional in character, a secondary development at the literary level. B. Renaud argued this point on literary grounds,[241] but form-critical considerations provide a more solid foundation. As has already been mentioned, within prophetic speech לכן often marks the transition from the indication of the situation to the prediction within a prophecy.[242] This causes one to suspect that new predictions begin at v. 8, 11, 16, a suspicion confirmed by the fact that each of the sections introduced by לכן depicts future events. An exception to this observation is found in v. 10 which, following v. 8-9, returns to the situation described in v. 4-7. This has occasioned some scholars to connect v. 8-9 with v. 16-17, either by assuming that they have somehow been transferred from their original position following v. 15,[243] or by assuming that an original unit in v. 8-9, 16-17 was subsequently separated by the redactor.[244] However, the dissociation of v. 8-9 from v. 4-7, as well as their association with v. 16-17, is born more out of the desire to let v. 10 follow directly upon v. 7 than out of the inappropriateness of v. 8-9 as the continuation of v. 4-7. Theological factors also play a role here in that the wife's intent to return to her first husband (v. 9) is apparently ignored in v. 10. But this only shows that v. 10 did not originally follow v. 9 and not that it originally followed v. 7. Indeed, the similar formulation of v. 7b and v. 9b argues decisively against separating these verses.[245] Thus v. 4-9 and v. 10-15 derive from originally separate oral units. Whether the first actually concluded with v. 9 or whether the original continuation has been lost cannot be said with certainty, but the personal pronoun at the beginning of v. 10 makes it as good as certain that a portion of this latter unit has been sacrificed for the sake of the redactional composition since the pronoun will have required an antecedent.

---

[238] The phrase "for/that she is not my wife and I am not her husband" (v. 4a) is not a divorce formula as maintained by C. Kuhl, "Neue Dokumente zum Verständnis von Hosea 2 4-15" and C. H. Gordon, "Hos 2 4-5 in the Light of New Semitic Inscriptions"; cf. the objections of R. Gordis, "Hosea's Marriage and Message," 20 n. 30a = 249 n. 30a, and also H. H. Rowley, "The Marriage of Hosea," 227; Rudolph, 65; G. A. Yee, *Composition*, 105. The recent study of M. A. Friedman ("Israel's Response") does not overcome these objections.

[239] "Literarische Struktur von Os 2,4-17."

[240] D. J. A. Clines ("Hosea 2") is also concerned strictly with the literary structure of the passage, although his mention of a redactor (p. 86) leads one to suspect that he considers the unity to be redactional.

[241] "Genèse et unité rédactionell de Os 2."

[242] K. Koch, *Biblical Tradition*, 192 = *Formgeschichte*, 235.

[243] Cf. Rudolph, who holds that the antithetical formulations in v. 7 and v. 9b induced the rearrangement.

[244] So L. Ruppert ("Hosea 1-3," 168-170), who also considers v. 19 to be the original continuation of v. 16-17.

[245] So also Wolff; D. J. A. Clines, "Hosea 2," 84-85.

That v. 16-17 do not constitute the original continuation of v. 15 has been hinted at above. Since both v. 16-17 and v. 11-15 are separate predictions introduced by לכן, an original connection is excluded. This view is reinforced by the concluding phrase נאם יהוה "utterance of Yahweh" in v. 15. Verses 16-17 thus form the prediction of a prophecy whose indication of the situation has not been transmitted. As such, they preserve only a portion of the orally delivered prophecy.

What can be said about the continuation in v. 18-25? It is generally recognized that these verses form a conglomeration of originally independent sayings or fragments thereof which have been concentrated here to flesh out the renewed relationship between Yahweh and Israel introduced in v. 16-17. They are divided into three sections, v. 18-19, 20-22, 23-25, by the phrase (והיה) ביום ההוא "(and it shall be) on that day" (v. 18, 20, 23), twice accompanied by נאם יהוה "utterance of Yahweh" (v. 18, 23). These sections are in turn composite in nature, as indicated by grammatical inconsistencies within each one. Thus, Israel is directly addressed in the second feminine singular in v. 18, but referred to in the third person in v. 19. In v. 20 the third masculine singular suffixes refer to Israel, whereas in the continuation, v. 21-22, Israel is again addressed in the second feminine singular. Finally, the third feminine singular suffix in v. 25 lacks an antecedent in the immediately preceding verses. The future orientation of these sayings makes it probable that they, too, like v. 16-17, all derive from the predictive portions of various salvation oracles.

Inasmuch as the various sayings of v. 16-25 were originally independent, the Hoseanic authorship must be examined for each one individually. The authenticity of v. 16-17 is today generally acknowledged, but this was not always the case. Marti argued that v. 15b-25 conflict with v. 4-15a both in tone and in content. Whereas anger occasions the total destruction of the land in v. 4-15a, v. 15b-25 are dominated by hope for the future with no mention of the desolation. Consequently, Marti considered these latter verses a later addition interpreting the desolation as the exile and stating, in contradiction to Hosea, that the exile was not the end but a transition period leading to a wonderful new era. Marti's comments, however, are hampered by the lack of form-critical considerations. Thus, he failed to isolate the originally independent oracles or parts of oracles, and hence to recognize the secondary character of the literary composition over against the oral presentation. Moreover, v. 4-15 are not as one-sidedly disastrous as Marti believed. Verse 5 is not a prediction but a threat which may or may not be carried out depending on the wife's response (v. 4b). Yahweh's actions are calculated to bring about the return of his unfaithful spouse (v. 8-9), not her total destruction.

A general methodological comment is also in order here. When attempting to assess the authenticity of a given prophecy within the corpus of a given prophetic book, it is vital that one does not become a captive of nomenclature. Simplifications that speak of pre-exilic prophecy as prophecy of disaster (Unheilsprophetie) and (post-)exilic prophecy as prophecy of salvation (Heilsprophetie) are likely to be as misleading as they are helpful, if not more so, in that they gloss over and blur the diversity and complexity of the phenomena so designated. It should also be obvious that such a schematic generalization cannot be employed as a criterion for making particular decisions concerning authenticity. Neither can it be maintained that both types of prophecy are mutually exclusive. There are no a priori grounds for denying to a given prophet who prophesied the fall of the nation and the exile of his people the ability to look beyond the national catastrophe. Hence, the mere fact that conditions following exile are predicted does not mean that the prophecy is (post-)exilic. A distinction must be made between presupposing *an* exile and presupposing *the* exile. Only the latter indicates a (post-)exilic date.

As for v. 18, J. Vollmer questions whether the contrast between אישׁי "my man" and בעלי "my lord/Baal" was intended by Hosea,[246] but this grossly underestimates the vigor with which Hosea fought against the syncretism with the Baal cults so prevalent in his day.[247] The same consideration argues for the authenticity of v. 19, the Hoseanic origin of which is today generally recognized.[248] The authenticity of v. 20, however, has been questioned on the grounds that a covenant between Israel and the animal world plays no role in Hosea's prophecy elsewhere; that רמשׂ "creeping things" is a late word; and that v. 20b finds its closest parallels in the late Judean additions 1:5, 7.[249] The first argument rests on an erroneous understanding of the parties to the covenant.[250] Yet even if this understanding were correct, the argument still proves nothing, since it presupposes that an idea must be represented twice before it can be genuine (an obvious fallacy) and fails to demonstrate that the idea is inconsistent with Hosea's ideas elsewhere. This is in fact not the case. That רמשׂ is a late word tacitly assumes a late date for 1Kgs. 5:13, which is uncertain.[251] The word is certainly no later than the pre-exilic text Hab. 1:14. Indeed, the argument represents a faulty evaluation of the evidence in that it fails to take seriously the incomplete attestation of the Hebrew language which the Old Testament traditions provide. "Creeping things" were without a doubt part of the landscape from the moment Israel entered the land, and also long before, so that it is quite improbable that there was no word for them until *ca.* 600 BC. As for the third argument, that v. 20b has terminological parallels in 1:5, 7 is certain; that it is therefore late is gratuitous. Hos. 1:5 is a genuine Hoseanic fragment,[252] and given that the series in 1:7b contains five members over against only three in 2:20, it is probable that the author of 1:7 has drawn upon 2:20 and expanded it.

The v. 21-22 are generally recognized as deriving from Hosea, and in fact nothing speaks against this view.[253] However, v. 23-25 have been subjected to doubts because the names of Hosea's children are interpreted in a manner different from Hos. 1 but in line with 2:1-3 (1:10-2:1) which is held to be a non-Hoseanic addition. Moreover, Yahweh's transcendence in v. 23-24 is said to contrast with Hosea's conception of Yahweh's direct action.[254] None of these arguments is compelling. That the names of Hosea's children are used differently here than in Hos. 1 does not necessarily imply that the usage does not stem from Hosea. Hos. 1 applies to contemporary Israel, whereas 2:23-25 (and 2:1-3) refer to the future restoration of Israel, so that there is no contradiction as to the meaning of

---

[246] *Geschichtliche Rückblicke,* 90.

[247] Cf. 2:7, 9, 12, 15, to mention only verses within the current literary complex, and G. I. Emmerson, *Hosea,* 25-26.

[248] Jeremias is an exception, but see below.

[249] J. Vollmer, *Geschichtliche Rückblicke,* 90; B. Renaud, "Os 2," 14-15. Cf. also W. Thiel, "'Bund' in den Prophetenbüchern," 13, who also argues that the change to the third person plural speaks against a Hoseanic origin. But this fails to take into account the composite character of the passage as a whole.

[250] See the *Comment.*

[251] See the discussion of M. Noth, *Könige I/1-16,* 80-81.

[252] So also Wolff; Rudolph; Mays. Andersen-Freedman go so far as to see it as original in its present context.

[253] Jeremias is again an exception, but again see below.

[254] J. Vollmer, *Geschichtliche Rückblicke,* 91; B. Renaud, "Os 2," 15.

the names. Reference to 2:1-3 is also inconclusive, since the authorship of this passage is contested. However, the fact that the phrase "Not-my-people" is altered to "sons of the living God" (cf. 11:1) rather than to "my people," as would he expected from a later hand, argues strongly for Hoseanic authorship.[255] And that Hosea should have conceived of Yahweh as giving Israel its grain, new wine, and fresh oil (2:10) in some way other than via the soil and rain is unlikely in the extreme.

One other argument has been advanced for the inauthenticity of Hos. 2:18-25. J. Jeremias considers these oracles to be non-Hoseanic on the basis of a historical theology of the Old Testament. In other words, the theological ideas expressed in these verses had not yet surfaced in the Israel of Hosea's day but reflect the thought of a later age. But is such an argument at all legitimate? Can a reconstructed history of theological development serve as a tool in determining authorship? Here one must examine the method by which such a history is established. Vital in this connection is the recognition that historical theology is a descriptive, not a prescriptive discipline. One cannot merely presuppose an evolutionary, or even a linearly progressive development of thought which is then superimposed upon the history of Israel on the basis of the (arbitrary) selection of a particular document or prophet as the first to evidence a particular thought. Rather, one must seek to retrace the intellectual journey with all its twists, turns and regressions, constantly guarding against tampering with the evidence to suit the reconstruction rather than adjusting the reconstruction to suit the evidence. For prophetic texts this means that the question of authenticity must be treated prior to and independent of any proposed history of ideas. If on other grounds a text can be shown to be "unauthentic," then historical theology can be helpful in the chronological ordering of that text, but this is a second step which must be strictly distinguished from the prior decision concerning authenticity.

The review of the various arguments brought against the authenticity of v. 16-25 has demonstrated that none of them proves the case. On the contrary, these verses fit admirably into the total context of Hosea's prophecy. Consequently, there are no grounds for denying them to Hosea.[256]

Comment

It is a decided handicap that the original indication of the situation that preceded the prediction in v. 16-17 has been lost, since this impedes the retracing of Hosea's thought. However, a reasonable degree of probability can be obtained if it is assumed that where an indication of the situation is lacking, this is due to similarity with one of the previous indications of the situation or with the immediate context. The motivation for such a procedure might have been to avoid extensive, or what appeared to the compiler(s) to be unnecessary repetition. It is also probable that greater emphasis was placed upon the predictive portion of a prophecy inasmuch as it was this portion that described the fate of the people and hence the fate of the tradents.

---

[255] Cf. Wolff; Rudolph. Mays is hesitant but leans on the whole towards Hoseanic authorship.

[256] See already the similar judgment of W. Baumgartner, "Heilseschatologie," 122: "Es liegt ... m.E. kein Grund vor, auch nur einen Vers von 2,16-25 Hosea abzusprechen."

Application of this principle to the present passage suggests that v. 16-17 are predicated upon Israel's unfaithfulness. She has gone whoring after her lovers (v. 4, 7, 15; cf. 1:2), whom she mistakenly holds to be her benefactors (v. 7b). She considers herself dependent on the various Baals for the produce of the land and so puts on her best dress in order to celebrate the various festivals dedicated to them (v. 13, 15). This no doubt brought with it the ascription of spheres of influence to the Baals, each personifying the natural forces he was viewed as controlling, and consequently a certain degree of disharmony and conflict inherent in the polytheistic religion of Canaan. Thus Israel "forgot Yahweh." She substituted a multiplicity of lesser deities for the sole lord of the land. It is Yahweh, and Yahweh alone, who provides for all here needs and causes the crops to grow. But Israel failed to recognize this (v. 10-11).

It is against this background that the "therefore" of v. 16 must be understood. Yahweh resolves to win back his bride. Much has been made of the sexual connotations of the root פתה, especially in the piel, which can be used for the seduction of a virgin (Ex. 22:15; cf. Judg. 14:15; 16:5). In light of the following "speak to her heart," these overtones are undeniable (cf. Gen. 34:3; Judg. 19:3). More generally, the verb means "to persuade" either in a positive sense (Prov. 25:15)[257] or in a negative sense as "deceive" (1Kgs. 22:20-23 = 2Chr. 18:19-21). Here the verb can only have a positive meaning, which has been rendered "win over" in an attempt to capture both its sexual and non-sexual aspects. To win over Israel Yahweh will lead her into the wilderness. in the solitude of the wilderness she will no longer be subject to the corrupting influence of the Baals (cf. v. 8-9). No longer distracted by the attractions of her lovers, Yahweh will enjoy her full and undivided attention. He will woo her and convince her that he is her one and only husband, the sole provider of the gifts of the land which she no longer enjoys. Whether Hosea had a literal return to the wilderness in mind or was speaking metaphorically of an exile in a foreign land is difficult to decide. If one dates this prophecy in the last years of Jeroboam II's reign before the rise of Assyria under Tiglath-pileser to the dominant political and military force in the region, one will probably be inclined to see a literal return to the wilderness here (Wolff). This view is further supported by the fact that there is no clear mention of an exile in the early chapters of Hosea.[258] However, prior to Tiglath-pileser's ascension to the throne Amos expressly predicts that Israel will go into exile (Amos 5:5, 27; 6:7; 7:11, 17; cf. 4:3; 6:14),[259] and the imagery of Hos. 2:16-17 admits of a metaphorical interpretation, so that this cannot be excluded with certainty.

In any event Israel's sojourn in the wilderness is a temporary one. It is motivated not by a love of the desert (cf. 2:5 [3]; 13:15), but by a desire to take Israel back to her origins, where her relationship to Yahweh was one of devotion. Yahweh will give her back her vineyards (v. 17a). But her second entry will be fundamentally different from the first. Yahweh will transform the valley of Achor (= trouble) into a door of hope. The context suggests that Hosea knew of events which transpired at this valley on the occasion of the settlement of the land and which shared the character of Israel's unfaithfulness in the

---

257 Cf. Rudolph, 75 n. 1.

258 The phrase עלו מן הארץ in 2:2 (1:11) does not refer to a return from exile but rather to "botanical growth" in the land as the result of God's sowing (יזרעאל). The objection of Jeremias that this meaning is artificial is refuted by Isa. 53:2 where the same imagery is expressed using the same terms (Rudolph).

259 This argument is not intended to show a dependence of Hosea on Amos but rather the possibility of predicting an exile at this early date.

ensuing years. This is commensurate with the tradition in Josh. 7 concerning the sin of Achan, who in the course of the conquest kept for himself precious items properly devoted to Yahweh in the ban, thereby incurring Yahweh's wrath and bringing "trouble" upon Israel. Hosea need not be referring to this tradition, although this is the simplest explanation. Otherwise one must postulate a different tradition, but there is no compelling reason to do so. Achan's sin was at the very least disobedience to Yahweh, but it may also have entailed for Hosea the failure to recognize Yahweh as the true owner of the goods and provider of the land (cf. 2:10 [8]; 12:9 [8]). But such will not happen in the new settlement. Because of her renewed devotion brought about by Yahweh in creating favorable conditions between himself and Israel in the wilderness, Israel will enter the land in anticipation of a life of peace and prosperity.

This renewed devotion will also enable Israel to respond to Yahweh as in the days of her youth. The root נער "youth" is used by Hosea elsewhere only in 11:1, where it is also used in connection with the Exodus. The period of the Exodus is the period of Israel's youth, but it is a period encompassing the wilderness as well. This becomes quite clear in v. 17b where the phrases "the days (pl) of her youth" and "the day (sg) of her coming up from the land of Egypt" stand in parallelism. In the age to come Israel will again respond to Yahweh as she had during the period inaugurated by the Exodus. She will be won over by Yahweh's wooing and will agree to renew the marriage relationship.[260] In Hosea the marriage symbolism is tied to the covenant,[261] and so Israel's acceptance of Yahweh's marriage proposal is equivalent to her acceptance of his offer to renew the covenant relationship between them. This interpretation finds support in the conception expressed in Exodus that Israel entered into the covenant in response (ענה Ex. 19:8; 24:3) to Yahweh's offer. L. Perlitt considers these passages, or at least the references to covenant in them, to be deuteronomistic,[262] but the improbability of this view has been convincingly demonstrated by D. J. McCarthy, who maintains that the differences in outlook and expression between them and deuteronom(ist)ic literature indicate that they are predeuteronomic traditions within the stream flowing into the deuteronom(ist)ic literature.[263] Further support may be found in v. 20 where the response of v. 17b is interpreted as including a covenant between Yahweh and Israel.[264] Admittedly, this interpretation probably derives from the circle of Hosea's disciples,[265] but since Hosea knew of a covenant between Yahweh and Israel, there is no reason to doubt the accuracy of the redactional explication of what is implicit in Hosea's original statement. Hosea envisioned a new covenant (v. 20), and in v. 17b he expresses this in terms of the marriage imagery. He also expresses it in terms of a comparison with Israel's earlier response when Yahweh brought her up from Egypt. As a consequence of this reference to the Exodus, שמה "there" in v. 17b is generally taken as referring back to the wilderness mentioned in v. 16.[266] This results in the chronological priority of v. 17b over against

---

260   Cf. P. Humbert ("L'unité d'Osée 2,4-22," 165) who refers to ענה in Ex. 21:10 as denoting conjugal rights; Wolff; Rudolph; Jeremias.
261   See above p. 91 and n. 231.
262   *Bundestheologie*, 167-181, 190-203.
263   *Treaty and Covenant*, 266-272.
264   On this verse see below pp. 101-102.
265   See above pp. 26-28.
266   So Wolff; Rudolph; Mays; Jeremias.

v. 17a.[267] However, it is also possible that שמה refers to the valley of Achor, the last locality mentioned. On this view there is no need to skip over v. 17a, and the events of v. 16-17 are listed in order of occurrence. Furthermore, the covenant envisioned in v. 20 appears to be concluded in the land, and this agrees with v. 25 which also suggests a renewal of the covenant following the sowing of Israel in the land.[268] Thus, as the youthful Israel accepted Yahweh's offer to enter into covenant, Israel will again accept his offer of a new covenant. But whereas the first covenant was concluded in the wilderness following the Exodus, the new covenant will be concluded in the land at the beginning of the return.

As indicated above,[269] the purpose of the three subdivisions of v. 18-25 is to illuminate various aspects of the renewed relationship mentioned in v. 16-17. The first division, v. 18-19, depicts the purity of the relationship. The point is not that Israel no longer views Yahweh as the legal authority over her (בעל) but as the loving husband (איש) to whom she may lovingly submit.[270] Rather, v. 18 reflects Israel's recognition of the fundamental difference between Yahweh and Baal.[271] This difference is so profound that, once grasped, any and all application of the title "Baal," associated as it was with sexual rites and the conception of a fertility god who is himself a captive, becomes an impossibility because a parody. Yahweh is the only Lord of nature, and in his hand resides all fertility (2:10-11) without recourse to or need of auxiliary sexual rites (2:23-24). Verse 18 expresses the fundamental insight, v. 19 the means by which Israel will come to it. Yahweh himself will purge the Baals from Israel's collective remembrance. This effectively means that the cultic invocation and worship of the Baals will cease completely,[272] thereby rendering them irrelevant. Israel's worship of the Baals will come to an end - a complete reversal of Israel's current practice (2:15)!

In contrast to the first section, which deals with the renewed Yahweh-Israel relationship in terms of Israel's past adultery with Baal and hence is formulated in a predominantly negative manner, the second section, v. 20-22, deals directly and positively with the renewed relationship and consequently is far more sweeping in character. A new covenant will be made encompassing Yahweh, Israel, and the animal world. But who is party to the covenant? Some see here a covenant between Israel and the animals mediated by Yahweh, who thus becomes its guarantor.[273] Others see a covenant between Yahweh and the animals made for Israel's benefit.[274] However, both of these interpretations run counter to normal usage. In all other occurrences of the phrase כרת ברית ל the subject

---

[267] L. Ruppert ("Hosea 1-3," 170) therefore transposes them.

[268] On v. 25b as referring to a renewal of the covenant see below pp. 103-108, and on the use of שמה to refer to a location without implying motion towards it, cf. GKC §90d.

[269] See above p. 96.

[270] So Wolff; cf. Jeremias. This interpretation has been ably refuted by G. I. Emmerson, *Hosea*, 25-26.

[271] So also G. I. Emmerson, *ibid.*

[272] On the cultic associations of זכר, cf. W. Schottroff, *THAT* I, 513; H. Eising, *TDOT* IV, 74-75; and Hos. 12:6 (5).

[273] So H. W. Wolff, "Jahwe als Bundesvermittler," building on M. Noth, "Das alttestamentliche Bundschliessen im Licht eines Mari-textes" = "Old Testament Covenant-making in the light of a Text from Mari," and followed by M. de Roche, "The Reversal of Creation in Hosea," 406; G. I. Emmerson, *Hosea*, 30.

[274] So Rudolph; Mays; Andersen-Freedman; Jeremias; and E. Kutsch, "Der Begriff ברית," 138-139, who, of course, speaks not of a covenant but of an obligation laid upon the animals by Yahweh.

of the verb and the object of the preposition are *both* party to the covenant.[275] The same is true of the preposition עם in connection with כרת ברית.[276] Hence, the most reasonable conclusion is that all three - Yahweh, Israel, and the animal world - are parties to the covenant.[277] This interpretation finds further support in the continuation, v. 20b, which pictures the complete destruction of weapons. This goes beyond the man-animal relationship and yet forms an integral part of the comprehensive peace and security which derive from the covenant. In a reversal of the circumstances described in 2:14 and of the turbulent political events typical of Hosea's day, Yahweh will bring about peace between himself and creation, between man and animal, and by implication among the nations - at least as far as Israel is concerned - since war and hostilities will be banished from the land. The initiative is fully on the part of Yahweh, and he is also the one who alone causes Israel to dwell in safety and prosperity in total reliance on him.[278]

In v. 21-22 the imagery shifts to that of the marriage relationship, but this is another way of portraying the effects of the covenant made in v. 20, since marriage could be viewed as a covenant.[279] Yahweh will betroth Israel to himself. The imagery, however, does not appear to be exact in that ארש "betroth" refers to the giving of the מהר "compensation-gift"[280] to the father or guardian of the prospective bride. The compensation-gift was normally given by the groom's father, but could also be given by the groom himself.[281] Once the gift had been received, the girl or woman became the legal wife of the groom (Deut. 22:23-24) even though the marriage was not yet physically consummated (Deut. 20:7; 28:30). But who could be conceived of as Israel's father? Elsewhere Hosea pictures Yahweh as Israel's father (11:1), but in this analogy Israel is not his daughter but his son. Also, Yahweh as father would result in his giving gifts to himself. There can be no doubt that the gifts in v. 21-22 are given to the bride. This would seem to indicate that it was customary for the groom to give gifts to the bride on the occasion of their betrothal[282] and that this act could also be included in the verb ארש. In contrast to the compensation-gift, the betrothal-gift would have been a purely customary act entailing no legal ramifications since it did not find its way into Israel's legal codes. The groom Yahweh, then, will enter into a new covenant relationship of marriage with his

---

275   Ex. 23:32; 34:12, 15; Deut. 7:2; Josh. 9:6-16; 24:25; Judg. 2:2; 1Sam. 11:1; 2Sam. 5:3; 1Kgs. 20:34; 2Kgs. 11:4; 1Chr. 11:3; 2Chr. 21:7; 29:10; Ezra 10:3; Isa. 55:3; 61:8; Jer. 32:40; Ezek. 34:25; 37:26; Ps. 89:4; Job 31:1.

276   Hos. 12:2 (1); Gen. 26:28; Ex. 24:8; Deut. 4:23; 5:2; 9:9; 29:11, 13, 24; 1Kgs. 8:21; 2Chr. 6:11; 23:3; Neh. 9:8; Job 40:28.

277   Cf. the analogous covenant with Noah, Gen. 9:9-10.

278   On בטח cf. E. Gerstenberger, *THAT* I, 302-305; A. Jepsen, *TDOT* II, 89, 92-93.

279   Ezek. 16:8; Mal. 2:14.

280   For the interpretation of the מהר as a compensation-gift (*RSV* "marriage present") rather than a bride-price, cf. M. Burrows, *The Basis of Israelite Marriage.* Other studies on marriage in Israel include W. Plautz, "Die Form der Eheschließung im AT" and J. Scharbert, "Ehe und Eheschließung in der Rechtssprache des Pentateuch und beim Chronisten."

281   1Sam. 18:25-27; 2Sam. 3:14.

282   This appears to be the best interpretation of the מתן offered by Shechem for Dinah, Gen. 34:12, and possibly also of the gifts given to Rebecca, Gen. 24:53; cf. C. Westermann, *Genesis 12-36,* 477, 657. In the Mesopotamian realm a parallel practice, albeit with a definitely legal character, may be reflected in the *nudunnû* (cf. M. Burrows, *Israelite Marriage,* 46-50; A. van Praag, *Droit Matrimonial Assyro-Babylonien,* 160-170) or in the *dumāqū* (cf. A. van Praag, *op. cit.,* 170-172; A. van Selms, *Marriage and Family Life in Ugaritic Literature,* 73; Driver and Miles, *The Assyrian Laws,* 193-198.

bride Israel, and as an expression of his love he richly blesses her with precious gifts. צדק "righteousness" enables one to act in a manner commensurate with the needs and demands of the relationships - to God, man, and nature - which characterize life and also maintains and nurtures these relationships and their salvific aspects.[283] משפט "justice" denotes "the institutional order, the intact but dynamic form of community, its specific characteristics and actions, the positive order of existence *per se*."[284] חסד is here best understood as loyalty to the covenant mentioned in v. 20 and implicit in the marriage imagery.[285] רחמים "compassion" is the tenderness and affection springing from genuine solidarity, as of a mother with her children (רחם = womb). אמונה "faithfulness" constitutes "a way of acting which grows out of inner stability" and upholds the proper order among men and God.[286] Taking the initiative, Yahweh provides his bride with all the qualities and capabilities necessary to live in total harmony with him. Empowered by these qualities, she will truly come to know Yahweh[287] with an intimacy and resoluteness diametrically opposed to her past infidelities. It is nothing less than a completely intact existence in all its relationships that is envisioned.

The final section, v. 23-25, depicts the consequences of the new Yahweh-Israel relationship for the natural phenomena. Concomitant with the restored knowledge of Yahweh is the recognition of him as the sole source of the produce of the land (2:10-11). The danger of Israel attributing these gifts to the Baals has been eliminated, so Yahweh can again bestow them freely to his people. But more than this, the positive order of existence has been restored, which must have a positive effect on nature. Yahweh will cause the heavens to bring forth rain, which will cause the earth to yield its produce in response to Jezreel, which here stands for Israel. Israel's actions are now supportive of the positive order of existence, and this must have a positive effect on nature which Yahweh for his part further enhances. It is significant that no room is left within the interaction or the influence of the Baals. They are not so much as implied, let alone mentioned (cf. v. 18-19).

The period of chastisement is over. Israel has been wooed and responded positively; the covenantal relationship has been restored and Israel lives peacefully in the land. This entire process is now summed up in v. 25 by means of the names of Hosea's children. The connection with v. 23-24 is achieved by the idea contained in the name Jezreel, "God sows," which is now applied to Israel. Yahweh will sow his bride in the land. Further, she who knew no family solidarity will experience the full love and affection of the one who chastised her to bring her to himself. And finally, the people who broke the (previous) covenant with Yahweh will partake of a new covenant with him in which they fully recognize him as their God.

This last statement is based on the view that in v. 25b Hosea is playing upon the "covenant formula." There are two basic studies of the covenant formula, those of R. Smend and N. Lohfink.[288] The formula may be defined as the statement "I will be(come)

---

[283] Cf. G. von Rad, *Theology* I, 370-383 = *Theologie* I, 368-380; K. Koch, *THAT* II, 507-530.

[284] K. Koch, *The Prophets* I, 59 = *Die Profeten* I, 70.

[285] On חסד see above p. 45.

[286] A. Jepsen, *TDOT* I, 317.

[287] See below on the knowledge of God, pp. 111-116.

[288] R. Smend, *Die Bundesformel*; N. Lohfink, "Dt 26,17-19 und die 'Bundesformel.'" L. Perlitt (*Bundestheologie*, 102-115) also treats the covenant formula.

your God and you will be(come) my people" and occurs in whole or in part some 37 (38) times in the Old Testament.[289] In seeking to illuminate the origin of the covenant formula Smend begins with Deut. 26:17-19, which because of the mutual character of the underlying ceremony, is probably closest to the original setting in life. This original setting is to be seen in the covenant made by king Josiah in 621 BC.[290] A possible objection to this dating is that according to the present context in Deuteronomy the formula belongs in the Mosaic period and therefore may be earlier than Josiah's era. 2Kgs. 11:17; Josh. 24; and Hos. 1:9; 2:25 (23) may point in this direction. To counter this objection Smend argues that 2Kgs. 11 and Josh. 24 may be deuteronomistic and that, although Hosea presupposes the content of the covenant formula, it cannot be demonstrated that he presupposes the formula itself.[291] He then turns to an examination of the formula's presuppositions to see when it could have arisen. The presuppositions are twofold: 1) the belief that Yahweh and Israel belong together; and 2) the existence of the expressions "Yahweh the God of Israel" and "Israel the people of Yahweh."[292] For Smend the earliest possible date is the period following the occupation of the land when Yahweh and the people of Yahweh coming from Egypt united with the God of Israel and Israel settled in Palestine.[293] Still, the formula did not originate at this time. According to Smend, the Song of Deborah, although attesting the phrase "Yahweh the God of Israel" (Judg. 5:3, 5), does not presuppose the identity of Israel (v. 2, 3, 5, 7-9, 11) and the people of Yahweh (v. 11, 13; cf. v. 9). Israel is the sum total of the tribes, whereas the people of Yahweh is the militia and is limited to those who actually came to fight in the battle. The people of Yahweh come from Israel but are not coterminous with it. The non-participating tribes are hence chastised not because they failed to fulfill an existing obligation but because the Song of Deborah seeks to unite Israel with the people of Yahweh.[294]

Smend's interpretation, however, is not entirely convincing. Neither of the phrases "Yahweh the God of Israel" and "Israel the people of Yahweh" appears in the covenant formula, rendering it questionable whether they may legitimately be considered presuppositions of the formula. Even granting that the conceptions contained in these two constructions are prerequisites of the formula, and Smend actually seems to argue along these lines, it may still be objected that a commemorative victory song like the Song of Deborah looks back on events and judges them according to the standards of the age in which it is composed in order to encourage adherence to them; it is not primarily concerned with creating or altering them. This consideration harmonizes well with the most natural interpretation of the song, namely that the tribes that failed to respond to the call to arms are reproached because, as members of Israel, they should have joined the battle. Every member of Israel should be a member of the people of Yahweh in battle in the

[289] In its entirety: Ex. 6:7; Lev. 26:12; Deut. 26:17-19; 29:12; 2Sam. 7:24 (= 1Chr. 17:22); Jer. 7:23; 11:4; 27:7; 20:22; 31:1, 33; 32:38 (Smend erroneously 32:28); Ezek. 11:20; 14:11; 36:28; 37:23, 27; Zech. 8:8. First half only: Gen. 17:7, 8; Ex. 29:45; Lev. 11:45; 22:33; 25:38; 26:45; Num. 15:41; Ezek. 34:24. Second half only: Ex. 19:5; Deut. 4:20; 7:6; 14:2; 27:9; 1Sam. 12:22; 2Kgs. 11:17; Jer. 13:11 (cf. R. Smend, *Bundesformel*, 5; N. Lohfink, "Bundesformel," 517.
[290] R. Smend, *Bundesformel*, 8-9.
[291] *ibid.*, 10-11.
[292] *ibid.*, 11.
[293] *ibid.*, 16.
[294] *ibid.*, 11-13.

conception of the Song of Deborah (as Smend correctly saw) and hence in the prevalent conception of its day (*contra* Smend). The song presupposes Israel as the people of Yahweh; it does not seek to weld the two into a new self-understanding.[295]

Further evidence of the conception of Israel as the people of Yahweh is found in 1Sam. 9:16. Here, in an early tradition of Saul's rise to kingship,[296] it is reported that Yahweh revealed to Samuel his intent to appoint Saul "prince over my people Israel."[297] Similarly, 1Sam. 2:22-25, also an early tradition,[298] assumes the identity of Israel and the people of Yahweh in a context in which the cultic community is perhaps primarily in view.[299] Both passages indicate that Israel was conceived of as the people of Yahweh by the early monarchic period, and the matter-of-fact manner with which this is assumed makes it appear likely that the conception dates back to the pre-monarchic period. In either case the prerequisites for the existence of the covenant formula at least as soon as the early monarchic period are met,[300] and hence the dating of the conception and/or ceremony underlying Deut. 26:17-19 to the Josianic era, which even by Smend's own admission is only one possibility,[301] becomes rather arbitrary.

Lohfink's criticism of Smend on this score is also worth noting. He points out that the text relating the making of a covenant by Josiah, 2Kgs. 23:3, reveals no positive points of contact with Deut. 26:17-19, so that a connection cannot be established on these grounds. Still, it is possible that Deut. 26:17-19 reflects the words spoken in the covenant ceremony, but this does not mean that they were necessarily composed for this occasion.[302] Indeed, Lohfink also challenges Smend's quick dismissal of 2Kgs. 11:17 as deuteronomistic, and also cites 2Sam. 7:24 with its unique use of the verb קום in the formula as further evidence of its existence in the early monarchic period, unless one assumes it to be a late non-deuteronomistic addition. Both passages may contain positive evidence of the covenant formula prior to Josiah's day.[303]

---

[295] R. Smend is followed in his interpretation by N. Lohfink ("Ausdruck עם יהוה," 281-283), who further adduces 2Sam. 1:12 and Judg. 20:2 in support of this view. But 2Sam. 1:12 is by Lohfink's own admission insufficiently clear on its own merits, and the "people of God" in Judg. 20:2 are "all the people of Israel ... from Dan to Beer-sheba, including the land of Gilead" (save, of course, Benjamin) mentioned in 20:1.

[296] Cf. H. Greßmann, *Geschichtsschreibung*, 35; M. Noth, *Überlieferungsgeschichtliche Studien*, 62 and n. 1 = *The Deuteronomistic History*, 54 and 124 n. 1; A. Weiser, *Samuel*, 56; O. Eißfeldt, *Introduction*, 275 = *Einleitung*, 367; H. J. Stoebe, *Das erste Buch Samuelis*, 65-66, 200.

[297] On this title cf. W. Richter, "Die *nāgîd*-Formel," with literature.

[298] This passage belongs to the anti-Shilonic tradition concerning Eli and his sons, 1Sam. 2:12-17, 22-33, 35-36, according to M. Noth, "Samuel und Silo," 392-394. He is followed by H. J. Stoebe, *Das erste Buch Samuelis*, 86. Noth dates the tradition, which reflects Jerusalem polemics against Shiloh, shortly after Solomon's death, but the expulsion of the Elide Abiathar in favor of Zadok (1Kgs. 2:26-27, 35) would provide ample motivation for the tradition in Solomon's lifetime.

[299] Cf. L. Rost ("Land und Volk im AT," 146 = 91), who maintains that עם as a designation for the people refers to the body of men capable of participating in the cult, of deciding legal matters in the town gate, and of fighting in the event of war. Though this view holds for some instances, it is quite often too narrow; cf. N. Lohfink, "Ausdruck עם יהוה," 277 and n. 14, and his conclusions summarized on pp. 289, 294.

[300] Cf. the statement of N. Lohfink ("Ausdruck עם יהוה," 284) that "mindestens seit David der עם יהוה mit der - selber wechselnden - Größe 'Israel' identifiziert wird."

[301] *Bundesformel*, 9. However, he then proceeds to treat this date as established fact.

[302] N. Lohfink, "Bundesformel," 547-548.

[303] *ibid.*, 525-526. Lohfink later abandoned the use of 2Sam. 7:24 on the grounds that it is a secondary deuteronomistic addition ("sekundärdeuteronomistischer Zusatz"), without abandoning his main thesis ("Ausdruck עם יהוה," 298 n. 83).

The discussion to this point has done little more than demonstrate the possibility of
the covenant formula as early as the beginning of the monarchic period, and perhaps
earlier. But one will not want to lean too heavily upon 2Sam. 7:24 and 2Kgs. 11:17,[304] and
so a closer look at Deut. 26:16-19 is in order. What can he inferred from this text?

In his analysis of the passage, Smend felt that the text made an "overloaded
impression" and held that at least some of the infinitive clauses beyond v. 17abα, 18aα
must be secondary, although he considered it a hopeless task to try to determine exactly
which of these were original, if any, and which were not.[305] If this impression is correct,
then the text as it now stands would be the elaboration of a shorter and older text. More
recent studies, however, tend to view the text in its present form, at least as far as v. 17-
19 are concerned,[306] as a literary unity. The ability of the Hebrew infinitive construct to
shift logical subject without explicit mention of the new subject deprives arguments based
on this shift of a solid foundation.[307] In its current form the passage joins together Deut.
5-26 and Deut. 28. This is indicated by the pair חקים "statutes" and משפטים "ordinances"
which brackets Deut. 5-11 and 12-26 (5:1; 11:32; 12:1; 26:16) and the insertion between
these two terms of מצות "commandments" (26:17), a term characteristic of Deut. 28 (v.
1, 9, 13, 15, 45).[308] Hence, the text belongs to the deuteronomic redactional level, that is
to Proto-Deuteronomy, the book of the law found in the Temple in 621.[309] With Proto-
Deuteronomy we find ourselves chronologically in the general vicinity of Hosea's ministry,
which spanned the three decades leading up to the siege of Samaria, perhaps in the two
decades following the fall of Samaria in 722.[310] The book preserves older material and
traditions from the northern kingdom of Israel.[311] The circles responsible for the
preservation of these traditions, however, are unlikely to have been situated in the territory
of the former northern kingdom, as Alt supposed, but rather were probably refugees from
the north living in Judah who "formulated their old traditions into a programme of reform
and revival which they intended to be carried out by the Judean authorities with whom

---

[304] One might also mention 1Sam. 12:22, on which cf. D. J. McCarthy, *Treaty and Covenant*, 212.

[305] R. Smend, *Bundesformel*, 7.

[306] Whether v. 16 was originally more closely associated with Deut. 5:1-26:15 or 26:17-19 is a question which need not be decided here.

[307] On the infinitive construct cf. Joüon §124s, who cites Ex. 5:21; Deut. 24:4 as examples. N. Lohfink ("Bundesformel," 530 n. 43) adds Deut. 6:1, 24; 2Chr. 6:19-20, though the appropriateness of the last reference is questionable.

[308] Cf. N. Lohfink, "Bundesformel," 541-543; D. J. McCarthy, *Treaty and Covenant*, 184-185. L. Perlitt (*Bundestheologie*, 103) made the same observation for v. 16 simultaneously with and independently of Lohfink, and also interprets the entire passage as composed for its present location (*op. cit.*, 114).

[309] Cf. O. Eißfeldt (*Introduction*, 225-232 = *Einleitung*, 299-309), who attributes both Deut. 5:1-26:15* and Deut. 28 to the original Deuteronomy but is not specific on 26:16-19; and D. J. McCarthy (*Treaty and Covenant*, 157-187), who employs the term "central discourse."

[310] Cf. e.g. W. H. Schmidt, *Einführung*, 122-123. Less convincing is the view that the book was composed during the reign of Manasseh as a response to the disappointment of Hezekiah's abortive reform movement, because it is then more difficult to account for the presence of the book in the Temple in 621. That it was stealthily planted there is difficult to accept. It seems more probable that the book is to be more closely connected with Hezekiah's attempted reform, which the compilers no doubt supported. The book found its way into the Temple at this time, but was later forgotten (intentionally?) when Manasseh reversed his father's policies. It then lay dormant until its discovery by Hilkiah.

[311] A. Alt, "Heimat des Deuteronomiums," 273-275.

they believed the future of Israel to lie."[312] This will also hold true for Deut. 26:17-19, which reflects a cultic practice in Israel and the interpretation given to it. One might object that the prime innovation of Proto-Deuteronomy lies precisely in the cultic realm, namely in the centralization of the cult, and so it is quite possible that the current passage also represents an innovation. But the reorganization of the cult is for the most part an external matter. It deals with the centralization of the cult at a single locality and the resulting logistical and practical repercussions, but it does not touch the content of the cult so centralized. On the contrary, it presupposes that the cultic festivals will be observed in the accustomed manner, but only at "the place which Yahweh your God will chose." It is therefore highly probable that Deut. 26:17-19 preserves the recollection of an Israelite cultic practice, and given the general setting of the text and the structure of Proto-Deuteronomy, this practice will have been a ceremony of covenant renewal.

What did this cultic act entail?[313] To answer this question it is necessary to distinguish between those portions of the text which reflect the act itself and those which represent the deuteronomic interpretation of it. In this connection Lohfink has made a significant observation. In the vast majority of its occurrences the covenant formula only refers to Yahweh's becoming Israel's God and/or Israel's becoming Yahweh's people. Also, much of the vocabulary of the clauses which go beyond these statements reflects typical deuteronomic conceptions. Thus, on both form-critical and literary-critical grounds v. 17abα, 18aα are likely to reflect the cultic act, whereas the remainder of these verses most probably represent the deuteronomic interpretation.[314]

Deut. 26:17abα, 18aα relate that Israel has declared Yahweh to be their God and that Yahweh has declared Israel to be his people.[315] The actual declarations of the parties are not quoted but presupposed,[316] and hence must be inferred. From the report it may be deduced that Israel declared either "Yahweh is our/my God" or "You are our/my God" and that Yahweh declared "You (sg/pl) are my people."[317] The degree to which the second pair of declarations parallels the formulation in Hos. 2:25(23)b is striking and can hardly be accidental. The only deviation is that the declaration of the people in v. 25b reads simply "my God." But the lack of a personal pronoun may be ascribed to the adaption to the poetic prophetic discourse (if an explanation is required at all), and should the original formula have been "You are our God," the shift to the singular possessive pronoun (suffix

---

[312] E. W. Nicholson, *Deuteronomy and Tradition*, 94.

[313] We are not concerned here with the entire ritual in all its splendor and glory, but with a single act within this ritual.

[314] N. Lohfink, "Bundesformel," 544-546.

[315] The exact force of the hiphil of אמר, which occurs only here, has occasioned some discussion. Is it to be understood as an intensive with the meaning "declare" (R. Smend, *Bundesformel*, 7-8) or as a causative with the meaning "cause to say" (N. Lohfink, "Bundesformel," 531-534; D. J. McCarthy, *Treaty and Covenant*, 183 n. 54)? The context favors the first interpretation. This is made clear by Lohfink's attempt to meet the needs of the context with the causative rendering: a person A (subject of the verb) causes a person B (object of the verb) to make a declaration in which B brings a demand to A, whereupon A accepts the demand by swearing to fulfill it (*op. cit.*, 534). But why take such a complex detour?

[316] L. Perlitt (*Bundestheologie*, 106) has correctly stressed this point. It is another indication that the author assumes familiarity with the act involved, since if it were his own invention, he would certainly have prescribed the formulas to be spoken.

[317] Cf. R. Smend, *Bundesformel*, 8; L. Perlitt, *Bundestheologie*, 106. Perlitt also considers "we want to be your people" and "I want to be your God" to be a possibility. This would correspond to the demand brought by party B in Lohfink's interpretation (see n. 315) rather than the response of party A.

in Hebrew) may be explained as due to the influence of the personification of Israel in
Hosea's children which is sustained throughout the verse. The exigencies of Hosea's use
of the symbolic names in 2:25 (23) would also be an adequate explanation of the diver-
gences in the case of the first pair of declarations, "Yahweh is our/my God" and "Israel
is my people," though each party's direct address of the other seems more likely precisely
because of the parallel in Hosea. A corresponding attestation of the first pair, or of one
of its members, in a direct speech addressed to the other party is lacking.[318] Hence, the
interpretation offered above that in 2:25(23)b Hosea is playing upon the covenant formula
taken from a ceremony of covenant renewal in order to express the future renewal of the
covenant between Yahweh and Israel accords with the evidence.

The view has also been expressed that Hosea negates the covenant formula in 1:9.[319]
This interpretation is sometimes coupled with the emendation of v. 9bß to לא ואנכי
אלהיכם "and I am not your God."[320] But Wolff has correctly pointed out that the
emendation has no support in the textual transmission, and most modern commentators
have rightly agreed with him in retaining לֹא.[321] They interpret v. 9bß as a noun-clause
parallel to the noun-clause in v. 9bα, in which case a reference to the revelation of the
divine name in Ex. 3:14 is seen in the לא־אהיה "I am not/will not be." Wolff appeals to
the Massoretic maqqef and to Ⅎ (καὶ ἐγὼ οὐκ εἰμι ὑμῶν "and I am not your I am")
as supporting this view. But the maqqef proves nothing, and that the Ⅎ translated לא
אהיה as a proper name from Ex. 3:14 does not mean that Hosea intended it so. Still, the
interpretation is possible, although attempts to explain the resulting meaning fall back on
the verbal idea. It should be kept in mind, however, that the text deviates from the
covenant formula in the second member, so that Yahweh does not declare that he is not
Israel's God. The first half of the explanation of the symbolic name "Not-my-people"
presupposes that Israel has de facto ceased to be Yahweh's people. It has more the
character of an assessment of existing fact than that of a declaration intended to alter the
existing situation. Israel has already by his actions broken the covenant.[322] Nevertheless,
Yahweh does not state that he has ceased or will cease to be Israel's God. Such a
statement would be irreconcilable with Hosea's conception of the coming disaster as
leading ultimately to a new and better relationship between Yahweh and Israel (2:9, 16-
25; 11:11; 14:5-9 [4-8]). Rather, Yahweh communicates that he no longer intends to be
there for Israel. He will withdraw his blessing and preserving hand from his people because
they have in fact ceased to be his people. But he does this in order to reestablish them
as his people (cf. 3:5; 5:15; 14:2-4 [1-3]; and the passages previously cited). Through the
entire process, Yahweh continues to be Israel's God.

---

[318] R. Smend (Bundesformel, 8) refers to Josh. 24:17-18, but here the addressee is Joshua, not Yahweh.
[319] In addition to the standard commentaries cf. e.g. F. C. Fensham, "The Marriage Metaphor in Hosea for
the Covenant Relationship between the Lord and his People (Hos. 1:2-9)." R. Smend (Bundesformel, 24-25)
actually sees the birth of the full mutual formula in Hosea's negative formulation, though this is based on
an emended text; see the next note.
[320] R. Smend, Bundesformel, 38 n. 73. Others who emend the text include Wellhausen; Marti; Harper;
Nowack; Sellin; Robinson; Weiser.
[321] In addition to Wolff, cf. Rudolph; Mays; W. Kuhnigk, Nordwestsemitische Studien, 4-5; Andersen-
Freedman; Jeremias.
[322] Similarly Wolff, 24: "Jahwe stellt fest, daß der Bund zerbrochen ist."

Results

The examination of 2:16-25 has naturally revealed more about Hosea's expectations for the future period of renewal than about his conception of Israel's past history and the traditions upon which he based his view. Nevertheless, some information can be gleaned. Hos. 2:17a suggests that Hosea knew the tradition of the sin of Achan preserved in Josh. 7. Hosea's allusion is consistent with the assumption that he knew the tradition in its current form, but it should be remembered that this is nothing more than an assumption. But it is the simplest explanation of the evidence.

More significant is what can be inferred about the initial covenant between Yahweh and Israel. This Hosea associates with the Exodus in the period of Israel's youth (2:17b), that is, with the time of the undisturbed relationship between Yahweh and Israel in the wilderness before Israel went chasing after the Baals (11:1-2; cf. 9:10). The possibility that Hosea located the initial covenant at Shechem (Josh. 24) may therefore be excluded, since this covenant was concluded in the land and not in the wilderness. It is also unlikely that Hosea would have placed the initial covenant in the valley opposite Beth-Peor in the land of Moab (Deut. 1:1, 5; 4:46). Hosea associates the fall to Baal and Israel's becoming an abomination with this site (9:10), so that it is most improbable that the covenant known to him would have been concluded subsequent to this event. It could have been concluded prior to the Baal-Peor episode, but this contradicts the view of Deuteronomy (4:3). Alternatively, Hosea could have conceived of an initial arrival at Beth-Peor when Israel entered into covenant with Yahweh but then returned to the wilderness, followed by a second arrival at Beth-Peor when Israel succumbed to Baal-Peor. But this view is not only needlessly complicated, it also contradicts the presentation in Deuteronomy-Joshua in which Israel proceeds into the land following the conclusion of the covenant. These considerations, taken in conjunction with the common conception of Israel responding to Yahweh's offer to enter into covenant evidenced both in Hosea and Exodus (Hos. 2:17b; Ex. 19:8; 24:2), suggest that Hosea had this covenant in mind. Whether he associated the covenant with the name Sinai or Horeb cannot be determined since he nowhere explicitly mentions either.

It might be objected that the conception of Israel as the female partner of Yahweh as found in Hosea is not expressly associated with this covenant in the extant sources. Of course, the female imagery is connected with the symbolic character of Hosea's marriage. It could be that his use of this symbolism derives from an existing conception of the covenant between Yahweh and Israel as a marriage relationship and that Hosea shared this conception with his contemporaries.[323] But when Hosea speaks directly of a future covenant in 2:20, Israel is referred to with a masculine form. Especially significant is the fact that in the declaration of Yahweh in the ceremony of covenant renewal which Hosea draws upon, Israel is also masculine (2:25). It is certainly no accident that Hosea applies a negated form of this declaration to his second son and not to his daughter. It may be that features deriving from marriage imagery had become associated with the covenant tradition in the north, perhaps facilitated by the common use of בעל to refer to the god Baal and with the meaning "husband" (e.g. Gen. 20:3; Ex. 21:3,22; Deut. 22:22; 24:4). But

---

[323]   So K. Koch, *The Prophets* I, 88-90 = *Die Profeten* I, 100-102.

if this was the case (which is not certain), it did not lead to a consistent identification of Israel as Yahweh's female partner, as indicated by the observable male imagery associated with Israel in the covenant context drawn upon by Hosea. The imagery of Israel as the bride of Yahweh is therefore not a compelling argument against the identification of the covenant known to Hosea adopted here.

Confirmation was also found for the inference drawn from 8:1-3 that there was a ceremony of covenant renewal in Israel.[324] Hosea plays upon the mutual declarations of Yahweh and Israel in this ceremony, which can be reconstructed on the basis of the information provided by Deut. 26:17-19. His knowledge of the covenant is thus to be connected with the cult. Unfortunately, this passage contributes little to the question of the particular form of the covenant tradition known to Hosea beyond what has already been discussed. However, 2:16-17 does indicate that Hosea not only located this covenant in the wilderness, but also that he connected it with the Exodus. Israel's future positive response to Yahweh's offer of covenant will be like the initial response at the time when Yahweh brought Israel up from Egypt. It can therefore be inferred that the Exodus and covenant traditions as known to Hosea were connected.

Turning to the future period itself, this will be an age culminating in hitherto unknown peace and prosperity in the land. It begins with a return to the wilderness (2:16) where Israel is separated from her lovers (2:8-9). Cultic worship of the Baals will come to an end and they will cease to be remembered by name (2:18-19). Yahweh will enjoy Israel's full and undivided attention and will speak tenderly to her heart (2:16). The purity of their relationship will be reestablished, and Yahweh will then return his bride to the land to enjoy the abundance of its produce (2:17a, 23-24). The return will be accompanied by a new covenant establishing peace between Yahweh, Israel, and the animals, and banishing war from the land. Security will prevail, and all will live in accordance with righteousness, justice, loyalty, compassion, and faithfulness, because Yahweh himself will give these qualities to Israel through the new covenant and so heal her apostasy (cf. 14:5 [4]). These attributes will be bestowed upon Israel at the beginning of the return to the land, so that the return will certainly communicate to Israel the unimpaired knowledge of Yahweh. All will come to know him and partake of a lasting covenantal relationship with him (2:20-22) in the land of peace and plenty.

---

[324] See above p. 91.

CHAPTER 4

HOSEA AND THE KNOWLEDGE OF GOD

The question now arises as to the source of Hosea's knowledge of the early historical traditions of Israel. Our investigation has already indicated that his knowledge of the covenant tradition derived at least in part from a ceremony of covenant renewal. This ceremony could not be reconstructed in its entirety, but included Yahweh's declaration that Israel was his people and Israel's declaration that Yahweh was their God, a feature alluded to in the depiction of the renewed covenantal relationship between Yahweh and Israel envisioned by Hosea (2:25 [23]; cf. 1:9). The ceremony of covenant renewal does not appear to have been a regular part of the annual cycle of festivals in Israel.[1] Rather, it appears to have been associated with communal laments on occasions of (national) disaster which were understood as a sign that the covenant had been transgressed,[2] although it should not be concluded that every occasion for a communal lament was also an occasion for the renewal of the covenant.[3] The cult was thus a source for Hosea's knowledge of the covenant between Yahweh and Israel. Was this also the case for the historical traditions upon which he drew? To answer this question it will be helpful to take a look at the knowledge of God in Hosea.

A. THE LACK OF THE KNOWLEDGE OF GOD

The preceding investigation has clearly shown that Hosea saw the decline of his people in the Canaanization of Israel in both the religious and social spheres, with emphasis on the former. Of course, Hosea himself does not speak of "Canaanization," but rather of the lack of faithfulness, loyalty, and especially the lack of the knowledge of God. The causal relationship between lack of the knowledge of God and the downfall of Israel is set forth by Hosea at the very beginning of the literary complex preserved in Hos. 4-11 and this establishes the interpretational framework for all that follows. Hosea's most explicit statement of this relationship is found in 4:6a: "my people are destroyed because of[4] the lack of the knowledge." The presence of the definite article - *the* knowledge - indicates that Hosea is referring to a well-known concept, and this can only be the knowledge of God. The consequences of the absence of this knowledge are depicted in 4:1-3.[5] When there is no faithfulness, (covenant-)loyalty, or knowledge of God in the land,

---

1 Cf. the calendars in Ex. 23:14-17; 34:18-23; Deut. 16:1-17.
2 See above pp. 90, 91.
3 Cf. K. Baltzer, *Das Bundesformular,* 64-67.
4 Causative מן, cf. GKC §119z.
5 For a fuller treatment of this passage cf. D. R. Daniels, "Prophetic Lawsuit," 345-347.

then swearing, lying, killing, stealing, and adultery burst forth, and blood-guilt follows upon blood-guilt. In a similar vein, Yahweh bemoans the transitoriness of Israel's (covenant-) loyalty, which required that he proclaim through the prophets that "I desire (covenant-) loyalty and not sacrifice, and the knowledge of God rather than burnt offerings" (6:6). This represents Hosea's understanding of the content of all prophetic preaching.

In both 4:1-3 and 6:4-6 the close association of (covenant-)loyalty and the knowledge of God can be observed. Apparently the two are intimately related. The fact that in lamenting Israel's transitory (covenant-)loyalty Yahweh emphasizes the need for the knowledge of God and not merely the need for a more reliable loyalty (6:4-6) suggests that true (covenant-)loyalty derives from a proper knowledge of God. The knowledge of God is thus the more fundamental of the two and issues in (covenant-)loyalty. On the other hand, the absence of both is in some sense "fatal." In 4:1-3 it results in a catalogue of sins, each of which brings death (דמים "blood-guilt"; cf. 12:15 [14]). Similarly, in 6:4-6 the lack resulted in Yahweh's "killing them by the words of my mouth" (v. 5a). In the context these words are equivalent to the judgment (משפט) referred to in v. 5b[6] and quoted in v. 6. What, then, is the knowledge of God that is so vital for Israel's well-being but which is lacking with such devastating consequences?

B. THE CONTENT OF THE KNOWLEDGE OF GOD

In seeking to determine the content of the knowledge of God we are in the fortunate position of being able to draw upon the results of the studies of H. W. Wolff and W. Zimmerli.[7] Wolff has shown, primarily on the basis of Hos. 4:6, that דעת אלהים was a technical term for a body of knowledge entrusted to and cultivated by the priests.[8] This verse also presupposes that it was the task of the priests to communicate this knowledge to the people since it is the people who lack the knowledge in 4:6a.[9] Isa. 28:9 confirms this view. In this passage Isaiah has charged the priests and prophets with performing their duties while intoxicated with wine and strong drink. Their judgments and visions are therefore unreliable. The accused respond by attempting to belittle Isaiah with the disparaging questions, "Whom will he teach knowledge, and to whom will he explain the message? Those who are weaned from the milk, those taken from the breast?" Isaiah's

---

[6]   In v. 5b ומשפטי כאור is to be read with 𝕲 for ומשפטיך אור in 𝔐.

[7]   H. W. Wolff, "'Wissen um Gott' bei Hosea als Urform von Theologie"; W. Zimmerli, *Erkenntnis Gottes nach dem Buche Ezechiel.* See also the exchange between F. Baumann, "'Wissen um Gott' bei Hosea als Urform von Theologie?" and H. W. Wolff, "Erkenntnis Gottes im Alten Testament," as well as the articles of J. L. McKenzie, "Knowledge of God in Hosea"; J. Bergman and G. J. Botterwerk, *ThWAT* III, 497-512; W. Schottroff, *THAT* I, 695-697; and E. K. Holt, "דעת אלהים und חסד im Buche Hosea." Other works treat the issue at hand at best peripherally and include J. Hänel, *Das Erkennen Gottes bei den Schriftpropheten;* S. Mowinckel, *Die Erkenntnis Gottes bei den alttestamentlichen Profeten;* and G. J. Botterweck, "*Gott Erkennen*" *im Sprachgebrauch des Alten Testaments.*

[8]   "Wissen um Gott," 537-538 = 187-188.

[9]   The term therefore cannot be limited to the professional knowledge of the priests communicated to the laity only in connection with individual decisions as first suggested by J. Begrich, "Die priesterliche Tora," 85-86 = 257-258. See the further arguments offered below.

credentials for instructing little children who have just been weaned are questionable, let alone professionals trained in the priestly and prophetic vocations. Of importance for our purposes is the association of knowledge (דעה) with the priests and the statement that it is the priests' responsibility to teach this knowledge, presumably to the laity. Also of importance in this connection is Mal. 2:7. Here it is stated that "the lips of the priest should preserve knowledge, and instruction should be sought from his mouth."

The knowledge of God was thus in the hands of the priests, who were charged with teaching it to the people. What was its content? The parallelism of the knowledge of God with "instruction" (תורה) in Hos. 4:6; Mal. 2:7 might suggest that the two terms were more or less synonymous and refer to the knowledge necessary for making decisions pertaining to cultic matters, particularly regarding clean and unclean, holy and profane.[10] But it was not the duty of the priests to instruct the laity in such knowledge in any systematic or comprehensive manner. Decisions were rendered on a case by case basis (Hag. 2:11-13), and perhaps some general principles necessary for proper participation in the cult were generally known. But only the priests had access to the full body of this knowledge. Moreover, Hosea does not employ the term תורה in this restricted sense. For Hosea it denotes the revelation of the divine will in its entirety,[11] and hence refers to the entire corpus of legal material (cf. 8:1, 12) in which this will found expression. It thus includes not only "cultic law" but "civil law" as well (cf. 6:7-10).

Is the knowledge of God then to be equated with the knowledge of the sum total of Israel's legal traditions?[12] This is possible, but the conclusion rests more on an examination of תורה than of דעת אלהים, and other considerations point in a different direction. In Isa. 5:12-13 lack of knowledge (דעת) is equated with the failure to regard the work of Yahweh: "but the deed of Yahweh they do not consider, and the work of his hand they do not see; therefore my people goes into exile for lack of knowledge." This passage, which is the only one to associate דעת with a specified content, suggests that דעת אלהים should be associated with Israel's historical traditions.[13] At this point the line of reasoning links up with the results of the study of Zimmerli mentioned above. Zimmerli has shown that the "recognition formula" (Erkenntnisaussage),[14] which is attested already in the Yahwist, but also in deuteronomistic and priestly circles, as well as in the prophetic circles as early as the tradition preserved in 1Kgs. 20,[15] follows upon the depiction of the activity of Yahweh in history. Thus, according to the logic of the recognition formula, Yahweh's action in history mediated the knowledge of God.[16] This knowledge may then be cultivated and transmitted to those who did not directly participate in or witness the events by

---

[10] J. Begrich, "Die priesterliche Tora," 85 = 257.

[11] Wolff, Hosea, 176.

[12] H. W. Wolff ("Wissen um Gott," 547 = 197) appears to come to this conclusion when he identifies the "primary contents" of the knowledge as Yahweh's covenant and Yahweh's teaching (תורה).

[13] On the connection of "the work of Yahweh" with history see e.g. G. von Rad, Theology II, 154, 161-163 = Theologie [4]II, 161, 168-170; H. Wildberger, Jesaja 1-12, 188-189; K. Koch, The Prophets I, 154-155 = Die Profeten I, 166-168.

[14] The formula has the form "and you (they) will know that I am Yahweh" (כי אני יהוה [וידעת]ם) or a variant thereof; cf. W. Zimmerli, Erkenntnis Gottes, 5-6 = 42-43.

[15] ibid., 16-29 = 54-69.

[16] ibid., 12-13, 40, 56 = 49-50, 80, 98.

retelling Yahweh's historical deed(s).[17] Hence, an event must be completed, or at least in the process of occurring, in order to mediate knowledge. The cultic cultivation and teaching of this knowledge is thus necessarily confined to the recitation of the past acts of Yahweh in history. In this connection one will have to think of the primary events recounted in the traditions of Israel's early history, namely the Exodus from Egypt and the entry into the land, since in the Old Testament traditions both events are understood as demonstrating the power of Yahweh and his exclusive claim to be Israel's God,[18] and perhaps also the tradition(s) recounting the initial conclusion of the covenant between Yahweh and Israel in this period. We thus have in דעת אלהים primarily a term for Israel's historical traditions which the priests taught to the laity, and in תורה a term for Israel's legal traditions.[19]

Returning to Hosea, we have already seen that he viewed the Exodus period as imparting the knowledge of Yahweh as Israel's deliverer and sole provider (13:4-5). The same conception of the gift of the land as imparting the knowledge of Yahweh lies behind 2:10 (8). Here, however, the idea is expressed negatively. Israel does not know that Yahweh is the true giver of the grain, new wine, and fresh oil. Granted, Yahweh is here the bestower of the produce of the land rather than of the land itself, but that Hosea should have disassociated the two is quite unlikely. Only the Lord of the land could cause it to bring forth its fruit (2:24 [22]), and only the Lord of the land could give it to Israel (2:17 [15]; 13:6). Israel has effectively forgotten that it was Yahweh who proved himself Israel's Lord and Lord of the land when he gave the land to Israel. It can therefore with reasonable confidence be maintained that Hosea viewed not only the Exodus but also the entry into the land as events imparting the knowledge of God. Thus, from Hosea's vantage point the adoption of Canaanite practices and customs, especially participation in the Baal cults, as the expression of Israel's degeneration is conceivable for Hosea only where the proper knowledge of God is no longer present, and this means where the proper knowledge of the historical traditions attesting to Yahweh is no longer present. For Hosea the knowledge and understanding of Israel's historical traditions results in conduct commensurate with the God revealed in these traditions. Hence, דעת אלהים as the knowledge of God deriving primarily from historical tradition and תורה as legal instruction in appropriate conduct ensuing from this knowledge were inherently related to one another.

---

[17]   *ibid.*, 43-44 = 85.

[18]   For the Exodus see above on Hos. 13:4, pp. 75-76; for the conquest cf. Josh. 3:10; 4:24; and W. Zimmerli, *Erkenntnis Gottes*, 35 = 75.

[19]   This appears to be in agreement with the view of H. W. Wolff when, in modification of his earlier statement (see n. 12), he states that "Gegenstand der דעת אלהים bei Hosea diejenigen Ereignisse und Gegebenheiten sind, die den Jahwebund der israelitischen Stämme in der Frühzeit zwischen Ägypten und Landnahme begründet haben" ("Wissen um Gott," 549 = 199). He is followed in his evaluation by E. K. Holt, "דעת אלהים und חסד im Buche Hosea." On the other hand, the results reached here are at variance with the view expressed by H. Gese ("Das Gesetz," 57), who considers the terms to be inter-changeable designations for the entirety of the content of revelation ("die Gesamtheit des Offenbarungsinhaltes").

C. The Source of Hosea's Knowledge

The implication of these considerations is that knowledge of Israel's early historical traditions was mediated to the people by priests. Furthermore, the fact that Hosea can presuppose familiarity with these traditions among his audience suggests that the priests communicated this knowledge not in the form of private tutorials given to individuals or small groups, but on occasions when larger gatherings of lay persons were at the sanctuary. The degree of familiarity with these traditions which Hosea himself displays and which presumably his audience was expected to possess, coupled with the fact that the teaching of this knowledge constituted a primary duty of the priests, renders it extremely probable that we should think in terms of the three major festivals of Israel's cultic calendar. From 12:10 (9) it was inferred that Hosea associated the Exodus with the Passover celebration, and if the interpretation of the plural "days" in this verse as an indication that Passover had already been combined with the Feast of Unleavened Bread by Hosea's day is correct,[20] then the Exodus tradition may have been connected with this festival. As for the other traditions, an assignment to a particular festival is not possible on the basis of the evidence provided by Hosea. Neither can the specific mode by which these traditions were taught to the laity be discerned. It is possible that the traditions were enacted or recited by priests as an integral part of the ritual celebration, but there is no direct evidence in Hosea to confirm this view. Since Hosea no doubt also attended these festivals, at least prior to his prophetic condemnation of the northern cults, he will also have his knowledge of these traditions from this source. He may also have received more extensive instruction in these traditions as part of a prophetic schooling, but no direct confirmation of this supposition has been encountered in this study.

Nevertheless, if this line of reasoning is correct, it does throw a certain light on the question of whether Hosea derived his knowledge from a written or an oral source. That he knew of written documents containing legal material is certain (8:12), and it is quite possible that he also knew of written compilations of Israel's historical traditions. In the course of this investigation no evidence has been encountered that would stand in the way of this view. But the considerations just put forth suggest that it is necessary to distinguish between knowing of written documents and actually having read them and drawn upon them as written sources. If the previous line of argumentation is correct, then unless Hosea was a priest - and there is no indication that he was - no evidence has been found in the texts treated suggesting that he would have had access to such written documents as existed. All that can be said with confidence is that Hosea knew these traditions from the recounting of them by the priests. Whether these drew their knowledge of Israel's historical traditions from written sources is difficult to decide. Written legal material was associated with the covenant (8:1, 12), which in turn was connected with the Exodus-wilderness traditions.[21] The relationship between דעת אלהים and תורה previously

---

[20]   See above p. 47.

[21]   See above pp. 109-110.

elucidated[22] also supports a connection between historical and legal tradition. The fact that Hosea knew of written compilations of legal material may indicate that the historical traditions with which this material was associated were also present in written form. Also pointing in this direction may be the extent of the history covered in these traditions, and in particular the indications that they had been related to one another chronologically. Hosea knew of a cycle of tradition recounting the life of Jacob which located his initial encounter with Yahweh at Bethel when he was fleeing to Aram.[23] He sees the covenant connected with the Exodus and following upon it,[24] and places the Baal-Peor episode on the boundary between the wilderness and the entry into the land.[25] Also, the tradition of the valley of Achor is connected by Hosea with the entry into the land and not with life in the land following the settlement.[26] Such arrangement is perhaps more indicative of a written source.

On the other hand, there is evidence in the Old Testament indicating that written legal material could exist independently of the historical tradition with which it was associated. Moses receives two tablets of stone with the law and the commandment in which the people are to be instructed (Ex. 24:12: cf. 32:15-16; 34:1). Between Mount Ebal and Mount Gerizim the Israelites construct an altar and set up large stones upon which the law is written (Deut. 27; Josh. 8:30-35). Mention should also be made of the "words" which Joshua wrote in the book of the law of God when he concluded a covenant with the people and made statutes and ordinances (Josh. 24:25). It is therefore conceivable that the compilation of written legal material existed independently of the historical traditions with which it was associated and which presumably recounted the occasion when the laws were enacted. Still, the fact that written legal collections were in the hands of the priests itself indicates that the priests could have preserved in written form the historical traditions in their care. Thus, although conclusive proof that this was necessarily the case is not available from the evidence considered here, it is nevertheless a very real possibility that the historical traditions drawn upon by Hosea were preserved by the priests in written compilations.[27]

---

[22]   See above pp. 112-115.

[23]   See above p. 45.

[24]   See above pp. 109-110.

[25]   See above p. 59; cf. also pp. 47-48.

[26]   Hos. 2:17a. On the relationship of Hosea's source to the extant sources see below pp. 119-122.

[27]   Cf. the considerations of H. S. Nyberg, "Das textkritische Problem," 243-244, who also reckons with a primarily oral tradition and a concurrent written tradition, though he is certainly too negative in his scepticism regarding the extent to which the prophets committed (some of) their oracles to writing.

CHAPTER 5

SUMMARY AND CONCLUSIONS

A. THE HISTORY OF ISRAEL ACCORDING TO HOSEA

1. The Four Periods

The investigation has shown that Hosea conceived of Israel's history as divided primarily into four major periods. The first is the patriarchal period (12:4-7, 13 [3-6, 12]).[1] Here Hosea demonstrates a knowledge only of the Jacob traditions. Whether he also was familiar with traditions about Abraham and/or Isaac can no longer be discerned. The argument from silence is hazardous in this case since as far as we can tell he had no compelling reason to draw upon them if he knew them. His use of the Jacob traditions is motivated by the identity of the name Israel for both Jacob and the nation of which Hosea was a citizen and to which he proclaimed his message, a factor clearly lacking for the other patriarchal traditions. The patriarchal period does not figure prominently in Hosea's prophecies, assuming that the current book is an accurate gauge. But certain aspects of this period are quite significant for Hosea. He knew of a promise of land to Jacob, as implied by the oracle to Jacob in which he is told that he will return (12:7 [6]),[2] and this promise quite probably gave these traditions a lasting importance. This is even more apparent for the commands contained in the oracle. The instructions of this period are considered by Hosea to be valid for and binding upon the Israel of his day. This would seem to imply a certain degree of "canonicity" for these traditions. This inference is supported by the fact that Hosea probably knew these traditions in a particular chronological scheme of Jacob's life. Jacob received the oracle at Bethel when he was fleeing to Aram (12:5b-7, 13 [4b-6, 12]).[3] Still, one will not want to press the term "canonical" too far, and definitely will not want to understand it along the lines of a modern conception of canon.

The patriarchal period is followed by the Exodus-wilderness period (12:13-14 [12-13]; cf. 2:16-17 [14-15]).[4] For Hosea this is the period *par excellence* of Israel's history to date. It began with the Exodus from Egypt under prophetic guidance in the person of Moses (11:1; 12:10, 14 [9, 13]) and continued until the episode with Baal-Peor (9:10).[5] This period was one of harmony between Yahweh and Israel in which Yahweh cared and provided for his people and Israel came to know Yahweh (9:10; 13:4-5).[6] At this time, too,

---

1   See above pp. 42-46, 48-50.
2   See above p. 45.
3   See above p. 45.
4   See above pp. 47, 50, 100.
5   See above p. 59.
6   See above pp. 59, 75-76.

Yahweh entered into covenant with Israel (2:17[15]b),[7] and the form of the covenant known to Hosea included legal material (6:7; 8:1).[8] This period hence saw the establishment of the foundations for life in the land with Yahweh. Knowledge of Yahweh was imparted to Israel, and the parameters for the conduct issuing from this knowledge (4:1-2) were given expression in the covenant.

The Exodus-wilderness period is followed by the period of Canaanization which began with the Baal-Peor episode, had as its primary salvific event the entry into the land, and continues in Hosea's day. At Baal-Peor Israel became detestable (9:10) and then brought their wickedness and sin with them into the land (12:9 [8]). Like a contagious disease this sin spread epidemically, carried from altar to altar as these multiplied throughout the land (12:12 [11]; 8:11). Yahweh's efforts to check this development through the prophets proved futile and only revealed the advanced stage of the disease (6:5; 7:1; 9:7-9; 11:3-4). This period is associated by Hosea with the arable land, and so his attitude towards the entry into the land is thus naturally ambiguous. He is well aware that the land is a gift from Yahweh, but he is also aware that, contrary to Yahweh's intention, the abundance of his gift fed Israel's pride and apostasy (13:6). Hosea appears to have been of the opinion that the gift of the land also imparted the knowledge of Yahweh, but he can only formulate this negatively (2:10 [8]). The consequences of the sin beginning with Baal-Peor evidently impeded the proper communication of this knowledge. Never having fully internalized that Yahweh was the giver of the land, Israel soon forgot Yahweh as their sole provider (13:5-6; cf. 2:15[13]b). This period so closely associated with the land must therefore end with the loss of the land. Yahweh will revoke his gift and deprive Israel of the possibility of cultic worship and hence of apostasy (2:11-15 [9-13]; 3:4; 8:6; 9:4-5; 10:2, 5-6, 8). The king, too, will be taken away (3:4; 8:10; 10:3, 7; 13:10), and Ephraim will be exiled in Egypt and Assyria (7:16; 8:13; 9:3, 6; 11:5). The coming disaster, however, does not mark the end of Israel's history. Although destroying almost all aspects of Israel's life in the land, and especially the institutions of king and cult, it is a prelude to the final period of renewal. The disaster is interpreted theologically as a return to the wilderness (2:16 [14]), to a situation free from the influence of the Baals.[9] The cessation of cultic worship (2:19 [17]; 3:4) will bring about a complete distinction between Yahweh and Baal (2:18 [16]). The distinction being clear, Yahweh will then return Israel to the land (2:17 [15]), but this time there will be no acts of disobedience to mar the entry or disturb the peace and tranquility in the land. In the future period life in the land will begin with a new covenant which Yahweh will make with Israel and the animals (2:17b, 20, 25b [15b, 18, 23b]). Whether the new covenant, like the former, will also contain legal material is not certain. Hosea does not address this issue, but rather emphasizes that Yahweh will directly impart the qualities of righteousness, justice, (covenant-)loyalty, compassion, and faithfulness to Israel, and these will empower Israel to know Yahweh (2:21-22 [19-20]). Hostilities between man and beast and between man and man will come to an end (2:20 [18]), and Israel's new moral behavior supporting the positive order of existence will contribute to the lasting abundance of the produce of the land (2:23-24 [21-22]). Cultic elements recede noticeably into the background. Hos. 3:5 with its reference to seeking

---

7 See above pp. 100-101, 109-110.

8 See above pp. 86, 91.

9 See above pp. 99, 101.

Yahweh (cf. 5:6) can be taken as implying a renewed cult,[10] but the verse is rather vague. The allusion to a future ceremony of covenant renewal (2:25[23]b) may also indicate cultic activity in the coming age. But it may legitimately be questioned whether the new covenant, once concluded, will ever require renewal, since Hosea's depiction of the future age does not suggest that it will ever be broken. Yahweh will betroth Israel to himself "forever" (2:21 [19]).

It may also be questioned whether Hosea anticipated the reestablishment of the monarchy in the coming age. Although he envisions a reunited Israel under a single leader, he does not call this leader a king but rather head (2:2 [1:11]). It could be that Hosea did have a king in mind but avoided the term because of the negative associations which he connected with it as a result of the degenerate state of the monarchy as he himself experienced it. It could also be maintained that the statement "they made kings but not from me" (8:4) implies that some kings were crowned with Yahweh's approval. But approval is the wrong word. According to 13:11, Yahweh installed and withdrew kings as an expression of his wrath. Since the preceding verse alludes to the time when Israel first sought a king, Hosea in all probability has the entire succession of kings in view.[11] Given this fundamental criticism of the monarchy, it is most unlikely that Hosea understood the future head to be a king.[12] Elsewhere Hosea stresses the prophetic guidance which will be especially abundant in the future period (12:11 [10]), and it may be that the future head will be chosen from their ranks, perhaps as a second Moses (cf. 12:14 [13]; Num. 14:4).[13] In any case Wolff is certainly correct when he remarks that the designation "head" is used here to indicate a pre-monarchic form of leadership (cf. Ex. 18:25; Num. 1:16; Judg. 10:18; 11:8; and in transition to the monarchy 1Sam. 15:17). Thus, although Hosea does not envision the reestablishment of the monarchy in the coming era, he does retain the centralization of power in a single person.

2. The Traditions Known to Hosea

Hosea displays the knowledge of a wide range of historical traditions. Of the Jacob traditions he alludes to a birth narrative (12:4[3]a; cf. Gen. 25:21-26), Jacob's struggle with a divine being (12:4b-5a [3b-4a]; cf. Gen. 32:22-32), his initial encounter with Yahweh at Bethel (12:5b-7 [4b-6]; cf. Gen. 28:10-22), his flight to Aram (12:13 [12]; cf. Gen. 27:41-45), and his service for his wife (12:13 [12]; cf. Gen. 29:15-30). These traditions were furthermore known to him as part of a composition depicting the life of the patriarch.[14] But various discrepancies between Hosea's allusions and the accounts in Genesis are to

---

10   On the use of בקש in connection with the cult cf. G. Gerleman, *THAT* I, 333-335; S. Wagner, *TDOT* II, 236-239.

11   See p. 74 n. 136. Similarly Wolff; Mays; Jeremias. Rudolph objects that David would also be included in this criticism, but there is no evidence that Hosea entertained a positive view of David's rule. And when A. Gelston ("Kingship in the Book of Hosea," 83-84) objects that elsewhere Hosea has the contemporary north-Israelite monarchy in view, he sets up a false alternative. Criticism of contemporary kings and conditions does not preclude criticism of the institution which they represent.

12   See the similar positions of O. Procksch, *Geschichtsbetrachtung,* 28; G. von Rad, *Gottesvolk,* 83 = 91; A. Alt, "Heimat des Deuteronomiums," 267; Wolff, *Hosea,* 31; Mays, *Hosea,* 32-33.

13   This possibility is also considered by Andersen-Freedman.

14   See above pp. 45, 50-51.

be observed.[15] Most striking is the form of the divine speech to Jacob at Bethel, which deviates markedly from Genesis. According to Hosea, Jacob flees to Aram, according to Genesis to Haran.[16] Hosea also speaks of an angel and Jacob's weeping in connection with his struggle with a divine being, both features lacking in Genesis. The combination of similar and dissimilar features suggests that Hosea drew upon a source containing variant forms of the traditions preserved in Genesis. Since the corresponding traditions in Genesis are now commonly assigned to the Yahwist, it may be concluded that Hosea did not draw upon this source. It also means that there is no way to compare Hosea with an Elohistic source. It may be postulated that this was his source, but it cannot be demonstrated.[17]

This conclusion is substantiated by the traditions underlying Hosea's conception of the wilderness period. Here it was seen that he most likely drew upon a form of the wilderness traditions which, unlike the Yahwist, did not contain the murmuring motif or the golden calf tradition.[18] However, like the Yahwist, Hosea's source depicted the Exodus as imparting the knowledge of God (13:4-5) and Moses as a prophet (12:14 [13]). He also knew the tradition of apostasy at Baal-Peor (9:10; cf. Num. 25). Furthermore, in this source the Exodus tradition was connected with a covenant tradition.[19] As for the wilderness traditions, these appear to be more closely associated with the Exodus than with the covenant tradition (13:4-5; cf. 2:16-17 [14-15]). This would agree with the different settings in life for the two traditions. The Exodus tradition appears to have been associated with Passover, perhaps already in combination with the Feast of Unleavened Bread (12:10 [9]),[20] whereas the covenant tradition is probably to be connected with a ceremony of covenant renewal performed on occasions of communal lament in the face of national disaster (8:1; cf. 2:25 [23]).[21] The form of the covenant tradition known to Hosea included legal material, probably covering both cultic and moral actions (6:7; 8:1).[22] Thus, we are again confronted with both similarities and dissimilarities between the Yahwist and Hosea, so that the former cannot have served as the source for the latter. Unfortunately, Hosea's references to the covenant are too general to permit comparison with a specific form of the traditions preserved in our sources, and in the case of the Exodus and wilderness traditions the corresponding traditions available for comparison in Exodus-Numbers are all Yahwistic (or Priestly), so that comparison with an Elohistic source is again precluded.

On the other hand, the opinion is often expressed that the concerns and concepts of Hosea and Deuteronomy are quite similar,[23] but on closer inspection many of the points of contact turn out to be rather tenuous. Reference has been made to the centrality of

---

[15] See above pp. 42-46, 50-51.

[16] Jacob is also placed in Paddan-aram at this point, but according to the tradition in Genesis he does not flee but is sent there (Gen. 27:46ff).

[17] Contra O. Procksch, Geschichtsbetrachtung, 118-134; E. Sellin, "Geschichtliche Orientierung," 650; J. Vollmer, Geschichtliche Rückblicke, 82.

[18] See above pp. 59-61.

[19] See above pp. 100-101, 109-110; cf. also pp. 112-115.

[20] See above p. 47; cf. also p. 115.

[21] See above pp. 91, 103-108.

[22] See above pp. 86, 91.

[23] See e.g. H. W. Wolff, "Hoseas geistige Heimat," 93-94 = 248-249; and G. von Rad, Gottesvolk, 78-83 = 86-91.

the covenant for the relationship between Yahweh and Israel and to the conception of Israel as Yahweh's son (Hos 11:1; 2:1 [1:10]; Deut. 1:31; 8:5; 14:1).[24] But not the slightest trace of the marriage imagery which Hosea associates with the covenant is to be found in Deuteronomy,[25] and the father-son relationship is also used by Isaiah (1:2; 30:9). The conception of Moses as a prophet (Hos. 12:14 [12]; Deut. 18:15) has also been adduced,[26] but as has already been pointed out,[27] this conception is also present in the Exodus-Numbers account. The common occurrence of the phrase "grain, new wine, and oil" (Hos. 2:10, 24 [8, 22]; Deut. 7:13; 11:14; 12:17; 14:23; 18:4; 28:51; cf. also Hos. 7:14; 9:1-2; Deut. 33:28) for the produce of the land has been noted,[28] but the trilogy also occurs elsewhere (Num. 18:12; 2Kgs. 18:32; Jer. 31:12; Joel 1:10; 2:19; Hag. 1:11; Neh. 5:11; 10:40; 13:5, 12; 2Chr. 31:5; 32:28). Both Hosea and Deuteronomy emphasize the need for proper knowledge (Hos. 4:1, 6; 5:4; 6:6; Deut. 4:39; 7:9; 8:5; 9:3), but Isaiah is also aware of its great importance (1:2; 5:13; cf. 28:9). The basically negative attitude towards the monarchy in both has been pointed out, but also the difference in degree. Whereas Hosea rejects the institution completely (13:10-11),[29] Deuteronomy at least tolerates it (17:14-20).[30]

More substantial is the common use of the term "love" (אהב) in the context of the relationship between Yahweh and Israel, especially as the motivation for Yahweh's deliverance of Israel from Egypt (Hos. 11:1; Deut. 7:8; cf. 4:37; 10:15; 23:6).[31] But it has also been pointed out that Deuteronomy also emphasizes the need for Israel to love Yahweh (cf. e.g. 6:5; 10:12; 11:1; 13:22), whereas Hosea does not use this term to describe Israel's proper attitude towards Yahweh. This may be due to his conscious avoidance of the term,[32] perhaps because of its negative association with Israel's apostasy (3:1; 4:18; 8:9; 9:1, 10). Mention should also be made of the prevalent use of "forget" (שׁכח) characteristic of both. But whereas Hosea observes that Israel has forgotten Yahweh (2:15 [13]; 8:14; 13:6), Deuteronomy, as a consequence of the situation supposed and the purposes pursued, must naturally formulate this as an admonition not to forget Yahweh or his deeds (4:9, 23; 6:12; 8:11, 14, 19). For Hosea, forgetting Yahweh is expressed concretely in Israel's adultery with the Baals (2:15 [13]), and this connection with the marriage imagery of the covenant suggests that the terminology of forgetting Yahweh be associated with the covenant. This agrees well with the covenantal context of Deuteronomy and the fact that both Hosea and Deuteronomy know of a ceremony of covenant renewal (Hos. 2:25 [23]; Deut. 26:16-19). It also finds support in Ps. 50 and 78. Ps. 50, the setting of which is probably a ceremony of covenant renewal (v. 5),[33] equates those who forget God with the

---

24 G. von Rad, *Gottesvolk*, 80 = 88.
25 As von Rad himself noted in *Das fünfte Buch Mose*, 46.
26 G. von Rad, *Gottesvolk*, 80 = 88; H. W. Wolff, "Hoseas geistige Heimat," 94 = 249.
27 See above p. 51.
28 G. von Rad, *Gottesvolk*, 80 = 88.
29 See above p. 119.
30 Cf. A. Alt, "Heimat des Deuteronomiums," 267, who explains this difference as due solely to the practical necessity with which the author(s) of Deuteronomy saw himself confronted.
31 Cf. G. von Rad, *Gottesvolk*, 81 = 89.
32 So W. L. Moran, "Love of God in Deuteronomy," 77; cf. also A. Alt, "Heimat des Deuteronomiums," 272-273.
33 This is, of course, a hotly contested issue, but such an interpretation seems demanded by the psalm. For a recent discussion with literature cf. H.-J. Kraus, *Psalmen*, 527-530.

wicked who violate the statutes of his covenant (v. 16-22). Ps. 78 also associates forgetting God's deeds with failure to keep his covenant and to live according to his law (v. 7, 10-11). Unfortunately, the dating of these psalms varies widely, rendering their temporal ordering relative to Hosea and Deuteronomy problematic. However, it may confidently be stated that both are Judean psalms (cf. Ps. 50:2; 78:9, 67-70). Isaiah, too, can state that "you have forgotten the God of your salvation" in favor of a foreign god (17:10).[34] It would therefore seem that, although this terminology is prevalent in Hosea and Deuteronomy, it was also known within a cultic context in Jerusalem.

Lastly, it may be noted that, since the account of the golden calf (Deut. 9:7b-21) is a secondary addition,[35] the lack of reference to this episode would be common to both Hosea and Proto-Deuteronomy. However, although the references in 6:16; 9:22-29 may also be secondary,[36] if 9:7a is original to Proto-Deuteronomy, then the statement that Israel provoked Yahweh to anger in the wilderness would stand in contradiction to Hosea's conception of this period, perhaps supporting the location of the compilers of Proto-Deuteronomy in the south.[37] The evidence, then, reduces primarily to the common importance of the covenant, Yahweh's love for Israel as motivation for the Exodus, and a negative attitude towards the monarchy. But in each case differences can be observed, so that the evidence for a connection between Hosea and Proto-Deuteronomy is somewhat fragile. Cautiously stated, it may be that both drew upon a tradition in which the Exodus was expressly motivated by Yahweh's love. The relationship of the covenant tradition known to Hosea and Proto-Deuteronomy is more difficult to evaluate due to the uncertainty concerning the origin of the marriage imagery which Hosea uses in connection with the covenant.[38] But even so, if this imagery does in fact derive from the tradition and not from Hosea, then this would speak against a connection, whereas if it was not part of the tradition known to Hosea, there is still no positive evidence demanding a connection between the two, since what can be deduced from Hosea's prophecies is too general in nature to permit a specific correlation.

It remains to be noted that Hosea knew of a tradition connected with the valley of Achor within the context of the entry into the land, perhaps in the form preserved in Josh. 7.[39] Again, Hosea's allusion is unfortunately too general to permit further inferences.

The investigation of Hosea's understanding of the covenant ran across evidence suggesting that the tradition known to him was connected with cultic ceremonies of covenant renewal (8:1; 2:25 [23]), and the examination of the knowledge of God further suggested that the other traditions known to Hosea were connected with the cult.[40] They were communicated to the people at the sanctuary during the three great festivals. The Exodus (and wilderness?) tradition was associated with Passover, and since this was not originally one of the three agricultural festivals, it may very well have already been combined with the Feast of Unleavened Bread.[41] Hosea's reference to written legal

---

[34]   The authenticity of the verse is contested, but cf. H. Wildberger, *Jesaja 13-27*, 655-657, 659.
[35]   See M. Noth, *The Deuteronomistic History*, 16-17 = *Überlieferungsgeschichtliche Studien*, 17.
[36]   See M. Noth, *ibid.*
[37]   See above p. 106.
[38]   See above pp. 109-110.
[39]   See above pp. 99-100.
[40]   See above pp. 91, 103-108, 111, 112-115.
[41]   See above p. 47.

material (8:12) strongly suggests that the covenant tradition was already present in written form. Since this tradition was probably connected with the Exodus and wilderness traditions in Hosea's day, it is also possible that these traditions were also present in written form, although this is not certain. But whether Hosea drew directly upon written sources or was dependent on the oral presentation of the traditions by priests could not be determined on the basis of this study.[42]

The conclusion to be drawn from these considerations is that written compilations of legal traditions existed in Hosea's day, and probably, though not necessarily, of historical traditions as well. Since the Exodus, covenant, and wilderness traditions were related to one another, they are likely to have formed portions of a single work which would then have included historical and legal traditions. It may also be that Hosea's association of Jacob and the Exodus in Hos. 12, especially v. 13-14 (12-13), indicates that the Jacob traditions were also part of the same work, although this conclusion is not necessary. On the other hand, if the interpretation of 12:12 (11) as referring to the initial entry into the land from the vicinity of Baal-Peor is correct,[43] then this would indicate a connection between the wilderness traditions and those recounting the entry into the land. In any case we must certainly reckon with an oral, perhaps even a written compilation including Exodus, covenant, and wilderness traditions, perhaps also settlement traditions, and maybe even Jacob traditions. Hosea thus evidences a connected understanding of Israel's early history based on traditions which in certain instances were known to him in a form variant to that preserved in the Pentateuch. Unless one assumes that these connections were Hosea's own creation, which is rather unlikely given the fact that Hosea expects his audience to understand his allusions, then it must be concluded that prior to the middle of the eighth century connected presentations of Israel's early history were in existence and known in Israel.

What are the implications of this result for Pentateuchal studies? Clearly the process of collection and integration of these traditions must have produced theologically motivated presentations of the formative period of Israel's history at a date significantly earlier than the late seventh century.[44] Neither can one speak globally of a "silence" among the preexilic prophets concerning these traditions. Hosea is anything but silent in this regard, and the "silence" of the other prophets is often the result of dubious decisions stemming from the conviction that these prophets simply could not have made such references. The circularity of the reasoning should be apparent, and the results of this study conclusively demonstrate its invalidity.

The results reached here also have implications for the specific models proposed by R. Rendtorff, E. Blum and J. van Seters. If Rendtorff's model is retained in full, this would mean that a continuous presentation of Israel's early history developed in the south a good century and a half later than its counterpart(s) in the north. Though this is not impossible, the supposition does not command great confidence. Still, his basic model could be adjusted to account for the evidence from Hosea by moving the timeframe suggested by Rendtorff to an earlier period. As for Blum's proposal, the results of this study again call into question the dating of the first connection of the patriarchal narratives with other

---

[42] See above pp. 115-116.
[43] See above pp. 47-48.
[44] *Contra* H. H. Schmid, J. van Seters, R. Rendtorff and others; see above pp. 16-20.

Pentateuchal traditions to the early post-exilic period, without, however, being able to refute the model definitively, since Blum speaks specifically of a literary connection. It could still be argued that the various complexes of tradition were understood as recounting related periods of Israel's early history although they were still independent of one another at the literary level. The argument, however, does appear somewhat forced.

The implications for van Seters' position are less clear, since the results of the current study cannot decide the issue of the date of the Yahwist. Nevertheless, it does become clear that the writing of Israel's history from the patriarchal period to the conquest did not commence with an exilic Yahwist and that the scribal tradition was not as unified as van Seters assumes. Presentations spanning the early period existed prior to the Deuteronomistic history, so that, assuming for the sake of argument an exilic Yahwist, he would no doubt have drawn upon such sources and would thus have functioned in part as a redactor combining earlier works, a conception spurned by van Seters. In this regard it is regrettable that van Seters has yet to address the question of the possible extent of the two pre-Yahwistic stages suggested by him for the Abraham traditions in the remainder of the Pentateuch, a question of no little importance for his overall scheme. It may very well be that the focus on Abraham is too narrow and has skewed the results. In any event the evidence provided by Hosea poses new and significant problems for those advocating a late date for the Yahwist.

B. THE HISTORY OF ISRAEL AS SALVATION HISTORY

The foregoing survey of Hosea's conception of Israel's history as evidenced in his prophecies reveals that he conceived of Yahweh as actively involved in all of this history. At a crucial point in Jacob's life, as he was leaving the land and fleeing to Aram, Yahweh spoke to him and promised him that his return would occur with his aid (12:7 [6]). Yahweh delivered Israel from Egypt and cared for Israel in the wilderness (11:1; 12:10 [9]; 13:4-5). He provided Israel with prophetic guidance and entered into covenant with his people (12:14 [13]; 6:7; 8:1). Even after the Baal-Peor episode and in the ensuing period of Canaanization Yahweh repeatedly sought to bring Israel back to himself by means of the prophets (6:5; 9:8; 11:3-4). But Israel persisted in its sin, rendering disaster the only means of removing the source of Israel's sin and hence inevitable. In the disaster, too, Yahweh is at work. It is he who destroys Israel (13:9). He becomes like a wild animal devouring its prey (13:7-8; 5:14) or like dry rot eating away at the house (5:12). He deprives them of children (9:11-12) and removes kings (13:11). Yahweh visits their deeds upon them (4:9; 8:13; 9:9; 12:3 [2]) in order to complete the effects of their sin (9:7). His activity in bringing about the disaster is thus intended to bring an end to the negative repercussions engendered by Israel's sin in order to start anew. Through the disaster he will heal his people of their apostasy (2:18-19 [16-17]; 14:5 [4]) and renew the relationship between them (2:20-23 [18-21]).

This overall conception of Israel's history justifies the application of the term salvation history to Hosea's perception of Yahweh's activity in this history.[45] This is not to say that Israel's history was characterized by continuous progress towards the goal of an unimpaired relationship with Yahweh in the land. Yahweh's historical deeds reach a preliminary high-point in the Exodus, covenant, and wilderness period. But the moment Israel begins to inherit the land, they begin to move away from the state of salvation intended by Yahweh. Israel's history in the land is a history of the increase of wickedness and sin. Yet Yahweh did not abandon his people in this period, but through the prophets sought to communicate his will for his people (6:6; cf. 9:8) and so to realize the salvation which he planned for them. This is also the underlying purpose of withdrawing the gift of the land. In so doing, Yahweh intends to remove the obstacles hindering the full realization of salvation for his people and also to provide them with the positive attributes needed to enjoy the communion with him inherent in his salvation. The nature of Israel's history as salvation history and the continuance of that history is dependent not on Israel's conduct but on the continuity of Yahweh's will for his people. Israel's history hence has a goal, and Yahweh's action in this history a unifying purpose.

It is thus not appropriate to limit the term salvation history to a particular period or periods of Israel's history for Hosea.[46] Although he considers the Exodus-wilderness period the pristine period of Israel's history so far, there is no indication that this period was based on fundamentally different presuppositions concerning the significance of the human factor from those obtaining in the previous or subsequent eras.[47] Jacob's return is expressly predicated upon his keeping justice and loyalty (12:7 [6]), and the coming disaster is a consequence of Israel's lack of moral conduct. By contrast, Israel's actions in the Exodus-wilderness period were positive. They brought joy to Yahweh (9:10), and so there is no reason to postulate that the human factor played no role in the course of events in this period. There is no indication that this constituted the pristine era of Israel's past history *despite* Israel's actions. Nevertheless, this period does receive a special character because Yahweh is particularly active in establishing the foundations of Israel's relationship with him. In the Exodus Yahweh brought his people to himself in the wilderness, imparted to them knowledge of himself, and established the covenant to help define that relationship and the type of conduct properly ensuing from that knowledge.[48] But the divine activity in history did not close with this period. It continues in the subsequent period. But now the human factor is no longer a positive but a negative force and so exercises a negative influence on the course and character of history, inducing Yahweh to massive intervention.

---

[45]   *Contra* G. Fohrer, "Prophetie und Geschichte," 487-495 = 273-284; B. Albrektson, *History and the Gods,* 68-97. The conception of salvation history adopted here agrees largely with, but goes beyond that expressed by R. Rendtorff, "Hermeneutik des AT," 39-40 = 23-24; cf. also *idem,* "Geschichte und Überlieferung," 89-93 = 33-37; and the broader considerations of K. Koch, "Der Tod des Religionsstifters," 114-117.

[46]   *Contra* G. von Rad, *Theology* I, 121-127 = *Theologie* [1]I, 127-133, and II, *passim.*

[47]   As maintained by G. von Rad, *ibid.*

[48]   Cf. the remarks on the nature of covenant expressed by D. J. McCarthy, "Covenant-relationships," 102.

C. Hosea's Eschatology

The final period envisioned by Hosea is the future period of renewal in which a new work of Yahweh ultimately brings about salvation for Israel to an extent hitherto unknown. This period may therefore appropriately be called the eschatological age in Hosea's thinking. From his overall conception of Israel's history it is also apparent that Hosea saw a definite historical continuity between Yahweh's past activity and his coming work of salvation. There is no indication that he expected the coming work to usher in a period of "historylessness."[49] The very continuity of purpose informing all of Yahweh's activity in Israel's history renders such a notion inconceivable for Hosea. The realization of an intact relationship with Yahweh in the land was and is the goal of Israel's history and of Yahweh's work in it. And if Yahweh's past deeds sought the fulfillment of this goal within a very definite and concrete historical context, then it is to be expected that his future work of salvation aimed at the fulfillment of the same goal should also be within a historical context. It is the same people, Israel, who partake of the new age, and the setting is again the land. Similarly, the prophetic office will be continued in the new age (12:11 [10]), and leadership will again be centralized in the hands of a single authority, albeit not a king (2:2 [1:11]). The basic presupposition concerning the significance of human conduct also evidences continuity. Nothing suggests that this will be rendered irrelevant. On the contrary, the agricultural abundance typical of the coming age is a response to Jezreel, that is, to the positive moral action of Israel.[50]

At one point, however, there is a difference between the coming age and Israel's past history. It has been repeatedly noted that Hosea understood the Exodus as imparting to Israel the knowledge of God. This knowledge was then passed on in the form of historical tradition, most probably the Exodus and wilderness traditions revealing Yahweh as Israel's sole deliverer and provider (13:4-5). He further saw the gift of the land, properly understood, as also imparting the knowledge of Yahweh as Israel's sole benefactor (2:10-11 [8-9]). Whoever possesses this knowledge enters into communion with Yahweh and comprehends him as the sole basis of his life. As a consequence, he acts in an appropriate manner, in a manner attesting faithfulness and loyalty as set out in the precepts of the covenant (cf. 4:1-2; 6:7-10). In the coming age the process will be reversed. The covenant will not merely define righteousness, justice, loyalty, compassion, and faithfulness; these will themselves be mediated (2:21-22 [19-20]). Rather than these qualities being dependent on the proper knowledge, the knowledge of Yahweh will result from these qualities. Thus, when Israel responds positively to Yahweh's offer to enter into a new covenant, she will be blessed with all the attributes necessary to know Yahweh. As a consequence, the new entry into the land will effect the knowledge of God in Israel to an extent far exceeding the first entry, stained as this was with apostasy, and so Israel will be able to enjoy the full benefits of the gift of the land.

---

49 *Contra* G. Fohrer, "Prophetie und Geschichte," 494 = 283.
50 Cf. K. Koch, *The Prophets* I, 92-93 = *Die Profeten* I, 104-105.

The eschatological age will therefore be one of unsurpassed splendor. An undisturbed harmony will prevail between Yahweh, Israel, and the animal world, and there will be a blessed absence of hostility in the land. The inhabitants will live in security and prosperity (2:20 [18]), able to enjoy their vineyards and the produce of the land (2:17, 24 [15, 22]) and to recline in Yahweh's shade (14:8 [7]). There will also be a degree of prophetic activity communicating the divine will such as has never been before (12:11 [10]). The coming eschatological age will hence be the crowning climax of Israel's history.

A comparison of what Hosea looks back on with what he looks forward to reveals both similarities and differences. A covenant is made, but whereas the first covenant was concluded in the wilderness, the new covenant will be made in the land.[51] Similarly, the return to the land follows upon a sojourn in the wilderness as had the first entry, but there is no mention of a new Exodus. Hos. 2:17(15)b anticipates Israel's agreement to enter into covenant with Yahweh as they had in the period of the Exodus. There will thus be a new marriage (cf. 2:21-22 [19-20]), but not a new Exodus. One might be inclined to press Hos. 11:11 with its prediction of a return from Egypt into service. Reference might also be made to Hosea's view that Israel would "return to Egypt" (8:13; 9:3, 6; 11:5; cf. 7:16). This statement is sometimes interpreted as the revocation of all of salvation history, but this view was rejected above in favor of the view that Hosea had in mind a literal return of parts of Israel to Egypt.[52] It is therefore all the more astonishing that, although he expects both a return to and a subsequent return from Egypt, Hosea does not speak in terms of a new Exodus. In light of the significant differences between the earlier period in which the salvific foundations were set and the final climax of Israel's history in which the foundations are relaid, it is questionable whether one can accurately speak of Hosea's eschatology as a typological interpretation of Israel's salvation traditions.[53] Such correspondence as does exist is so general and imprecise that it is difficult to envision a strict application to the future age of the particular forms of the covenant, wilderness, and settlement traditions known to Hosea. The old saving traditions were the norm for Hosea's depiction of the coming age[54] only in the sense that through them he discerned the ultimate salvific will of Yahweh for his people and the forms inherent to its realization.[55]

D. Hosea's Relationship to Historical Tradition and Metahistory

Hosea's conception of the history of Israel also indicates that his relationship to Israel's early historical traditions was one of continuity. He understands these traditions as recounting Yahweh's past activity in establishing the basis of Israel's life and faith. They are traditions which attest Yahweh's salvific work in Israel's history and as such remain for

---

51   See above pp. 100-101.
52   See above p. 69.
53   *Contra* G. von Rad, *Theology* II, 112-119 = *Theologie* [4]II, 121-129. Cf. also *ibid.*, 357-387 = 380-412; and *idem,* "Typological Interpretation," 181-182 = 25-26 = "Typologische Auslegung," 23-24 = 11-12.
54   Cf. G. von Rad, *Theology* II, 118 = *Theologie* [4]II, 128.
55   Cf. J. Jeremias, "Gott und Geschichte im AT," 391: "Sie (= die Geschichte) ... weist zugleich Wege, wie ideale Gottesgemeinschaft zu finden ist."

Hosea salvation traditions.[56] But Hosea is also acutely aware of the great extent of Israel's sin. So great is the destructive force of the vast mass of sin hovering, as it were, over Israel that the salvific foundations established by Yahweh have been rendered ineffective. Forgiveness would amount to nothing more than postponement because Israel is caught up in apostasy (11:7) and their deeds prevent true repentance (5:4; cf. 7:10; 11:5). For the foundations to be restored the sin must be removed, the consequences brought to completion. Hence the coming disaster as a work of salvation! Hosea does not arbitrarily annul the historical traditions in order to make room for the coming disaster,[57] but rather recognizes Israel's own conduct as a factor influencing the course of events. And Hosea perceives that Israel's conduct has been and is an impediment to the realization of the salvation whose foundations Yahweh had laid. It is therefore misleading to term those portions of Hosea's message eschatological which invalidate these foundations, since this conception applies primarily to the current state of Israel.[58] The immoral actions of Israel, inconsistent with the knowledge of Yahweh, negate these foundations and sever the relational bond with him.

Hosea thus argues metahistorically.[59] He understands the guiding principle motivating Yahweh's activity in the history of Israel to be Yahweh's desire to establish an undisturbed and harmonious relationship with his people. Yahweh began his work with the promise to Jacob (if not before). He continued it in the Exodus from Egypt which laid a historical foundation for the relationship with Israel as a people. Prophetic care and guidance was provided and the proper means of upholding the relationship issuing from the Exodus were given more tangible definition in the covenant. The parameters for the full enjoyment of all the richness and blessing ensuing from an intact relationship were set. Israel had been given knowledge of Yahweh and the basic institutions through which the qualities accompanying this knowledge, which included righteousness, justice, loyalty, compassion, and faithfulness (4:1, 6; 6:4; cf. 2:21-22 [19-20]), might be mediated. The Exodus-wilderness period was a period in which Israel experienced a harmonious relationship with Yahweh, but not the full blessings which this entailed because these were connected with the land. The land was the selected stage for the fullness of life with Yahweh. But with the entry into the land Israel began to be filled with a spirit of harlotry (1:2; 2:4 [2]; 4:12; 5:4). Israel became defiled (6:10; 5:3), infested with the abominable nature of their lover (9:10; 7:1) and hence incapable of a genuine relationship with a holy God (11:9; 5:4; 7:10). They forgot Yahweh as the God of the Exodus who revealed himself in historical events, and so went chasing after the sexual powers of fertility supposedly offered by the Baals and neglected the knowledge of Yahweh. Hosea thus perceives the cause of Israel's demise to be the lack of the knowledge of Yahweh and the accompanying qualities.

This being the case, Israel's restoration must in some way remove the deficiency. Hosea thus naturally has recourse to that phase of Israel's history in which these attributes were initially imparted to Israel: the great past events of salvation history. But he looks to these traditions not to project them (typologically) into the future but to understand the basic will of Yahweh for his people and the forms and institutions fundamental to the

---

56   Similarly, H.-D. Neef, *Heilstraditionen*, 249-252.
57   *Contra* J. Vollmer, *Geschichtliche Rückblicke*, 119-124.
58 . *Contra* G. von Rad, *Theology* II, 118 = *Theologie* [4]II, 128.
59   With K. Koch, *The Prophets* I, 87-88 = *Die Profeten* I, 99-100; see also above p. 11.

fulfillment of that will. From these traditions Hosea discerns Yahweh's desire for an exclusive covenantal relationship with his people in the land. The coming loss of the land is hence understood in terms of the wilderness period when the relationship between Yahweh and Israel was exclusive (2:16 [14]; 13:4-5). There will be a surge in prophetic activity (12:11 [10]) and a new covenant (2:20-22 [18-20]), both institutions deriving from this period. The covenant will mediate the attributes so desperately needed by Israel to empower them to moral action. Israel will so come to a true knowledge of Yahweh. Thus restored, the return to life in the land in fellowship with Yahweh can proceed. But this time it will be free of all ambiguity. The tension characteristic of the first entry into the land, the (impaired) mediation of the knowledge of God and yet apostasy from Yahweh, will not obtain. Only the salvific aspects will remain because of Yahweh's prior provision of the appropriate attributes. Only when one appreciates Hosea's attention to the positive foundations set by Yahweh and the negative effects of Israel's behavior and its consequences can one appreciate Hosea's understanding of the course and meaning of history.

The recognition of Hosea's metahistorical perception of Israel's history renders it unnecessary and inappropriate to set up the word of Yahweh and historical tradition as alternatives to a proper understanding of his prophecy.[60] Both are primary factors, as is his own empirical experience of the conditions prevailing in Israel and of the course of cultic and political events.[61] Hosea's use of historical traditions, especially those recounting her early history, is thus anything but inconsequential. They are more than merely illustrative material,[62] although they also function in this manner. They form an integral part of his message and go to the very heart of his proclamation. With them he repeatedly demonstrates Yahweh's claim upon Israel and the nature and extent of Israel's sin. It is certainly no accident that whenever Hosea draws upon these traditions he is concerned with exposing Israel's apostasy. This is the essence of Israel's sin, and these traditions are the primary means for exposing it. With them he describes the great benefits which Yahweh had bestowed upon Israel, and with them he contrasts Israel's downfall, the incomprehensible abuse of the benefits received. This is not to say that Hosea knows of no other way to address the issue, but when he strives to penetrate to the heart of the matter, he consistently employs the traditions of Israel's early history. Similarly, in his prediction of the future period of renewal he is compelled to draw upon these traditions to comprehend Yahweh's activity in history and his goal for Israel. These traditions testified to Yahweh's efforts to establish an intact relationship characterized by the knowledge of him and the benefits and institutions accompanying it. Here again Hosea is not confined to describing the restoration exclusively in terms drawn from these traditions. But in such instances the descriptions focus on the renewed life in the land. They are concerned primarily with life following restoration, not with the means by which Yahweh will bestow upon Israel those benefits attending the proper knowledge of him. The interpretation of the means of restoration occurs within the framework of Israel's early

---

60 *Contra* G. Fohrer, "Modern Interpretation," 314-316 = 25-27; J. Vollmer, *Geschichtliche Rückblicke,* 123-124, 209-210.
61 With K. Koch, *The Prophets* II, 194 = *Die Profeten* II, 197.
62 *Contra* O. Procksch, *Geschichtsbetrachtung,* 14; J. Rieger, *Bedeutung der Geschichte,* 114; E. Sellin, "Geschichtliche Orientierung," 649; G. Fohrer, "Modern Interpretation," 314 = 25; *idem,* "Prophetie und Geschichte," 495 = 286; J. Vollmer, *Geschichtliche Rückblicke,* 124, 210.

traditions of the Exodus-wilderness period, the covenant, and the settlement in the land. Thus, although Hosea is not restricted to these traditions in the sense that every prophecy must in some way be explicitly related to them, they are nevertheless essential within the total context of his proclamation because they constitute one of the pillars supporting his underlying metahistorical understanding of Israel's history.

In sum it may reasonably be stated that historical tradition forms the lens through which Hosea perceives God and Israel. His basic perception of Israel's sin is focused by his interaction with the early traditions. His conception of Israel's past history is informed by the conviction that in her early history Yahweh had revealed himself as Israel's sole deliverer and provider, thereby imparting the knowledge of himself and the accompanying salvific benefits; by his awareness of Israel's sin; and by his understanding of Israel's early historical traditions in this light. In this process Hosea is quite respectful of the traditions. Nowhere can it be shown that he understood or employed them in a manner blatantly contradictory to their obvious content.[63] But in contrast to his contemporaries, Hosea emphasizes not the special status of Israel documented in these traditions, but rather the sin of Israel, and its consequences, in failing to abide by the special responsibilities deriving from these traditions.[64]

A process similar to that informing Hosea's perception of Israel's current situation also informs his conception of the future course of salvation history beyond the coming catastrophe. The prevailing sin must be eradicated at its source if the goal of Israel's history is to be realized. To accomplish this the lacking knowledge of God must be instilled in Israel anew and the forms and institutions governing a harmonious relationship with Yahweh reestablished. Here it becomes especially apparent that Israel's early historical traditions play a fundamental role in shaping Hosea's understanding and formulation of his proclamation. The meaning and purpose of coming events become apparent to him only against the background of the need of the future age as discerned in Yahweh's past activity in Israel's early history, coupled with Israel's response to the salvific benefits received. The prescribed cure, like the diagnosis, is determined with the aid of historical tradition.

---

[63] *Contra* J. Vollmer, *Geschichtliche Rückblicke,* 124-126; cf. G. Fohrer, "Prophetie und Geschichte," 495 = 286.

[64] Cf. G. von Rad, *Theology* II, 186 = *Theologie* [4]II, 192-193.

BIBLIOGRAPHY

1. Commentaries and Similar Works

These works are cited by author's name only except for purposes of clarity. All references are *ad loc.* unless accompanied by a page reference.

Andersen, F. I. and Freedman, D. N., *Hosea*. AB 24; Garden City, NY: Doubleday, 1980.

Deissler, A., *Zwölf Propheten. Hosea. Joel. Amos.* Neue Echter Bibel. Würzburg: Echter Verlag, 1981.

Duhm, B., "Anmerkungen zu den Zwölf Propheten," *ZAW* 31 (1911) 1-43, 81-110, 161-204 = in book form *Anmerkungen zu den Zwölf Propheten.* Giessen: Alfred Töpelmann, 1911.

Ehrlich, A. B., *Randglossen zur hebräischen Bibel V.* Leipzig: J. C. Hinrichs, 1912; reprinted Hildesheim: Georg Ohms, 1968.

Harper, W. R., *Amos and Hosea.* ICC; Edinburgh: T. & T. Clark, 1905.

Hitzig, F., *Die zwölf kleinen Propheten.* Leipzig: S. Hirzel, 1838, [4]1881.

Jacob, E., "Osée," in: E. Jacob, C.-A. Keller and S. Amsler, *Osée, Joël, Abdias, Jonas, Amos.* CAT 11a; Neuchatel: Delachaux et Niestlé, 1965.

Jeremias, J., *Der Prophet Hosea.* ATD 24/1; Göttingen: Vandenhoeck & Ruprecht, 1983.

Keil, C. F., *Die zwölf kleinen Propheten.* BC 3/4; Leipzig: Dörffling und Franke, 1866.

Marti, K., *Das Dodekapropheton.* KHC 13; Tübingen: J. C. B. Mohr (Paul Siebeck), 1904.

Mauchline, J., *Hosea.* IB 6; Nashville: Abingdon Press, 1956.

Mays, J. L., *Hosea.* OTL; Philadelphia: Westminster Press, 1969.

Nowack, W., *Die kleinen Propheten.* HKAT; Göttingen: Vandenhoeck & Ruprecht, 1922.

Nyberg, H. S., *Studien zum Hoseabuche.* Uppsala Universitets Årsskrift 1935:6; Uppsala: Almqvist und Wiksells, 1935.

Robinson, Th. H., "Hosea," in: Th. H. Robinson and F. Horst, *Die zwölf kleinen Propheten.* HAT 14; Tübingen: J. C. B. Mohr (Paul Siebeck), [3]1964.

Rudolph, W., *Hosea.* KAT XIII/1; Gütersloh: Gerd Mohn, 1966.

Sellin, E., *Das Zwölfprophetenbuch.* KAT 12/1; Leipzig: A. Deichert, [1.2]1929.

Ward, J. M., *Hosea. A Theological Commentary.* New York: Harper & Row, 1966.

Weiser, A., *Das Buch der zwölf kleinen Propheten.* ATD 24; Göttingen: Vandenhoeck & Ruprecht, [4]1963.

Wellhausen, J., *Die kleinen Propheten.* Berlin: Georg Reimer, [3]1898.

Wolff, H.W., *Dodekapropheton 1. Hosea.* BKAT XIV/1; Neukirchen-Vluyn: Neukirchener Verlag, 1965, [3]1976.

2. Reference Works.

AHw   W. von Soden, *Akkadisches Handwörterbuch.* Wiesbaden: Otto Harrassowitz 1965ff.
ARM   *Archives royales de Mari.* ed. by A. Parrot and G. Dossin. Paris: Imprimerie
       Nationale, 1950ff.
Bauer-Leander   H. Bauer and P. Leander, *Historische Grammatik der Hebräischen Sprache.*
       2 vol. Halle: Max Niemeyer, 1922.
BDB   F. Brown, S. R. Driver and C. A. Briggs, *A Hebrew and English Lexicon of the
       Old Testament.* Oxford: Clarendon Press, 1907 = 1978.
BrSyn C. Brockelmann, *Hebräische Syntax.* Neukirchen Kreis Moers: Verlag der
       Buchhandlung des Erziehungsvereins, 1956.
CAD   *The Assyrian Dictionary of the Oriental Institute of the University of Chicago.* ed.
       by I. J. Gelb, *et al.* Chicago: Oriental Institute, 1956ff.
Dalman, G. H., *Aramäisch-Neuhebräisches Handwörterbuch zu Targum, Talmud und
       Midrasch.* Göttingen: Vandenhoeck & Ruprecht, 1938; reprinted Hildesheim:
       Georg Olms, 1967.
GKC   *Gesenius' Hebrew Grammar.* ed. by E. Kautsch; tr. A. E. Cowley. Oxford:
       Clarendon Press, 1910.
HAL   W. Baumgartner, B. Hartman and E. Y. Kutscher, *Hebräisches und Aramäisches
       Lexikon zum Alten Testament.* Leiden: E. J. Brill, 1967ff.
Jastrow, M., *A Dictionary of the Targumim, the Talmud Babli and Yerushalmi, and the
       Midrashic Literature.* 2 vol. New York: Pardes Publishing House, 1950; reprinted
       Brooklyn, NY: P. Shalom Publishers, 1967.
Joüon, P., *Grammaire de l'Hébreu Biblique.* Rome: Pontifical Biblical Institute 1923 =
       1982.
KBL   L. Köhler and W. Baumgartner, *Lexicon in Veteris Testamenti Libros.* Leiden: E. J.
       Brill, 1958.
König, F. E., *Historisch-Kritisches Lehrgebäude der Hebräischen Sprache.* Leipzig: J. C.
       Hinrichs, 1897.
Lambdin, T. O., *Introduction to Biblical Hebrew.* New York: Charles Scribner's Sons, 1971.
Liddell-Scott   H. G. Liddell and R. Scott, *A Greek-English Lexicon.* 9th rev. ed. by H. S.
       Jones and R. McKenzie. Oxford: Clarendon Press, 1940.
Oxford Bible Atlas. ed. by H. G. May. London & New York: Oxford University Press,
       1984.
Payne Smith, J., *A Compendious Syriac Dictionary.* Oxford: Clarendon Press, 1984.

3. *Secondary Literature Cited.*

Ackroyd, P. R., "Hosea and Jacob," *VT* 13 (1963) 245-259.

Aharoni, Y., *The Land of the Bible.* rev. ed. Philadelphia: Westminster Press, 1979.

Albertz, R., "זעק ṣ'q schreien," *THAT* II, 568-575.

Albrektson, B., *History and the Gods.* CB OT Series 1; Lund: C. W. K. Gleerup, 1967.

Albright, W. F., *Samuel and the Beginnings of the Prophetic Movement.* Cincinnati: Hebrew Union College Press, 1961.

---, *Yahweh and the Gods of Canaan.* Winona Lake, IN: Eisenbrauns, 1968.

Alt, A., "Hosea 5,8-6,6. Ein Krieg und seine Folgen in prophetischer Beleuchtung," *Neue kirchliche Zeitschrift* 30 (1919) 537-568 = KS II, 163-187.

---, "Die Heimat des Deuteronomiums," KS II, 250-275.

---, *Kleine Schriften zur Geschichte des Volkes Israel.* 3 vol. Munich: C. H. Beck, 1959 (vol I & II 1953 = 1959).

Andersen, A. A., *The Book of Psalms.* 2 vol. NCB; London: Oliphants, 1972.

Andersen, F. I., "Note on Genesis 30₈," *JBL* 88 (1969) 200.

André, G., "טמא ṭāme'," *ThWAT* III, 352-366.

Audet, J.-P., "Le Sens du Cantique des Cantiques," *RB* 62 (1955) 197-221.

Bach, R., *Die Erwählung Israels in der Wüste.* Diss. Bonn, 1951.

Baltzer, K., *Das Bundesformular.* WMANT 4; Neukirchen-Vluyn: Neukirchener Verlag, 1960.

Barth, C., "Zur Bedeutung der Wüstentradition," *SVT* 15 (1965) 14-23.

Baumann, E., "ידע und seine Derivate," *ZAW* 28 (1908) 22-41, 110-143.

---, "'Wissen um Gott' bei Hosea als Urform von Theologie?" *EvTh* 15 (1955) 416-425.

Baumgartner, W., "Kennen Amos und Hosea eine Heilseschatologie?" *Schweizerische Theologische Zeitschrift* 30 (1913) 30-42, 95-124, 152-170.

Beer, E., "Zu Hosea XII," *ZAW* 13 (1893) 281-293.

Begrich, J., "Die priesterliche Tora," in: *Werden und Wesen des Alten Testaments.* ed. by P. Volz, F. Stummer, and J. Hempel. BZAW 66; Berlin: Alfred Töpelmann, 1936, 63-88 = GS, 232-260.

---, "Berît. Ein Beitrag zur Erfassung einer alttestamentlichen Denkform," *ZAW* 60 (1944) 1-11 = GS, 55-66.

---, *Gesammelte Studien zum Alten Testament.* TB 21; Munich: Chr. Kaiser, 1964.

Bentzen, A., "The Weeping of Jacob, Hos. XII 5A," *VT* 1 (1951) 58-59.

Bergman, J. and Botterweck, G. J., "ידע jāda'," *ThWAT* III, 479-512.

Beyerlin, W., *Herkunft und Geschichte der ältesten Sinaitraditionen.* Tübingen: J. C. B. Mohr (Paul Siebeck), 1961.

Blum, E., *Die Komposition der Vätergeschichte.* WMANT 57; Neukirchen-Vluyn: Neukirchener Verlag, 1984.

Boer, P. A. H. de, "Genesis XXXII 23-33" *Nederlansch Theologisch Tijdschrift* 1 (1946/47) 149-163.

Botterweck, G. J., *"Gott Erkennen" im Sprachgebrauch des Alten Testaments*. BBB 2; Bonn: Peter Hanstein, 1951.

---, see also under Bergman, J.

Briggs, C. A., *Psalms*. 2 vol. ICC; Edinburgh: T. & T. Clark, 1906 & 1907 = 1952 & 1951.

Bright, J., *Jeremiah*. AB 21; Garden City, NY: Doubleday, 1965.

Burrows, M., *The Basis of Israelite Marriage*. American Oriental Series 15; New Haven: American Oriental Society, 1938.

Buss, M. J., *The Prophetic Word of Hosea*. BZAW 111; Berlin: Alfred Töpelmann, 1969.

Caquot, A., "Osée et la Royauté," *RHPR* 41 (1961) 123-146.

Childs, B. S., *The Book of Exodus*. OTL; Philadelphia: Westminster Press, 1974.

Clements, R. E., *Prophecy and Tradition*. Oxford: Basil Blackwell, and Atlanta: John Knox Press, 1975.

Clines, D. J. A., "Hosea 2: Structure and Interpretation," in: *Studia Biblica 1978*. JSOTS 11; Sheffield: JSOT Press, 1979, 83-103.

Coats, G. W., *Rebellion in the Wilderness*. Nashville: Abingdon Press, 1968.

Coote, R. B., "Hosea XII," *VT* 21 (1971) 389-402.

Cross, F. M., Jr., *Canaanite Myth and Hebrew Epic*. Cambridge, MA and London: Harvard University Press, 1973.

Dahood, M. J., *Ugaritic-Hebrew Philology*. Biblica et Orientalia 17; Rome: Pontifical Biblical Institute, 1965.

---, *Psalms II*. AB 17; Garden City, NY: Doubleday, 1968.

---, *Psalms III*. AB 17A; Garden City, NY: Doubleday, 1970.

Dalman, G., *Arbeit und Sitte*. 7 vol. Gütersloh, 1928; reprinted Hildesheim: Georg Olms, 1964 = AuS.

Daniels, D. R., "Is There a 'Prophetic Lawsuit' Genre?" *ZAW* 99 (1987) 339-360.

Day, J., "Pre-Deuteronomic Allusions to the Covenant in Hosea and Psalm lxxviii," *VT* 36 (1986) 1-12.

Diedrich, F., *Die Anspielungen auf die Jacob-Tradition in Hos 12,1-13,3*. Würzburg: Echter Verlag, 1977.

Donner, H., *Israel unter den Völkern*. SVT 11; Leiden: E. J. Brill, 1964.

Driver, G. R., "Babylonian and Hebrew Notes," *Die Welt des Orients* 2 (1954-59) 19-26.

--- and Miles, J. C., *The Assyrian Laws*. Oxford: Clarendon Press, 1935; reprinted Aalen: Scientia, 1975.

Duhm, B., *Die Psalmen*. KHC; Tübingen: J. C. B. Mohr (Paul-Siebeck), ^{2}1922.

Eichrodt, W., *Theology of the Old Testament*. 2 vol. London: SCM Press, and Philadelphia: Westminster Press, 1961 & 1967 = *Theologie des Alten Testaments*. 3 vol. 5 & 6 ed. Stuttgart: Ehrenfried Klotz, and Göttingen: Vandenhoeck & Ruprecht, 1959 & 1964.

Eising, H., "זָכַר *zākhar*; etc.," *TDOT* IV, 64-82.

Eißfeldt, O., "Der Gott Bethel," *ARW* 28 (1930) 1-30 = KS I, 206-233.

---, "Jahwe Zabaoth," in: *Miscellanea Academica Berolinensia*, Berlin 1950, II/2, 128-150 = KS III, 103-123.

Eißfeldt, O., "Psalm 80," in: *Geschichte und Altes Testament*. Fs A. Alt. Tübingen: J. C. B. Mohr (Paul Siebeck), 1953, 65-78 = KS III, 221-232

---, *Kleine Schriften*. 6 vol. Tübingen: J. C. B. Mohr (Paul Siebeck), 1962ff.

---, *The Old Testament. An Introduction*. New York: Harper & Row, and Oxford: Basil Blackwell, 1965 = *Einleitung in das Alte Testament*. Tübingen: J. C. B. Mohr (Paul Siebeck), ^{3}1964.

Eitan, I., "Biblical Studies," *HUCA* 14 (1939) 1-22.

Elhorst, H. J., "Das Ephod," *ZAW* 30 (1910) 259-276.

Elliger, K., "Ich bin der Herr - Euer Gott," in: *Theologie als Glaubenswagnis*. Fs K. Heim. Hamburg: Furche-Verlag, 1954, 9-34 = *Kleine Schriften zum Alten Testament*. TB 32; Munich: Chr. Kaiser, 1966, 211-231.

Emmerson, G. I., "The Structure and Meaning of Hosea VIII 1-3," *VT* 25 (1975) 700-710.

---, *Hosea. An Israelite Prophet in Judean Perspective*. JSOTS 28; Sheffield: JSOT Press, 1984.

Eslinger, L. M., "Hosea 12:5a and Genesis 32:29: A Study in Inner Biblical Exegesis," *JSOT* 18 (1980) 91-99.

Fensham, F. C., "The covenant-idea in the book of Hosea," *OTWSA* 7-8 (1964-65) 35-49.

---, "The Marriage Metaphor in Hosea for the Covenant Relationship Between the Lord and his People (Hos. 1:2-9)," *JNSL* 12 (1984) 71-78.

Fohrer, G., "Umkehr und Erlösung beim Propheten Hosea," *ThLZ* 11 (1955) 161-185 = *Studien zur ... Prophetie*, 222-241.

---, "Der Vertrag zwischen König und Volk in Israel," *ZAW* 71 (1959) 1-22 = *Studien zur ... Theologie und Geschichte*, 330-351.

---, "Remarks on the Modern Interpretation of the Prophets," *JBL* 80 (1961) 309-319 = (in German) *Studien zur ... Prophetie*, 18-31.

---, "Tradition und Interpretation im Alten Testament," *ZAW* 73 (1961) 1-30 = *Studien zur ... Theologie und Geschichte*, 54-83.

---, "Prophetie und Geschichte," *ThLZ* 89 (1964) 481-500 = *Studien zur ... Prophetie*, 265-293.

---, "Altes Testament - 'Amphictyonie' und 'Bund'?" *ThLZ* 91 (1966) 801-816, 893-904 = *Studien zur ... Theologie und Geschichte*, 84-119.

---, *Studien zur alttestamentlichen Prophetie, 1949-1965*. BZAW 99; Berlin: Alfred Töpelmann, 1967.

---, *Studien zur alttestamentlichen Theologie und Geschichte*. BZAW 115; Berlin: Walter de Gruyter, 1969.

Foresti, F., "Hos. 12: A Prophetical Polemic against the Proto-Elohistic Pentateuchal Tradition," *Ephemerides Carmeliticae* 30 (1979) 179-200.

Frankena, R., "The Vassal-Treaties of Esarhaddon and the Dating of Deuteronomy," *OTS* 14 (1965) 122-154.

Frey, H., "Der Aufbau der Gedichte Hoseas," *Wort und Dienst* NF 5 (1957) 9-103.

Friedman, M. A., "Israel's Response in Hosea 2:17b: 'You are my Husband,'" *JBL* 99 (1980) 199-203.

Fritz, V., *Israel in der Wüste*. Marburger Theologische Studien 7; Marburg: N. G. Elwert, 1970.

Galling, K., *Die Erwählungstraditionen Israels*. Giessen: Alfred Töpelmann, 1928.

Gelston, A., "Kingship in the Book of Hosea," *OTS* 19 (1974) 71-85.

Gerleman, G., "בקשׁ *bkš* pi. suchen," *THAT* I, 333-336.

Gerstenberger, E., "בטח *bṭḥ* vertrauen," *THAT* I, 300-305.

Gertner, M., "The Masora and the Levites. Appendix: An Attempt at an Interpretation of Hosea XII," *VT* 10 (1960) 272-284.

Gese, H., "Geschichtliches Denken im Alten Orient und im Alten Israel," *ZThK* 55 (1958) 127-145 = *Vom Sinai zum Zion*, 81-98.

---, "Bemerkungen zur Sinaitradition," *ZAW* 79 (1967) 137-154 = *Vom Sinai zum Zion*, 31-48.

---, *Vom Sinai zum Zion*. Munich: Chr. Kaiser, 1974.

---, "Das Gesetz," in: *Zur biblischen Theologie. Alttestamentliche Vorträge*. Munich: Chr. Kaiser, 1977, 55-84.

---, "Jakob und Mose: Hosea 12:3-14 als einheitlicher Text," in: *Tradition and Re-Interpretation in Jewish and Early Christian Literature*. Fs J. C. H. Lebram. Studia Post-Biblica 36; Leiden: E. J. Brill, 1986, 38-47.

Ginsberg, H. L., "Hosea's Ephraim, More Fool than Knave. A New Interpretation of Hosea 12:1-14," *JBL* 80 (1961) 339-347.

Glueck, N., Ḥesed *in the Bible*. Cincinnati: Hebrew Union College Press, 1967; reprinted Ktav Publishing House, 1975 = *Das Wort* Ḥesed *im alttestamentlichen Sprachgebrauche als menschliche und göttliche gemeinschaftsgemäße Verhaltungsweise*. BZAW 47; Giessen: Alfred Töpelmann, 1927.

---, *Explorations in Eastern Palestine, IV*. AASOR 25-29 (for 1945-49) 1951.

Gnuse, R., "Calf, Cult and King: The Unity of Hosea 8:1-13," *BZ* 26 (1982) 83-92.

Good, E. M., "The Composition of Hosea," *SEÅ* 31 (1966) 21-63.

---, "Hosea and the Jacob Tradition," *VT* 16 (1966) 137-151.

---, "Hosea 58-66: An Alternative to Alt," *JBL* 85 (1966) 273-286.

Gordis, R., "Hosea's Marriage and Message. A New Approach," *HUCA* 25 (1954) 9-35 = *Poets, Prophets and Sages*. Bloomington & London: Indiana University Press, 1971, 230-254.

Gordon, C. H., "Hos 2 4-5 in the Light of New Semitic Inscriptions," *ZAW* 54 (1936) 277-280.

---, "Zu ZAW 1936, 277ff.," *ZAW* 55 (1937) 176.

Greßmann, H., *Die älteste Geschichtsschreibung und Prophetie Israels*. SAT II/1; Göttingen: Vandenhoeck & Ruprecht, ²1921.

Grimm, D., "Erwägungen zu Hosea 12₁₂ 'in Gilgal opfern sie Stiere,'" *ZAW* 85 (1973) 339-347.

Gunkel, H., *Genesis*. Göttingen: Vandenhoeck & Ruprecht, ³1910 = ⁹1977.

Gunkel, H., *Die Psalmen*. Göttingen: Vandenhoeck & Ruprecht, ³1929 = ⁵1968.

Hänel, J., *Das Erkennen Gottes bei den Schriftpropheten*. BWAT NF 4; Stuttgart: W. Kohlhammer, 1923.

Hasel, G., "זָעַק *zāʿaq*; etc.," *TDOT* IV, 112-122.

Henry, M.-L., *Prophet und Tradition. Versuch einer Problemstellung*. BZAW 116; Berlin: Walter de Gruyter, 1969.

Hesse, F., "Die Erforschung der Geschichte Israels als theologische Aufgabe." *KuD* 4 (1958) 1-20.

---, "The Evaluation and the Authority of Old Testament Texts," in: *Essays in Old Testament Hermeneutics*, ed. by C. Westermann, 285-313 = *Probleme alttestamentlicher Hermeneutik*, 266-294 = Fs F. Baumgärtel. Erlangener Forschungen, Reihe A, Band 10; Erlangen: Universitätsbund, 1959, 74-96.

---, "Kerygma oder geschichtliche Wirklichkeit? Kritische Fragen," *ZThK* 57 (1960) 17-26.

---, *Das Alte Testament als Buch der Kirche*. Gütersloh: Gerd Mohn, 1966.

---, "Bewährt sich eine 'Theologie der Heilstatsachen' am Alten Testament?," *ZAW* 81 (1969) 1-18.

---, *Abschied von der Heilsgeschichte*. ThSt 108; Zürich: Theologischer Verlag, 1971.

Hillers, D. R., *Treaty-Curses and the Old Testament Prophets*. Rome: Pontifical Biblical Institute, 1964

---, "A Note on Some Treaty Terminology in the Old Testament," *BASOR* 176 (1964) 46-47.

Holladay, W. L., "Chiasmus, The Key to Hosea XII 3-6," *VT* 16 (1966) 53-64.

Holt, E. K., "דעת אלהים und חסד im Buche Hosea," *SJOT* 1 (1987) 87-103.

Huffmon, H. B., "The Treaty Background of Hebrew *YĀDAʿ*," *BASOR* 181 (1966) 31-37.

Humbert, P., "La logique de la perspective nomade chez Osée et l'unité d'Osée 2,4-22," in: *Vom Alten Testament*. Fs K. Marti. Giessen: Alfred Töpelmann, 1925, 158-166.

Hyatt, J. P., *Exodus*. NCB; London: Oliphants, 1971.

Jacob, E., "La Femme et le Prophéte. Apropos d'Osée 12,13-14," in: *Maqqél Shâqédh*. Hommage á W. Vischer. Montpellier: Causse, Graille, Castellnau, 1960, 83-87.

---, "Der Prophet Hosea und die Geschichte," *EvTh* 24 (1964) 281-290.

Jepsen, A., "Berith. Ein Beitrag zur Theologie der Exilszeit," in: *Verbannung und Heimkehr*. Fs W. Rudolph. Tübingen: J. C. B. Mohr (Paul Siebeck), 1961, 161-179.

---, "אָמַן *ʾāman*; etc.," *TDOT* I, 292-323.

---, "בָּטַח *bāṭach*; etc.," *TDOT* II, 88-94.

Jeremias, C., "Die Erzväter in der Verkündigung der Propheten," in: *Beiträge zur alttestamentlichen Theologie*. Fs W. Zimmerli. Göttingen: Vandenhoeck & Ruprecht, 1977, 206-222.

Jeremias, J., "Hosea 4-7. Beobachtungen zur Komposition des Buches Hosea," in: *Textgemäß*. Fs E. Würthwein. Göttingen: Vandenhoeck & Ruprecht, 1979, 47-58.

---, "Gott und Geschichte im Alten Testament. Überlegungen zum Geschichtsverständnis im Nord- und Südreich Israels," *EvTh* 40 (1980) 381-396.

Jeremias, J., "Zur Eschatologie des Hoseabuches," in: *Die Botschaft und die Boten.* Fs H. W. Wolff. Neukirchen-Vluyn: Neukirchener Verlag, 1981, 217-234.

Johnson, A. R., "HESED and HASID," in: *Interpretationes ad vetus testamentum pertinentes.* Fs S. Mowinckel. Oslo: Fabritius & Sønner, 1955, 100-112.

---, *The Cultic Prophet in Ancient Israel.* Cardiff: University of Wales Press, ²1962.

Jüngling, H.-W., "Aspekte des Redens von Gott bei Hosea," *ThPh* 54 (1979) 335-358.

Kellenberger, E., ḥäsäd wä'ᵉmät *als Ausdruck einer Glaubenserfahrung. Gottes Offen-Werden und Bleiben als Voraussetzung des Lebens.* AThANT 69; Zürich: Theologischer Verlag, 1982.

Kinet, D., "Eschatologische Perspektiven im Hoseabuch," in: *Eschatologie. Bibeltheologische und philosophische Studien zum Verhältnis von Erlösungswelt und Wirklichkeitsbewältigung.* Fs E. Neuhäusler. St. Ottilien: EOS Verlag, 1981, 41-55.

Kittel, R., *Die Psalmen.* KAT; Leipzig: A. Deichert, ⁵,⁶1929.

Knierim, R., "The Vocation of Isaiah," *VT* 18 (1968) 47-68.

---, "Offenbarung im Alten Testament," in: *Probleme biblischer Theologie.* Fs G. von Rad. Munich: Chr. Kaiser, 1971, 206-235.

Koch, K., "Gibt es ein Vergeltungsdogma im Alten Testament?" *ZThK* 52 (1955) 1-42 = *Um das Prinzip der Vergeltung in Religion und Recht des Alten Testaments.* ed. by K. Koch. WdF 125; Darmstadt: Wissenschaftliche Buchgesellschaft, 1972, 130-180.

---, "Tempeleinlassliturgien und Dekaloge," in: *Studien zur Theologie der alttestamentlichen Überlieferungen.* Fs G. von Rad. Neukirchen-Vluyn: Neukirchener Verlag 1961, 45-60.

---, "Der Tod des Religionsstifters," *KuD* 8 (1962) 100-123.

---, *The Growth of the Biblical Tradition. The Form-Critical Method.* New York: Charles Scribner's Sons, 1969 = *Was ist Formgeschichte? Methoden der Bibelexegese.* Neukirchen-Vluyn: Neukirchener Verlag, ²1967; expanded ⁴1981. References to the German original are to the fourth edition.

---, "Die Entstehung der sozialen Kritik bei den Profeten," in: *Probleme biblischer Theologie.* Fs G. von Rad. Munich: Chr. Kaiser, 1971, 236-257.

---, *The Prophets.* 2 vol. Philadelphia: Fortress Press, 1983 & 1984 = *Die Profeten.* 2 vol. Stuttgart: W. Kohlhammer, 1978 & 1980.

---, "צדק *ṣdq* 'gemeinschaftstreu/heilvoll sein,'" *THAT* II, 507-530.

---, "מועד *mô'eḏ*," *ThWAT* IV, 744-750.

---, "Geschichte/Geschichtsschreibung/Geschichtsphilosophie II. Altes Testament," *TRE* XII, 569-586.

Köckert, M., "Prophetie und Geschichte im Hoseabuch," *ZThK* 85 (1988) 3-30.

Kraetzschmar, R. *Die Bundesvorstellung im Alten Testament in ihrer geschichtlichen Entwicklung.* Marburg: N. G. Elwert, 1896.

Kraus, H.-J., *Psalmen.* 2 vol. BKAT XV; Neukirchen-Vluyn: Neukirchener Verlag, ⁵1978.

---, *Klagelieder.* BKAT XX; Neukirchen-Vluyn: Neukirchener Verlag, ⁴1983.

Krszyna, H., "Literarische Struktur von Os 2,4-17," *BZ* 13 (1969) 41-59.

Kümpel, R., *Die Berufung Israels. Ein Beitrag zur Theologie des Hosea.* Diss. Bonn, 1973.

Kuhl, C., "Neue Dokumente zum Verständnis von Hosea 2 4-15," *ZAW* 52 (1934) 102-109.

Kuhnigk, W., *Nordwestsemitische Studien zum Hoseabuch.* Rome: Biblical Institute Press, 1974.

Kutsch, E., "Gesetz und Gnade," *ZAW* 79 (1967) 18-35.

---, "Der Begriff בְּרִית in vordeuteronomistischer Zeit," in: *Das ferne und nahe Wort.* Fs L. Rost. BZAW 105; Berlin: Alfred Töpelmann, 1967.

---, "'Bund' und Fest. Zu Gegenstand und Terminologie einer Forschungsrichtung," *ThQ* 150 (1970) 299-320.

Lambert, W. G., "History and the Gods: A Review Article," *Or* NS 39 (1970) 170-177.

Lehming, S., "Versuch zu Ex. XXXII," *VT* 10 (1960) 16-50.

Lindblom, J., *Hosea literarisch untersucht.* Acta Academiae Aboensis Humaniora V:2; Åbo Akademi, 1928.

Lohfink, N., "Dt 26,17-19 und die 'Bundesformel,'" *ZThK* 91 (1969) 517-553.

---, "Beobachtungen zur Geschichte des Ausdrucks עַם יהוה," in: *Probleme biblischer Theologie.* Fs G. von Rad. Munich: Chr. Kaiser, 1971, 275-305.

---, "כַּעַס *kā'as*, etc.," *ThWAT* IV, 297-302.

Lubsczyk, H., *Der Auszug Israels aus Ägypten.* Erfurter Theologische Studien 11; Leipzig: St. Benno, 1963.

Maass, F., "טהר *ṭhr* rein sein," *THAT* I, 646-652.

---, "טמא *ṭm'* unrein sein," *THAT* I, 664-667.

Mazar, A., "The 'Bull Site' - An Iron Age I Open Cult Place," *BASOR* 247 (1982) 27-42.

McCarthy, D. J., *Old Testament Covenant. A Survey of Current Opinions.* Oxford: Basil Blackwell, 1972 = an expanded version of *Der Gottesbund im Alten Testament. Ein Bericht über die Forschung der letzten Jahre.* SBS 1; Stuttgart: Katholisches Bibelwerk, 1966.

---, "*bᵉrît* in Old Testament History and Theology," *Bib* 53 (1972) 110-121.

---, "*Bᵉrît* and Covenant in the Deuteronomistic History," *SVT* 23 (1972) 65-85.

---, "Covenant-relationships," in: *Questions disputées d'Ancien Testament.* ed. by C. Brekelmans. Gembloux, Belgium: Duculot & Leuven University Press, 1974, 91-103.

---, *Treaty and Covenant.* AnBib 21a; Rome: Biblical Institute Press, ²1981.

McKenzie, J. L., "Knowledge of God in Hosea," *JBL* 75 (1955) 22-27.

McKenzie, S. L., "The Jacob Tradition in Hosea xii 4-5," *VT* 36 (1986) 211-222.

Mendenhall, G. E., *Law and Covenant in Israel and the Ancient Near East.* Pittsburg: The Biblical Colloquium, 1955 = *BA* 17 (1954) 26-46, 49-76 = *Recht und Bund in Israel und dem Alten Vordern Orient.* ThSt 64; Zürich: EVZ-Verlag, 1960.

Miles, J. C., see Driver, G. R.

Moran, W. L., "A Note on the Treaty Terminology of the Sefire Stelas," *JNES* 22 (1963) 173-176.

---, "The Ancient Near Eastern Background of the Love of God in Deuteronomy," *CBQ* 25 (1963) 77-87.

Mowinckel, S., *Psalmenstudien I.* Oslo 1921; reprinted Amsterdam: P. Schippers, 1961.

Mowinckel, S., *Le Décalogue*. Paris: Félix Alcan, 1927.

---, *Die Erkenntnis Gottes bei den alttestamentlichen Profeten*. Tilleggshefte, Norsk
   Theologisk Tidsskrift; Oslo Grøndahl & Søns Forlag, 1941.

---, *The Psalms in Israel's Worship*. 2 vol. Oxford: Basil Blackwell, 1962.

Neef, H.-D., *Die Heilstraditionen Israels in der Verkündigung des Propheten Hosea*. BZAW
   169; Berlin and New York: Walter de Gruyter, 1987.

Nicholson, E. W., *Deuteronomy and Tradition*. Oxford: Basil Blackwell, 1967.

---, *God and His People. Covenant and Theology in the Old Testament*. Oxford: Clarendon
   Press, 1986.

Nötscher, F., "Bundesformular und 'Amtsschimmel,'" *BZ* NF 9 (1965) 181-214.

Noth, M., *Die israelitischen Personennamen im Rahmen der gemeinsemitischen Namengebung*.
   Stuttgart: W. Kohlhammer, 1928; reprinted Hildesheim: Georg Olms, 1966.

---, *Überlieferungsgeschichtliche Studien*. Schriften der Königsherger Gelehrten Gesellschaft.
   Geisteswissenschaftliche Klasse 18 (1943) 43-266 = Tübingen: Max Niemeyer Verlag,
   ³1967 = *The Deuteronomistic History*. JSOTS 15; Sheffield: JSOT Press, 1981.

---, *A History of Pentateuchal Traditions*. Englewood Cliffs, NJ: Prentice-Hall, 1972;
   reprinted Scholars Press, 1981 = *Überlieferungsgeschichte des Pentateuch*. Stuttgart:
   W. Kohlhammer, 1948.

---, "Das alttestamentliche Bundschliessen im Lichte eines Mari-textes," Annuaire de
   l'institut de Philologie et d'Histoire Orientales et Slaves, Tome 13 (1953) 433-444 =
   Gesammelte Studien zum Alten Testament. TB 6; Munich: Chr. Kaiser, 1957, expanded
   ³1966, 142-154 = "Old Testament Covenant-making in the Light of a Text from Mari,"
   in: *The Laws in the Pentateuch and other Studies*. Oliver & Boyd, 1966; reprinted
   London: SCM Press, 1984, 108-117.

---, *Das zweite Buch Mose*. ATD; Göttingen: Vandenhoeck & Ruprecht, 1959.

---, "Samuel und Silo," *VT* 13 (1963) 390-400.

---, *Könige I/1-16*. BKAT IX/1; Neukirchen-Vluyn: Neukirchener Verlag, ²1983.

Nyberg, H. S., Das textkritische Problem des Alten Testaments am Hoseabuche
   demonstriert," *ZAW* 52 (1934) 241-254.

Otto, E., "Jakob in Bethel. Ein Beitrag zur Geschichte der Jakobüberlieferung," *ZAW* 88
   (1976) 165-190.

Pannenberg, W. (ed.), *Offenbarung als Geschichte*. KuD Beiheft 1; Göttingen:
   Vandenhoeck & Ruprecht, ²1963.

Pedersen, J., "Passahfest und Passahlegende," *ZAW* 52 (1934) 161-175.

Perlitt, L., *Bundestheologie im Alten Testament*. WMANT 36; Neukirchen-Vluyn:
   Neukirchener Verlag, 1969.

---, "Mose als Prophet," *EvTh* 31 (1971) 588-608.

Plautz, W., "Die Form der Eheschließung im Alten Testament," *ZAW* 76 (1964) 298-318.

Plöger, O., *Die Klagelieder*. HAT 18; Tübingen: J. C. B. Mohr (Paul Siebeck), ²1969.

Praag, A. van, *Droit matrimonial assyro-babylonien*. Archaeologisch-Historische Bijdragen
   12; Amsterdam: N. V. Noord-Hollandsche Uitgevers Maatschappij, 1945.

Procksch, O., *Geschichtsbetrachtung und geschichtliche Überlieferung bei den vorexilischen Propheten*. Leipzig: J. C. Hinrichs, 1902.

Rabin, C., "Hebrew *BADDIM* 'Power,'" *JSS* 18 (1973) 57-58.

Rad, G. von, *Das Gottesvolk im Deuteronomium*. BWANT 47 (3. Folge Heft 11); Stuttgart: W. Kohlhammer, 1929 = *Gesammelte Studien zum Alten Testament II*. TB 48; Munich: Chr. Kaiser, 1973, 9-108.

---, "The Form-Critical Problem of the Hexateuch," in: *The Problem of the Hexateuch and other essays*. Oliver & Boyd, 1966 = London: SCM Press, 1984, 1-78 = *Das formgeschichtliche Problem des Hexateuchs*. Stuttgart: W. Kohlhammer, 1938 = *Gesammelte Studien zum Alten Testament*. TB 8; Munich: Chr. Kaiser, 1958, 9-86.

---, "Grundprobleme einer biblischen Theologie des Alten Testaments," *ThLZ* 68 (1943) 225-234.

---, "Typological Interpretation of the Old Testament," *Int* 15 (1961) 174-192 = *Essays on Old Testament Hermeneutics*, ed. by C. Westermann, 17-39 = "Typologische Auslegung des Alten Testaments," *EvTh* 12 (1952) 17-33 = (in Auszüge) *Probleme alttestamentlicher Hermeneutik*, ed. by C. Westermann, 11-17.

---, *Old Testament Theology*. 2 vol. New York: Harper & Row, 1965 = *Theologie des Alten Testaments*. 2 vol. Munich: Chr. Kaiser, 1957 & 1960; [4]1965.

---, *Das fünfte Buch Mose*. ATD; Göttingen: Vandenhoeck & Ruprecht, 1964.

Renaud, B., "Genèse et unité rédactionelle de Os 2," *RevSR* 54 (1980) 1-20.

---, "Le livret d'Osée 1-3. Un travail complex d'édition," *RevSR* 56 (1982) 159-178.

---, "Osée 1-3: analyse diachronique et lecture synchronique. Problèmes de méthode," *RevSR* 57 (1983) 249-260.

Rendtorff, R., "Hermeneutik des Alten Testaments als Frage nach der Geschichte," *ZThK* 57 (1960) 27-40 = GS, 11-24.

---, "Geschichte und Überlieferung," in: *Studien zur Theologie der alttestamentlichen Überlieferungen*. Fs G. v. Rad. Neukirchen-Vluyn: Neukirchener Verlag, 1961, 81-94 = GS, 25-38.

---, "Die Offenbarungsvorstellungen im Alten Israel," in: *Offenbarung als Geschichte*. ed. by W. Pannenberg. KuD Beiheft 1; Göttingen: Vandenhoeck & Ruprecht, 1961, 21-41 = GS, 39-59.

---, "Geschichte und Wort im Alten Testament," *EvTh* 22 (1962) 621-649 = GS, 60-88.

---, "Tradition und Prophetie," *Theologia Viatorum* 8 (1961/62) 216-226.

---, "Traditio-Historical Method and the Documentary Hypothesis," in: *Proceedings of the Fifth World Congress of Jewish Studies*. Jerusalem: R. H. Hacohen Press, 1969, 5-11.

---, *Gesammelte Studien zum Alten Testament*. TB 57; Munich: Chr. Kaiser, 1975.

---, "The 'Yahwist' as Theologian? The Dilemma of Pentateuchal Criticism," *JSOT* 3 (1977) 2-10 = "Der 'Jahwist' als Theologe? Zum Dilemma der Pentateuchkritik," *SVT* 28 (1975) 158-166.

---, "Pentateuchal Studies on the Move," *JSOT* 3 (1977) 43-45.

---, *Das Überlieferungsgeschichtliche Problem des Pentateuch*. BZAW 147; Berlin and New York: Walter de Gruyter, 1977.

Rendtorff, R., *Das Alte Testament. Eine Einführung.* Neukirchen-Vluyn: Neukirchener Verlag, 1983.

Reventlow, H. Graf, *Hauptprobleme der alttestamentlichen Theologie im 20. Jahrhundert.* EdF 173; Darmstadt: Wissenschaftliche Buchgesellschaft, 1982.

Richter, W., "Die *nāgîd*-Formel," *BZ* 9 (1965) 71-84.

Rieger, J., *Die Bedeutung der Geschichte für die Verkündigung des Amos und Hosea.* Giessen: Alfred Töpelmann, 1929.

Ringgren, H., "טָהַר *ṭāhar*," *ThWAT* III, 306-315.

Robinson, H. W., "The Hebrew Conception of Corporate Personality," in: *Werden und Wesen des Alten Testaments.* ed. by P. Volz, F. Stummer and J. Hempel. BZAW 66; Berlin: Alfred Töpelmann, 1936, 49-62.

Roche, M. de, "The Reversal of Creation in Hosea," *VT* 31 (1981) 400-409.

---, "Yahweh's *rîb* Against Israel: A Reassessment of the So-Called 'Prophetic Lawsuit' in the Preexilic Prophets," *JBL* 102 (1983) 563-574.

Rost, L., "Die Bezeichnungen für Land und Volk im Alten Testament," in: Festschrift Otto Procksch. Leipzig: A. Deichert, 1934, 125-148 = *Das kleine Credo,* 76-101.

---, *Israel bei den Propheten.* BWANT 71 (4. Folge 19); Stuttgart: W. Kohlhammer, 1937.

---, "Weidewechsel und altisraelitischer Festkalender," *ZDPV* 66 (1943) 205-216 = *Das kleine Credo,* 101-112.

---, *Das kleine Credo und andere Studien zum Alten Testament.* Heidelberg: Quelle & Meyer, 1965.

Rowley, H. H., "The Marriage of Hosea," *BJRL* 39 (1956) 200-233.

Rudolph, W., *Klagelieder.* KAT XVII/3; Gütersloh: Gerd Mohn, 1962.

---, *Jeremia.* HAT 12; Tübingen: J. C. B. Mohr (Paul Siebeck), [3]1968.

Ruppert, L., "Herkunft und Bedeutung der Jakob-Tradition bei Hosea," *Bib* 52 (1971) 488-504.

---, "Beobachtungen zur Literar- und Kompositionskritik von Hos 1-3," in: *Künder des Wortes.* Fs J. Schreiner. Würzburg: Echter Verlag, 1982, 163-182.

---, "Erwägungen zur Kompositions- und Redaktionsgeschichte von Hosea 1-3," *BZ* 26 (1982) 208-223.

Sakenfeld, K. D., *The Meaning of Ḥesed in the Hebrew Bible. A New Inquiry.* HSM 17; Missoula: Scholars Press, 1978.

Sauer, G., "יעד *j'd* bestimmen," *THAT* I, 742-746.

Sawyer, J. F. A., "שָׁוְא *šāw'*, Trug," *THAT* II, 882-884.

Scharbert, J., "Ehe und Eheschließung in der Rechtssprache des Pentateuch und beim Chronisten," in: *Studien zum Pentateuch.* Fs W. Kornfeld. Vienna: Herder, 1977, 213-225.

Schmid, H. H., *Der sogenannte Jahwist.* Zürich: Theologischer Verlag, 1976.

---, "In Search of New Approaches in Pentateuchal Research," *JSOT* 3 (1977) 33-42.

---, "Auf der Suche nach neuen Perspektiven für die Pentateuchforschung," *SVT* 32 (1980) 375-394.

Schmidt, H., "Hosea 6,1-6." in: *Beiträge zur Religionsgeschichte und Archäologie Palästinas.* Fs E. Sellin. Leipzig: A. Deichtert, 1927, 111-126.

---, *Die Psalmen.* HAT; Tübingen: J. C. B. Mohr (Paul Siebeck), 1934.

Schmidt, W. H., *Einführung in das Alte Testament.* Berlin and New York: Walter de Gruyter, [3]1985.

Schottroff, W., "זכר *zkr* gedenken," *THAT* I, 507-518.

---, "ידע *jd'* erkennen," *THAT* I, 682-701.

---, "פקד *pqd* heimsuchen," *THAT* II, 466-486.

Sellin, E., "Die geschichtliche Orientierung der Prophetie des Hosea," *Neue Kirchliche Zeitschrift* 36 (1925) 607-658, 807.

Selms, A. van, *Marriage and Family Life in Ugaritic Literature.* London: Luzac, 1954.

Seters, J. van, "Confessional Reformulation in the Exilic Period," *VT* 22 (1972) 448-459.

---, *Abraham in History and Tradition.* New Haven and London: Yale University Press, 1975.

---, "Recent Studies on the Pentateuch: A Crisis in Method," *JAOS* 99 (1979) 663-673.

---, *In Search of History. Historiography in the Ancient World and the Origins of Biblical History.* New Haven and London: Yale University Press, 1983.

Smend, R., *Die Bundesformel.* ThSt 68; Zürich: EVZ Verlag, 1963.

Steingrimsson, S., "זמם *zmm*; etc.," *TDOT* IV, 87-90.

Stinespring, W. F., "Hosea, The Prophet of Doom," *Crozer Quarterly* 27 (1950) 200-207.

Stoebe, H. J., *Das erste Buch Samuelis.* KAT VIII/1; Gütersloh: Gerd Mohn, 1973.

Stolz, F., "כעס *k's* sich ärgern," *THAT* I, 838-842.

Thiel, W., "*HÊFÊR B^ERÎT.* Zum Bundbrechen im Alten Testament," *VT* 20 (1970) 214-229.

---, "Die Rede vom 'Bund' in den Prophetenbüchern," *Theologische Versuche* 9 (1977) 11-36.

Torczyner, H., "Dunkle Bibelstellen," in: *Vom Alten Testament.* Fs K. Marti. Giessen: Alfred Töpelmann, 1925, 274-280.

Utzschneider, H., *Hosea. Prophet vor dem Ende.* OBO 31; Freiburg, Switzerland: Universitäts-Verlag, and Göttingen: Vandenhoeck & Ruprecht, 1980.

Valeton, J. J. P., "Bedeutung und Stellung des Wortes ברית im Priestercodex," *ZAW* 12 (1892) 1-22.

---, "Das Wort ברית in den jehovistischen und deuteronomischen Stücken des Hexateuch sowie in den verwandten historischen Büchern," *ZAW* 12 (1892) 224-260.

---, "Das Wort ברית bei den Propheten und in den Ketubim - Resultat," *ZAW* 13 (1893) 245-279.

Vaux, R. de, *Ancient Israel.* 2 vol. New York: McCraw-Hill, 1961 = 1965 = *Les Institutions de l'Ancien Testament.* 2 vol. Paris: Cerf, 1958 & 1960.

---, *The Early History of Israel.* Philadelphia: Westminster Press, 1978 = *Histoire ancienne d'Israël: Des Origines à l'Installation en Canaan.* Paris: J. Gabalda et Cie, 1971, and *Histoire ancienne d'Israël: La Period des Juges.* Paris: J. Gabalda et Cie, 1973.

Vogels, W., "'Osée-Gomer' car et comme 'Yahweh-Israël' Os 1-3," NRTh 103 (1981) 711-727.

Vollmer, J., Geschichtliche Rückblicke und Motive in der Prophetie des Amos, Hosea und Jesaja. BZAW 119; Berlin and New York: Walter de Gruyter, 1971.

Vries, S. J. de, "The Origin of the Murmuring Tradition," JBL 87 (1968) 51-58.

Vriezen, Th. C., "La Tradition de Jacob dans Osée XII," OTS 1 (1942) 64-78.

Vuilleumier, R., "Les Traditions d'Israël et la liberté du Prophet Osée," RHPR 59 (1979) 491-498.

Wallis, G., review of H. H. Schmid, Der sogenannte Jahwist, ThLZ 106 (1981) 23-25.

Wagner, S., "בקשׁ biqqesh; etc.," TDOT II, 229-241.

Weinfeld, M., "כָּבוֹד kāḇôḏ, ThWAT IV, 23-40.

Weiser, A., Die Psalmen. ATD; Göttingen: Vandenhoeck & Ruprecht, ⁴1955.

---, Einleitung in das Alte Testament. Göttingen: Vandenhoeck & Ruprecht, ⁴1957.

---, Samuel. Seine geschichtliche Aufgabe und religiöse Bedeutung. FRLANT 81; Göttingen: Vandenhoeck & Ruprecht, 1962.

Westermann, C., Basic Forms of Prophetic Speech. London: Lutterworth Press, 1967 = Grundformen prophetischer Rede. Munich: Chr. Kaiser, 1960.

---, (ed.), Essays on Old Testament Hermeneutics. Atlanta: John Knox, 1963 = Probleme alttestmentlicher Hermeneutik. TB 11; Munich: Chr. Kaiser, 1960.

---, Genesis 12-36. BKAT I/2; Neukirchen-Vluyn: Neukirchener Verlag, 1981.

---, "כבד kbd schwer sein," THAT I, 794-812.

Wildberger, H., Jesaja 1-12. BKAT X/1: Neukirchen-Vluyn: Neukirchener Verlag, ²1980.

---, Jesaja 13-27. BKAT X/2; Neukirchen-Vluyn: Neukirchener Verlag, 1978.

Willi-Plein, I., Vorformen der Schriftexegese innerhalb des Alten Testaments. BZAW 123; Berlin and New York: Walter de Gruyter, 1971.

Wolff, H. W., "Das Thema 'Umkehr' in der alttestamentlichen Prophetie," ZThK 48 (1951) 129-148 = GS, 130-150.

---, "'Wissen um Gott' bei Hosea als Urform von Theologie," EvTh 12 (1952/53) 533-554 = GS, 182-205.

---, "Erkenntnis Gottes im Alten Testament," EvTh 15 (1955) 426-431.

---, "Hoseas geistige Heimat," ThLZ 81 (1956) 83-94 = GS, 232-250.

---, "Jahwe als Bundesvermittler," VT 6 (1956) 316-320 = GS, 387-391.

---, "The Understanding of History in the Old Testament Prophets," in: Essays in Old Testament Hermeneutics, ed. by C. Westermann, 336-355 = "Das Geschichtsverständnis der alttestamentlichen Prophetie," EvTh 20 (1960) 218-235 = Probleme alttestamentlicher Hermeneutik, ed. by C. Westermann, 319-340.

---, Gesammelte Studien zum Alten Testament. TB 22; Munich: Chr. Kaiser, 1964.

Woude, A. S. van der, "פָּנִים pānîm Angesicht," THAT II, 432-460.

---, "צָבָא ṣāḇā', Heer," THAT II, 498-507.

Yee, G. A., Composition and Tradition in the Book of Hosea. A Redaction Critical Investigation. SBLDS 102; Atlanta: Scholars Press, 1987.

Zenger, E., "'Durch Menschen zog ich sie ...' (Hos 11,4). Beobachtungen zum Verständnis des prophetischen Amtes im Hoseabuch," in: *Künder des Wortes*. Fs J. Schreiner. Würzburg: Echter Verlag, 1982, 183-201.

Zimmerli, W., "Promise and Fulfillment," *Int* 15 (1961) 310-338 = *Essays on Old Testament Hermeneutics*, ed. by C. Westermann, 89-122 = "Verheißung und Erfüllung," *EvTh* 12 (1952/53) 34-59 = *Probleme alttestamentlicher Hermeneutik*, ed. by C. Westermann, 69-101.

---, "Ich bin Yahweh," in: *Geschichte und Altes Testament*. Fs A. Alt. Tübingen: J. C. B. Mohr (Paul Siebeck), 1953, 179-209 = GS, 11-40.

---, *Erkenntnis Gottes nach dem Buche Ezekiel*. Zürich: Zwingli Verlag 1954 = GS, 41-119.

---, "'Offenbarung' im Alten Testament," *EvTh* 22 (1962) 15-31.

---, GS = *Gottes Offenbarung*. TB 19; Munich: Chr. Kaiser, 1969.

Zohary, M., *Plants of the Bible*. Cambridge: Cambridge University Press, 1982.

INDEX OF SELECT BIBLICAL REFERENCES

BEIHEFTE ZUR ZEITSCHRIFT FÜR DIE
NEUTESTAMENTLICHE WISSENSCHAFT

Judentum, Urchristentum, Kirche
Festschrift für Joachim Jeremias
Herausgegeben von Walther Eltester
2., berichtigte, ergänzte und vermehrte Auflage
Groß-Oktav. XXX, 259 Seiten. 1 Abbildung. 1964. Ganzleinen DM 79,–
ISBN 3 11 005594 5 (Band 26)

WOLFGANG HUBER
Passa und Ostern
Untersuchungen zur Osterfeier der alten Kirche
Groß-Oktav. XII, 255 Seiten. 1969. Ganzleinen DM 74,–
ISBN 3 11 002585 X (Band 35)

ULRICH FISCHER
Eschatologie und Jenseitserwartung im hellenistischen Diasporajudentum
Groß-Oktav. VIII, 272 Seiten. 1978. Ganzleinen DM 81,–
ISBN 3 11 007595 4 (Band 44)

FREDERICK DAVID MAZZAFERRI
The Genre of the Book of Revelation from a Source-critical Perspective
1989. Large-octavo. XIX, 486 pages. Cloth DM 168,–
ISBN 3 11 011518 2 (Band 54)

ULRICH MELL
Neue Schöpfung
Eine traditionsgeschichtliche und exegetische Studie zu einem soteriologischen Grundsatz paulinischer Theologie
Groß-Oktav. XV, 436 Seiten. 1989. Ganzleinen DM 148,–
ISBN 3 11 011831 9 (Band 56)

Preisänderungen vorbehalten

Walter de Gruyter **Berlin · New York**